The Dynamics of Advertising

Studies in Consumption and Markets
Edited by
Colin Campbell, Department of Sociology, University of York, UK
and
Alladi Venkatesh, Graduate School of Management, University of California, Irvine, USA

Consumption has become a major focus of research and scholarship in the social sciences and humanities. Increasingly perceived as central to any successful understanding of the modern world, the meaning of the individual and collective consumption of goods is now a crucial issue at the heart of numerous contemporary debates on personal identity, the social and cultural structure of postmodern societies, and the historical development of modern industrial society.

This new interdisciplinary series will publish work on consumption-related topics in the fields of sociology; anthropology; material-culture studies; social, economic and cultural history; media and cultural studies; psychology; communication; human geography; marketing; economics; and art and design.

The series will publish the results of empirical research which employs an ethnographic, historical, or case-study approach. Theoretical and conceptual discussions will also be included, either those which represent original perspectives on the study of consumption or those which constitute critical commentaries on existing theories.

Volume 1   *The Dynamics of Advertising*
      Barry Richards, Iain MacRury and Jackie Botterill

Forthcoming Volumes
    Food and Cultural Studies
    Bob Ashley, Joanne Hollows, Steve Jones and Ben Taylor

    Ordinary Consumption
    Edited by Jukka Gronow and Alan Warde

This book is part of a series. The publisher will accept continuation orders which may be cancelled at any time and which provide for automatic billing and shipping of each title in the series upon publication. Please write for details.

The Dynamics
of Advertising

Barry Richards,
Iain MacRury and
Jackie Botterill
University of East London, UK

harwood academic publishers
Australia • Canada • France • Germany • India
Japan • Luxembourg • Malaysia • The Netherlands
Russia • Singapore • Switzerland

Amsteldijk 166
1st Floor
1079 LH Amsterdam
The Netherlands

British Library Cataloguing in Publication Data

A catalogue record for this book is available from the British Library.
ISBN: 90-5823-084-8 (hardcover)
ISSN: 1562-6709

Table of Contents

List of Figures

Acknowledgements

The University of East London has in various ways supported the work on which this book is based. The award of a research assistantship and later a research fellowship to Iain MacRury, and of a research studentship to Jackie Botterill, has underpinned the work of the Centre for Consumer and Advertising Studies. We are grateful to our colleagues in the Departments of Human Relations and Sociology for their support, and for the intellectual environment within which our efforts towards interdisciplinarity and towards a creative but rigorous use of psychoanalytic concepts in social research have taken shape.

We are especially indebted to Mica Nava of the UEL Department of Cultural Studies, who was co-founder with Barry Richards of the Centre for Consumer and Advertising Studies, and whose writing on advertising and consumption has been very helpful in opening up space for a more complex understanding of the social meanings of advertisements. Our empirical research was greatly assisted by the existence and helpfulness of the History of Advertising Trust archive (see Chapter 1, Note 1) at Raveningham in Norfolk, specifically by the Trust's Secretary Michael Cudlipp and Archivist Margaret Garrod, who on our numerous visits there have facilitated our exploration of the rich collection of materials which the Trust is building up. The US advertisement sample was collected at the archive of the John W. Hartman Center at Duke University, and thanks are due to the Center for a travel grant to Iain MacRury and to its Director Ellen Gartrell for her expert assistance and hospitality. Larry and Suzanne Viner at the Advertising Archive in Cricklewood, London, have also been very helpful in response to our requests for help in locating certain kinds of advertisements from certain periods. For their efforts in the work of coding, thanks to Helen Ure, Maggie Brennan and Linda Huxford.

We are very grateful to Michael Brewer of Abram Hawkes plc, whose awareness of the intellectual frailty of much commercial research led him to invite us to contribute to the advertising study reported in Chapter 10, and from whom we have learnt much about the place of commercial research in the marketing process. Amanda Fajak of Abram Hawkes has helped us towards a detailed understanding of the relationship of our academic research to marketing contexts.

Permission to reproduce advertisement images has been granted by the following: DMB&B (Fig. 6.1), Marie Curie Cancer Care (Fig. 6.2), Vauxhall (Fig. 6.3), Peugeot (Figs. 6.4 and 7.3), Café Direct (Fig. 6.5), Gore (Fig. 6.6), BMP DDB (Figs. 7.2 and 8.13), Mazda (Fig 8.1), Daewoo (Fig. 8.2), Hyundai (Fig. 8.7), DaimlerChrysler (Fig. 8.8), Publicis (Fig. 8.14), HSBC (Fig. 9.9), Royal Bank of Scotland (Fig. 9.10), NatWest Group (Figs. 9.11 and 9.12), Lloyds TSB Group (Fig. 9.13), Co-operative Bank (Figs. 9.14 and 9.15), American Express (Fig. 10.5) and Visa International (Fig. 10.7).

Chapter 1

INTRODUCTION: 'DYNAMIC AND SENSUOUS REPRESENTATIONS OF CULTURAL VALUES'

We choose the phrase 'the dynamics' of advertising in order to speak of two things. One is the impact that advertising has on the individual—the psychological tensions and conflicts that may be activated, and the reliefs, hopes and pleasures which may be offered, in a brief encounter with an advertisement. The other is the part that advertising is playing in the process of cultural change—the stimulus or the resistance that particular advertisements may offer to certain trends, the part that advertising as a whole is playing in the complex developments transforming our culture.

The link between these two areas of dynamic tension and change, between the psychic and the social, is in cultural values. By this we mean the categories which people use when they are evaluating something, such as an experience they have just had, a consumer good on offer, or a communication of any sort. These values are used by us as individuals to organise our experience of ourselves, while they are also integral to large-scale processes of change in society.

We began with the assumption—which we think is amply supported by our data—that advertisements are suffused with cultural values. In poster form, they are one of the most prominent carriers of these values in public space. On TV and in the press, we think of the commercials as a 'break', and see advertisements as extra to and different from the programming and editorial material which is what we think we really watch and read. Nonetheless, advertisements form part of the continuous stream of words and images. They are as laden with values as the programmes and articles which they seem, at times, to 'interrupt'. As the American historian Jackson Lears (1994) has said, advertisements have become 'perhaps the most dynamic and sensuous representations of cultural values in the world'.

Advertisements are therefore an important focus for a study of cultural values, and for an attempt to answer the question of whether these values are changing, and if so in what directions. In seeing values as rooted deeply in both inner psychological life and global cultural trends, we are setting out a *psycho-social* approach to the study of culture and cultural change. As the reader will see, we develop what we think is an innovative and fruitful psycho-social approach, one based on combining ideas from British psychoanalysis with some from contemporary social theory.

Through this psycho-social approach to the study of values (or socio-psychoanalytic approach, we might equally say), we try to provide answers to some questions of importance to all those interested in understanding the nature of contemporary society. Is the move into what some call the 'postmodern' world involving deep changes in the values of our culture? If there is some change, in what areas and at what speed is it taking place? Where do we now find credible sources of authority? And in what general terms do we define our needs and wants—how do we now pursue happiness, or the mitigation of unhappiness?

It is our belief that the study of advertisements can contribute to the exploration of these complex questions. Despite their ephemerality, and their belonging to what many see as the trivial or ignoble business of selling branded goods, they command an influential place in everyday culture. Their influence is a testimony to what money can buy. The money poured into advertising secures it a prominent place in most people's daily experience (hours of prime-time TV, acres of roadside hoardings, pages of glossy magazines, and so on), and also makes it likely that the messages broadcast from these hilltops of the information society will be well crafted. The creative and technological resources deployed in advertising are considerable; the dramatic power of some of the images is very great. An important part of the intense crafting process is the extensive research which is often involved in several phases of the marketing process, including pre-testing a number of possibilities, then post-testing the ones chosen to run. While some opinion in the advertising industry may be sceptical of the value of such work, the ratio of research to output is very high in advertising, and many other professionals would envy the extent to which advertising agencies can adjust their products in the light of feedback from research.

This is not to say that advertisements are necessarily effective in persuading us to buy the goods they promote; the commercial efficacy of advertisements is a separate issue from their cultural impact. A particular advertisement or campaign may have had no appreciable effect on sales figures, yet may have been very well known, or notorious, or may simply have added to the vocabulary or imagery available to a general public for use in conversation, daydreaming, and thinking about everyday experience. As part of the general pool of public symbols, it is available—as we argue later on—for use by individuals in their daily work of identity development and maintenance.

One important category of advertising is in fact based upon the assumption that whether or not advertisements directly affect consumer behaviours, they do act upon our general stock of perceptions and ideas about social institutions and social values. This is corporate advertising, where the purpose of the advertisement is to enhance the image of the corporation or of the general brand, not of any specific product. The purpose of this is either to influence social values (e.g. an oil or power-generating company seeking to influence ideas about the environment and what may or may not be damaging to it), or—more usually—to establish a connection between the company or brand and an already-established positive value, such as ecological responsibility.

It is also the case that some kinds of product advertising depend for their commercial effectiveness on having a wide cultural effect. Advertisements for expensive goods—prestige cars, designer sunglasses, gold watches and the like—are 'aimed' at only a small percentage of the population, if they are considered purely as appeals to buy. However it is sometimes pointed out that even though, say, less than 1% of the population is potentially in the market for a particular type of car, the advertiser hopes that many of the other 99% will register their advertisements, because the purchasers of such cars like to feel that others know the *meaning* of what they have bought.

We are moving here to discuss the nebulous yet powerful aura of the 'brand'. In this era of identity, many deep psychic and social forces are organised around identities of various sorts. In commercial culture this trend has been reflected in the growing importance of brand and corporate identities. One aspect of the research reported in this book is a study of how brands are gathering places for important values, and of how the competitive 'conversations' that we can see going on between brands in their advertising can be a contribution to the play of values in culture as a whole.

Our view of advertising in general is that it constitutes a kind of public conversation, an exchange of symbols, images, words and phrases. Although at one level it is a one-way communication—from advertisers and their agencies to us the public—in another, deeper sense it is a place where popular culture is in communication with itself, and is therefore being both reproduced and changed. The advertising agencies' role is to attend closely to the multifarious sights and sounds generated daily in popular culture, in its specifically national forms and in those global aspects of it which arrive on the national scene, and to pick out those which seem to be helpful in the construction of an advertising message. These chosen elements are then fed instantly back into the popular culture, perhaps with a different nuance, or combined with different elements, or in some other context which adds to or inflects their meanings. Given—as we noted above—the loudness and the skill with which advertisements speak, this circulation of words and images plays a significant part in the constant negotiation and sharing of meanings which comprises popular culture. In this respect it should be clear why advertising professionals are seen as being amongst the new 'cultural intermediaries', people whose work involves the production, transmission or mediation of meanings, whether carried by words or images.

We do not underestimate the extent to which advertising's role in the conversational process has been a negative one, in that the meanings which it has picked out for confirmation and enhancement have often been elitist, sexist or racist ones, or have valorised the selfish or the superficial. The advertising industry, like other parts of the modern marketing apparatus, has on the whole exhibited an extraordinary tunnel vision, such that it has for much of the time been able to judge itself only by its commercial objectives or by its own limited notions of aesthetic excellence, even though its practitioners have been aware that—to modify a notorious statement by Margaret Thatcher—there *is* such a thing as society, and that they are a part of it.

So in describing advertising as a public conversation, we are not seeking to sanitise its image. Some of the voices which have been heard in that conversation have been self-satisfied, and on occasions some may have been ugly and divisive. We do however want to place it firmly in the contexts of popular culture and social change of which it is an integral part, and we are critical of those traditions of thought which see it as an essentially malign force imposed from without on a public who are inevitably degraded by it. We do not hold a brief either for the industry or its traditional critics, but are attempting to develop a complex understanding of public communication in which the assessment of advertising will be multi-dimensional.

Overall this book has three main aims. One is to review existing work on advertising by social scientists and cultural theorists. We provide a critical summary of much of this work, identifying those approaches which seem to us to be more adequate to the task of understanding the complexities of advertising. We consider the existing work in relation to some current debates about contemporary social change, particularly about the nature of what some writers have called 'postmodernity', or what others including ourselves prefer to call 'late modernity'.

The second aim is to set out a new approach to understanding advertising, based on a psychodynamic analysis of how advertisements are actually 'read'. This approach is part of a broader understanding of cultural processes, especially in relation to popular culture, and of how they are related to the psychic lives of individuals. Our work on advertising is one component in the development of a 'psychoanalytic sociology' of contemporary culture.

Thirdly we describe some particular research into advertisement content, using a new method of content analysis based on a psycho-analytic approach to cultural values. We offer some reflections on what our findings tell us about some recent cultural trends. They suggest that no matter how dense and vibrant with signs and symbols the late modern world has become, material goods and practical services, and the uses we make of them, continue to have deep significance in the construction and maintenance of personal and social identities.

The combination of these aims has resulted, we hope, in a book that will be of interest and value to all students on courses studying popular culture, media and communications, the sociology of postmodernity, and the emergent field of psychoanalytic studies. Since it has grown out of our own work in the interdisciplinary field of psycho-social studies, we hope that it will also be of potential interest to interdisciplinary students and scholars who are not working specifically on issues concerned with advertising or public communication but for whom our efforts to integrate psychoanalytic concepts with social theory might provide some useful models for developing interdisciplinary understanding.

Another divide we have sought to bridge is between, on the one hand, the qualitative, interpretive methods favoured both by psychoanalyti-cally-influenced approaches and by cultural studies, and on the other the quantitative methods which are the traditional approach of the social or psychological scientist. We have developed methods for quantitatively assessing the presence of certain psychological forma-tions, an undertaking which many people working within the psycho-analytic tradition on which we are drawing would probably regard as invalid.

We are sure, though, that it is necessary to find a new approach to the gathering of evidence about the impact of advertising, and about many broader issues concerning cultural change. Academic debates about the nature and significance of the postmodern tend to oscillate between the unrestrained play of high theory on the one hand, and the offering of vignettes about contingently-chosen cultural phenomena (observations which an author happens to like or to find significant) on the other. We have sought to create a 'middle ground', that is a large but focused body of systematic evidence, drawn from the close scrutiny of over 2500 advertisements. While based methodologically on conventional social science research methods, this approach is addressed to the major theoretical issues of the day concerning the nature of contemporary culture, and is also enriched by an intuitive approach to case studies which form an important supplementary kind of evidence.

There are basically two ways of embarking on a systematic study of a culture. One can either examine its texts and artefacts, or talk to its subjects. Most academic studies of advertising have tended more towards the first method—they have studied advertisements themselves, or the recorded history of the advertising industry or the writings of its practitioners. In the work reported here, we have remained primarily oriented to this method. Amassing good samples of old advertisements can be very difficult, and, as the commercial value of old images becomes more widely recognised, can be expensive. On the whole, though, text-based research is less costly than setting up a large number of interviews. However, we have begun in this study to introduce where possible some measure of the second, ethnographic type of method. A complete research strategy needs to incorporate both, and having developed here a method for analysing what is presented to the public we will in any future work be giving more attention to the study of the appropriations of that material by individuals. Commercial studies of advertising have tended heavily towards this second approach, mainly by the use of focus groups to assess public perceptions of and responses to particular advertisements. Another bridging aspiration of our work was to make some connections, if possible, between academic and commercial understandings of what advertising does. More specifically, the divide to be crossed here is between commercial work on the one side and the studies of advertising conducted in social science and cultural studies departments on the other; academic work in marketing and business studies departments of universities may be closer to the concerns and techniques of the commercial researcher.

Some work of recent years in cultural studies, especially semiotics, has made an impact in the commercial research field, but it is our perception that there is very little exchange across this divide. There are good reasons for this. Although much data is collected by commercial researchers which is potentially of value to academics (e.g. the focus group is a simple tool for the production of huge amounts of ethnographic data), it is acquired at considerable expense by companies who then probably see it as a commercial asset and are unwilling to release it. When, after a period of time, its commercial sensitivity has declined, there is the question of the retrieval costs—who, even if asked, is going to take the time to dig the records out, check them and present them to academic researchers?[1]

It is even less surprising that there has been little influence or input in the other direction, from academia to commerce, because the agendas of academics are typically very different from those of practitioners. Even when academic work is not premised upon assumptions highly critical of the whole business of marketing, it is likely to be looking for a very different kind of significance in data—for what an image or a statement tells us about society, rather than about the efficacy of a particular advertising message in influencing consumer behaviour.

However the practical efficacy of a message is determined at least in part by its place in the cultural web of meanings, and the study of social trends has an accepted place in the backroom operations of marketing. So we have sought to try out our approach to the analysis of advertising messages in commercial contexts. Two occasions on which that has been possible are reported on, in Chapters 8 and 10. We were eager to learn more about the contexts in which commercial research is conducted, and how its findings are used, and curious about how our own ideas would be received by marketing professionals. In a longer-term perspective, we would see the strengthening of socially-responsible marketing practices as a feasible and desirable goal, and we hope that well-rounded academic studies of advertising might make an input towards that end. Once the necessity or inevitability of something like advertising is accepted, then it is important to ask which values are being circulated or celebrated in advertisements, and whether advertisers face having to choose between those most likely to be commercially effective and those most likely to contribute to a better society. Our belief is that such choices are not logically necessary, and that in late modern society a large pool of broadly positive social values is available from which advertisers can select the commercially optimal ones.

At the same time it must be said that the tasks of commercial research are clearly distinct from those of academic research *per se*, and our commitment in this book is primarily to developing an understanding of advertising which can contribute to the overall understanding of contemporary culture. Within this framework, we were able to gather some data in commercial contexts which we think can be used to that end, and to use our general experience of commercial research to inform our theorising.

Some readers will be not be equally interested in all three of the aims outlined earlier. The following guide to the structure and contents of the book will hopefully help to indicate which chapters will be of most interest to different readers.

Chapter 2 provides a brief overview of some issues in the history of advertising, with a particular focus on the relationships between advertising agencies and their clients, and between advertising, the mass media, and the research industry. These issues relate to advertising inside and outside the UK, and we discuss some aspects of the American history. We aim to situate advertising in the array of social trends, institutions and practices which have shaped it, and the tensions amongst them. An awareness of these is, we believe, essential to a sound understanding of advertising and advertisements.

In Chapter 3 we review the major studies of the history of advertisements in the English-speaking world. There are not many such studies, and those that exist have all been of advertisements in the U.S. or Canada. (These include the one previous study comparable to ours, which was in some respects a model for our own research, namely that of Leiss *et al.* (1990). Their wide-ranging book remains an exemplary overview of the whole field of social studies of advertising, though in the present volume we intend to break new ground, theoretically and empirically, and to provide an updated critique of the existing literature.) Insofar as they address the same issues, these studies agree broadly that there has been a historical trend in the content of advertisements towards locating the things advertised in the context of symbolically richer messages, in which the actual commodity has in some ways become less important. At the same time there is a recurrent argument that there is a cyclical quality to the history of advertising strategies, as fundamentally opposed forces fluctuate in relative strength. Here, as in our review of some topics concerning the advertising industry in Chapter 2, we find that one set or another of dynamic tensions are often understood to be at the heart of advertising.

Chapter 4 is an extensive critical review of theoretical, academic studies of advertising in the social sciences and studies of culture. Again, we seek to combine a synoptic guide to the literature with a particular argument which is of importance in the development of our own analysis. Summarising a number of studies old and new, we identify a long tradition of generally hostile commentary upon advertising. Advertising is seen by this tradition as central to the debasement of culture produced by either 'mass society' or 'capitalism', according to the ideological position of the critic. While acknowledging the strengths of some of this commentary, we identify a tendency towards a one-dimensionality characteristic of this tradition of critical writing, and note that it usually gives audience responses only marginal attention. (There is, it might be suggested, a complementarity of omissions between this academic work and commercial research, which ruminates endlessly on audience responses to the exclusion of any consideration of the overall impact of advertising.) Our own approach has some strong affinities with the value bases from which the academic critiques derive, but we attempt to proceed in our own study with fewer preconceptions, and with more attentiveness to the emotional and cultural meanings which advertisements have for their readerships. We indicate the affinities between our approach and a minority of other previous work, such as that of Leiss *et al.* (1990), Nava *et al.* (1992), and Fowles (1996), who uses advertising to reflect upon the nature of popular culture and of the contemporary world. We find in these writers a more measured and complex sense of the social significance of advertising with which we are much in sympathy, though they do not pursue the depth-psychological enquiry into the meanings of advertising images with which our approach is centrally concerned.

Our own theoretical framework is developed in Chapters 5 and 6. The range of theoretical sources we draw on is distinctive. At the heart of our approach is an interweaving of psychoanalytic object-relations theory with some recent sociological theory, especially in the sociology of consumption and theories of late modernity. In Chapter 5 we extract from the literature on postmodernity/late modernity the concepts of risk and reflexivity as being of particular relevance to a psycho-social study of advertisements. Then we identify in recent developments in psycho-analytic cultural theory two contrasting accounts of the psychology of late modernity. In one, the 'postmodern' is seen as involving a shrinkage of the self, producing the defensive 'culture of narcissism' much discussed over the last twenty years. In the other, it is seen as bringing an enhancement of the self, as expressed in the positive category of 'identity' and in descriptions of the expansion of individual autonomy and self-determination. These different accounts of the contemporary consumer and of consumer culture will yield different predictions about trends in the content of advertisements. Against this background we discuss how the notion of 'identity', so important in so many debates about the psycho-social nature of contemporary culture, can be defined in a particularly rich way through a combination of Bourdieu's sociology with Kleinian psychoanalysis. We also suggest the term 'identity work' to refer to individuals' engagement with the flux of identity change and its management.

In Chapter 6 we set out the main psychodynamic ideas of relevance to the study of advertisements. We introduce the concepts of association, unconscious phantasy and anxiety, defence and containment, and deploy them in an account of how readers of advertisements can use the texts presented to them in their day-to-day management of their own emotions and anxieties, either to defend against them or to contain (manage) them. We take a short series of examples, all concerning the theme of guilt, to illustrate the use of these ideas.

Taken together, Chapters 2 to 6 provide a grounding in the literature of social and historical studies of advertising, a review of debates in social and cultural theory relevant to advertising, and an introduction to the psycho-social approach which we believe can deepen understanding of contemporary culture (Richards, 1994).

Chapter 7 sets out the methods we used in our own empirical study of advertisements. We have coded the content of a large and system-atically-generated sample of advertisements (mainly British, but with a significant U.S. sub-set) in two major product sectors: cars and financial services (the latter sub-divided into credit cards and banks). We used a complex set of categories for describing the textual content of the advertisements, ranging from quite simple or gross features (e.g. the number of people portrayed) to more subtle assessments of the values carried by the advertisement. In this chapter we describe the coding forms, which were initially developed for use with print advertisements but then subsequently found to be applicable to TV advertising. We give a detailed account of how we linked the descriptive categories used to the theories outlined in the previous chapters, i.e. to the psychodynamic concepts of anxiety and containment, and to the idea of 'identity work'.

We also describe how samples of advertisements were assembled for coding, and outline an ancillary component of our research strategy, which involved conducting some interviews and focus groups to assess whether the responses of other readers of these advertisements could be described in terms of our categories. Finally we specify some questions which the research is intended to investigate, about the psycho-social and emotional qualities of contemporary culture and how these are carried in the texts of advertisements.

Chapters 8 to 10 describe and analyse the findings from the quantitative study of content. A large number of statistical analyses were run on the frequency data produced by the coding work, i.e. the records of whether particular features were or were not present in each of the advertisements in the sample. Statistically these are fairly simple procedures, typically involving the comparison of means or frequency counts between different sub-samples. Conceptually however they are at times quite intricate, as we tried to find ways of mapping our voluminous descriptive data onto the theoretical formulations we believe to be of importance in understanding both individual experience and cultural change. In these three chapters we try to take the reader through the various ways in which we think that the changing patterns of advertisement content provide some answers to the questions outlined in Chapter 7. We add some refinements to the data, derived from focus groups and depth interviews, and find that while there are some surprising and contradictory elements, the picture overall provides considerable support for a particular theorisation of contemporary cultural change.

Chapter 11 summarises the answers we have been able to produce, albeit necessarily incomplete and provisional ones, to the questions of how to understand advertising, and how to understand the cultural changes we are currently living through. While empirically tied to the domain of advertising, the conclusions we reach are, we contend, of the widest relevance to understanding those cultural changes. Since we now live in a 'promotional culture' (Wernick, 1991), the study of the most developed form of promotional communication, advertising, is considerably more than the study of advertising. Our conclusions are not, however, in the apocalyptic mode sometimes found in studies of the 'postmodern', and of advertising in particular. The complexity and ambivalence of much cultural life is persistently reflected in our data and our analysis.

Note

1. Some of our research was made possible by the existence of the History of Advertising Trust, which accepts unsorted archives from advertising agencies and other sources and conserves them, making them available for scholarly researchers. In the period that we have been using it, this archive has grown rapidly in size. While being the nearest thing in the UK to an official industry archive, it is dependent on the support of individual companies with an interest in the history of marketing.

Chapter 2

THE HISTORICAL DYNAMICS OF THE ADVERTISING INDUSTRY

Like other professional practices and cultural forms, advertising has developed within a field of tensions, a set of historical dynamics which have shaped it. While our interest in this book is primarily in the psycho-social dynamics of advertisements, rather than the industry as such, we will begin by outlining some of these historical tensions within the social relations of advertising, both as background to our own enquiry and because some of them, as we shall see, have a particular bearing on the project of researching and understanding advertisements as a major form of public communication. While we focus mainly on the UK, a similar account could probably also be given for other countries where advertising is highly developed.

We do not present a detailed factual history of advertising; a number of sources already exist which provide such a history in various countries. Of these, there are two main types: those which present straightforward factual, empirical, historical accounts of how advertising has developed, with little or no theoretical analysis or critique, and those which may cover a lot of detailed historical ground but do so in the context of setting out a particular theory or critique of advertising as a social institution. In the first category, the two most detailed sources on the history of advertising in Britain are E. S. Turner's *The Shocking History of Advertising* (1965) and Terry Nevett's *Advertising in Britain: A History* (1982). Extensive historical material on British advertising can also be found in J. A. C. Brown's *Techniques of Persuasion* (1963). We consider a number of works of the second category in Chapter 4, if they embody a theory of advertising's influence as public communication. The debates about the economic and commercial effects of advertising, and accounts of its intricate business relationships with the media, are beyond our scope, though we allude to them in the next section. A clear and careful discussion of advertising's role in relation to the overall process of marketing and to the development of the media can be found in Sinclair (1989), first published in 1987 but still a helpful guide to the issues.

Instead we sketch some aspects of the advertising industry and link these to a discussion of how the history and practice of the industry is enmeshed with the development of the commercial research industry.

The dynamics and history of advertisements themselves must be seen in the context of this complex aggregation of knowledges, practices, and institutions, in which the marketing of goods is linked to the study of people as consumers and as audiences, and is intrinsic to the development of the mass media. Social-scientific knowledge and the arts of persuasion are linked in the crafts of advertising; the tension between prescriptive rationality, as aspired to by research, and the indeterminacy of intuitive creativity is at the centre of advertising practice, as of many other aspects of life today. We will see that in the spaces which advertising occupies in everyday life and in the complex of marketing practices, a number of tensions are in play around the work of advertising creatives. Amongst these we give particular attention to the question of the knowability of advertising's effects. As advertising researchers we obviously believe these effects to be knowable, at least to some degree, and we scan the strategies used in commercial research to capture this knowledge.

In addition to this tension between the aim of research to *know* and the impossibility of definitive knowledge, there are other tensions which course through advertising practice. There are stark political and moral oppositions between the broad social roles ascribed to advertising by its defenders and detractors, between advertising as information and as manipulation. These feed into more specific tensions between regulation and restraint on one side, and creativity and commercial impulses on the other. There are tensions between advertising agencies and their clients, and between different approaches to advertising research.

In the following sections we describe and discuss these tensions and some of the interactions between them.

THE ADVERTISING SPACE AND ITS TENSIONS

Advertising is the most widespread form of public communication in late modern societies. It is a major presence in many areas of public space (especially in urban centres, retail spaces and stadia, less so in residential suburbs, public buildings and parks), and in most news and entertainment media. The power of market-based social relations, and the commercial culture which has built up around them, is such that some other types of public communication are now being modelled on advertising. Wernick's concept of 'promotional culture' brings out this exemplary role of advertising communication. One obvious and controversial example of this is the shaping of political communication by what, in present parlance, are called 'soundbites' (crisp focused statements intended to function in ways at least similar to advertising slogans) and by the principle of staying 'on-message' (the 'old' political axiom of sticking to the party line, revived by a linkage with the marketing principle of sustaining a clear and positive brand image). 'Promotional' language has also entered the field of education, especially the university sector where competition in the market for students is played out on websites and in glossy brochures.

There are manifest tensions around these developments. Embracing promotional techniques is seen by some as a beneficial 'professionalis-ation' of the institution or group concerned, and by others as an avoidable capitulation to market ideologies. These debates about the extension of advertising techniques reflect arguments about the basic social role of commodity advertising, in which the relationships of advertising both to the media it appears in, and the public to whom it appears, have been contested. From the beginning of the twentieth century, advertising revenue came to play an increasingly important role in the finances of newspapers and magazines. With the exception of public service broadcasting in the UK, it has underpinned the development of television and radio everywhere. Does advertising revenue secure the freedom of the media from state control, or tie them to commercial interests and therefore, it is argued, to unprincipled editorial and programming policies in order to gain the readerships and audiences which advertisers demand? In this latter position it is assumed that the search for markets will drive standards down; we consider some of the reasons for such an assumption in Chapter 4, though our concern there is more with the debates about the effects of advertising on the public. In that field we have on the one side the arguments that advertisements inform and entertain, and that consumers are not fundamentally vulnerable to manipulation by them, and on the other the contentions that advertisements are (perhaps by definition) instruments for the colonisation of the mind.

The extent to which advertisements may embody pretensions, and the fear and vanity to which they may speak, can sometimes seem very clear to us when we see advertisements from much earlier periods. Taken out of the context of shared preoccupations, we can see how contrived and specious their promises were. Such is the pace of social change that advertisements of even ten years ago can occasion this retrospective wisdom. They seem to have come from another world. Yet in a longer historical perspective, the variations in style we now see from one year or decade to another are developments within one type of public communication, and moreover one of recent emergence. Although obvious continuities exist between today's advertising and various types of publicity found in centuries past, advertising as the kind of social institution it is today emerged in the late nineteenth century, and arguably was not fully developed until the middle of the twentieth century. For it to be a dominant form of public communication, there have to be two major, linked conditions in place. Firstly there has to be a mass market in branded consumer goods (see e.g. Fraser, 1981), and secondly there have to be mass media in which space is available for advertising.

Both of these conditions began to develop in the late nineteenth century in the advanced capitalist countries. While some individual advertisements from earlier times may seem strikingly similar to recent ones, the impact of advertising as a whole in pre-modern and early modern times, both on individuals and on other social institutions, cannot be compared with its presence in contemporary culture. For one thing, advertising is an important cog in the economic engine, which is the focus for another set of arguments about its value. Top advertising agencies are multi-million dollar transnational corporations; in 1997 the top twenty-five agencies world-wide had a combined income of $17.4 billion. Does this money represent a gratuitous tax on the price of the goods and services it promotes, or a necessary investment in the stimulation of demand and the intensification of competition?

Large though their incomes are, these agencies account for only a small proportion of GDP in the countries concerned. But the social impact of advertising is arguably far greater than that of other industries of similar turnover. To understand its cultural influence we need to consider its relationship to the mass media, and to modern society's 'reflexive' development of knowledge about itself.

The origins of today's advertising agencies are to be found in the work of people who, in the nineteenth century, sold media space to advertisers. These were at first employees of the newspaper and magazine publishers, who later became independent and acted as intermediaries between the publishers and the advertisers, i.e. the manufacturers or other people with something to sell. The opportunity for this new specialism to emerge was given by the major growth in the possibilies for print advertising during the nineteenth century, as circulations of papers increased rapidly. This in turn was due partly to increased literacy, and to technological improvements in printing which made the reproduction of images possible and the whole thing cheaper.

The scope for advertising to grow as part of the general increase in printed communication was greatly increased by the abolition in the mid-nineteenth century of the government tax on advertisements, and in the 1890s by the newspaper publishers themselves coming to accept display advertisements covering several columns and with more varied content. This was part of the more populist, attractive style being adopted by some newspapers, and was a crucial step in the colonisation of everyday experience by commercial text and imagery.

This incursion into public space was by no means unimpeded, however. Simultaneous with the emergence of modern forms of advertising came pressures for its regulation and restraint, and the elaboration of another major tension in the history of advertising. As the historical texts describe, what would now be called pressure groups, with strong bases in the ruling elite, lobbied for controls on the advertising industry, on its freedom to place its products where it chose, especially in the countryside, and on its licence to make claims. While much of the agitation in the early decades of this century was aimed at the activities of patent medicine advertisers, from whom the modern advertising industry tried to differentiate itself (see Chapter 3), the pressures resulted in statutory frameworks being constructed within which all subsequent advertising had to develop. In its search for respectability the new industry had also embarked on self-regulation, culminating some time later in comprehensive codes of practice. Given this strong self-regulatory tendency, the tension between creative licence and societal restriction has not been a prominent one, though the case archives of the monitoring bodies are extensive and could reveal at which tension points advertisers have tended to infringe the codes. Also the contemporary case of tobacco advertising shows how persistent and ingenious advertising agencies can be in subverting some restrictive measures.

Tobacco advertising is, of course, a deeply controversial subject. While the main controversy is about the effectiveness of such advertising in causing smoking, there is another issue which tobacco advertising raises. On the one hand the restrictions upon it might be taken as an example of the fetters which government can and does place upon advertising (and which here have significantly limited the impact of advertising to expand markets), and thereby of the deeply controlled, socialised and reflexive nature of advertising. On the other, it might be argued that the ingenuity of the response (and the persistence of smoking) shows that the only really effective restraint, at least in this case, would be a total ban, and that the commercial imperatives at the heart of advertising cannot be reconciled with an agenda for collective well-being.

However, the overall significance of the high degree of regulation to which modern advertising has been subject is that the final products of the industry, the advertisements themselves, are the output of a complex and highly negotiated social process in which a series of very sensitive judgements are made about contemporary sensibilities. Even when, as in most cases, an individual advertisement will not have been directly subject to legal consultation or to the intervention of a regulatory code, it will bear the stamp of the whole set of social arrangements—statutes, codes, authorities, and above all the trained sensibilities of the advertising professionals—which has evolved in the process by which the proper limits of advertising have been negotiated. All advertisements which are actually used will be expressions of the overall discourse of compromise and resolution which has developed within the field of tensions around advertising's social presence. This is one reason why we think that they can be rich social documents, ephemeral but nuanced statements of the balance of social forces. Advertising is not an externality to the core realities of life, but is part of the social fabric, interwoven with and constrained by social values as an embedded and regulated component of everyday life. Insofar as our social values and individual identities are formed in the dynamics of market societies, between competition and promotion on the one hand and collectivity and regulation on the other, then the reflection of those social dynamics in the dynamics of advertising will be an important and revealing dimension of social life.

With the rapid growth in advertising activity around the turn of the century, the activities of the intermediaries increased. They began to offer a service to advertisers by giving information about the circulations of different publications, and about the social composition of their readerships. In other words they began offering early forms of audience research. (The subsequent development of audience research is beyond our scope in this book; see Abercrombie and Longhurst, 1998.) The intermediaries also started buying space in bulk, then selling it on. And most importantly, they developed copywriting and artwork skills. By 1900 some of these agencies were insisting on doing everything, and were clearly no longer just space brokers but were becoming recognisable as modern advertising agencies.

Nonetheless advertising is still in one sense basically the verbal and visual language of salesmanship which fills space reserved for it in the mass media. In this respect the central business of the advertising industry is the brokerage of media space. One might think that agencies are paid for their creative talents, but the major cost of advertising is the purchase of media space: comparatively, creative talent is cheap. While much academic attention is given to the content of advertisements, most in the business would acknowledge that the placement of advertisements, the number of times they are repeated, and the audiences they reach have as great, if not greater, impact than advertising aesthetics. An agency can produce a dramatic and powerfully persuasive advertisement, but if it is shown on the inside page of a newspaper with a small readership it is unlikely to realise its persuasive potential.

Here we come to an important aspect of the working relationships between advertising agencies and their clients, and within agencies. Agencies are sometimes frustrated that their creations are short-changed by clients who refuse to purchase what the agency believes to be the required amount for maximum impact. While the agency can lay out logical criteria as to why so much space is required, clients are well aware that it is in the agency's interest to sell as much space as possible (historically agency fees have been set as a percentage of the media space costs). Thus, in this way and many others, the client can be seen as a source of deep insecurity for the industry, for the client stands in a powerful position of judgement while also being able to influence the making of that which is judged.

However, the dependency is reciprocal. While clients may disagree with the directives of a given agency, corporations have come overall to rely on the industry. Local businesses, government, or indeed almost anyone who has the money could feasibly purchase space in the media, yet often advertising agencies are called upon to broker media space. There is also nothing preventing corporations from producing their own advertising in-house, but the majority do not. Fowles claims that early on advertisers came to feel that out-of-house production resulted in better advertising copy at lower cost (Fowles, 1996). Corporate clients tend to view advertising agencies as possessing expert advice on how to understand and speak to the consumer.

The efficacy of this expertise cannot be definitively assessed. It is simply very difficult to assess advertising's commercial impact: the effect of promotion on the general public's buying behaviour and attitudes is extraordinarily difficult to measure. So what agencies sell is media space, marketing advice, creative talent, and faith.

Lury and Warde (1997) argue that advertising sells not because it effectively influences consumer behaviour, but because it offers a palliative to advertisers' anxieties about the consumer. The stronger legitimation of advertising in the post-World War II period is linked to the enhanced emphasis placed upon market-led strategies. As Wernick

(1991) has argued, finding a market for a good increasingly precedes production. Bauman (1992) notes that the postmodern marketplace is not just involved in producing goods, but in producing consumers. With these changes in orientation, producers believe they require more specialised information about the consumer. The advertising industry's legitimation as a resource of specialist knowledge about the consumer thus places it in an important position within contemporary market dynamics.

According to Lury and Warde the consumer is basically an unknowable entity. This, however, serves to strengthen the advertising agencies' position, for they are able to present themselves as in a privileged position to foretell the minds and behaviours of consumers without undergoing a definitive test. The situation is somewhat unstable, however. The elusiveness of the consumer, and competition between agencies, sets the industry on a continual search for 'new' modes of research to confirm their knowledge of the consumer, or to seize competitive advantage.

DIFFERENCES AND DILEMMAS IN ADVERTISING RESEARCH

Having budded off from publishing, advertising had itself given birth to the market research industry, and has remained very closely associated with it. Market research refers to a wide range of activities—demographic and socio-economic research into markets for particular products, psychological studies of consumers' preferences and responses to particular goods, etc. Market research uses a wide range of methods—desk research, large-scale surveys (in relation to which we can note that political opinion polling is an application to politics of methods developed for commercial purposes), campaign recall and impact studies, intensive individual interviews and small group research (the 'focus' group) being amongst the main ones. Market research influences and is influenced by varying understandings of the human condition, as well as marketing and business philosophies.

Some of the first research was undertaken in the U.S. by the advertising agency JWT, which began in 1916 to commission social and demographic research. Seeking respected and effective research approaches, agencies turned to university specialists. In 1919, JWT hired the behaviourist psychologist John B. Watson as a consumer researcher. George Gallup, founder of the opinion polling agency, was an academic whose entry into applied research was at the invitation of the Young and Rubicam advertising agency to set up their research department. The first UK market research companies were set up in the 1920s and 1930s and had their origins in advertising agencies. At this time it was not uncommon for agencies to have their own research departments; however, just as the agencies had separated out from the publishers to serve the advertisers directly, so too have market researchers separated out from the agencies, who today typically commission research out-of-house. Research companies are also contracted directly by advertisers themselves, for advertising research as well as for the other kinds of research (such as new product development and brand tracking) which the market research industry has developed.

Lury and Warde usefully point to the role which advertising plays for the client, on the basis either of research-generated knowledge of the consumer, or of an assertion of the agency's intuitive understandings and creative capacity for apposite communication. This perspective offers a unique explanation of why clients are attracted to advertising and why the industry is often preoccupied with research methodology. Further, the argument rightly problematises research by pointing to the opacity of its object of study. The problem we find with this argument, however, is that in placing emphasis solely on the relationship between client and agency, it neutralises advertising as a form of social communication. Regardless of how advertising is construed in the relationship between clients and agencies, it remains a prominent form of public discourse. Further, the argument implies that all research is consistently invalid. Is the consumer really completely unknowable? One can agree that research is never complete, without conceding that it is wholly without substance.

The nature of research and its status in advertising is subject to some variation internationally. The British advertising industry has interacted significantly with that in the U.S., which has long dominated the international market. The UK advertising industry still uses the American industry as a point of comparison, sometimes to highlight what are considered problems with the UK product, and at other times to celebrate British inventiveness. Significant American ownership within the UK industry is not uncommon, although as Nixon (1997) points out, the strength of UK ownership has grown since the 1980s with the rise of such agencies as Saatchi and Saatchi. Further, some of the most prominent figures within the industry such as David Ogilvy have been British, and despite American ownership, British creative products are not imitations of American ones. Indeed, Lury (1996) claims that UK advertising has an international reputation for being the best in the world.

British advertising is also credited with having introduced in the 1960s an important development in the division of labour within the industry: the account planner. This new professional role was concerned with mediating the relationship between consumer research and the creative department. The account planner speaks to and for the consumer, bringing their insights to bear more directly on advertising design. This creates more space in the process of producing ads for how consumers felt and the meanings they created, as well as the older emphasis on what they did. The account planner listens intently to consumers, combing through their discourse:

> Listening and listening. Not just to what they say, but to what they mean. Listening for the expressions of need, of dissatisfaction, uncovering attitudes or behaviour patterns. (Leiss *et al.*, 1990)

However, as we have indicated, not all research is aimed at exploring the depths of the consumer's soul. Research paradigms and conceptions of the consumer have gone through several changes, or as Fox (1984, see Chapter 3) would have it, there have been a number of oscillations between two basic paradigms.

In the early development of market research, quantitative methods became predominant, as the popularity of behaviourism in psychology and the general influence of positivism in the social sciences justified quantification as the preferred mode to achieve 'objectivity'. Understandings of the human condition were influenced by classical economics—consumers were viewed as largely rational agents deliberately out to maximise their individual gains (Leiss *et al.*, 1990). In keeping with the notion of a rational subject, one of the dominant axioms to emerge at this time was Lasker's philosophy that promotion should provide people with a 'reason why' they should take interest in a product. This 'reason why' approach contrasted with the earlier emphasis placed on promotional 'appeal'. Drawing on conceptions of hypnosis, Scott had argued in 1913, in *The Psychology of Advertising*, that the consumer was not only a creature of 'reason', but also of 'persuasion', and that it was more important for advertising to be interesting and suggestive, rather than rationally purposive.

Research on advertisements is only one of a number of types of work done by market research companies, but the advertising industry has continued to have a close and influential relationship with research. The two have been seen as being in devilish alliance together against the innocent consumer, especially in that period of great paranoia, the 1950s. One major focus of this alarm was the use of 'motivation research' techniques.

The vogue of 'motivation research' (MR) in the 1940s and 1950s tipped the emphasis back towards the 'non-rational', and as Fox notes, placed greater emphasis on qualitative procedures:

> Motivation research replaced the older statistical techniques of polling and counting with esoteric methods borrowed from the social sciences, especially depth psychology and psychoanalysis. Instead of treating consumers as rational beings who knew what they wanted and why they wanted it, MR delved into subconscious, non-rational levels of motivation to suggest— beforehand—where ads should be aimed...depth interviews, projective techniques, word-association and sentence-completion games, and thematic apperception tests. (Fox, 1984)

'Motivation research' understood consumers as governed by irrationality and insecurity and moved by eroticism. Gender may also have influenced the shift to a more 'non-rational' model. Earlier quantitative studies had revealed women made the majority of purchases. The switch from 'reason why' to 'suggestion' and 'aestheticisation' was for the benefit of feminine consumers who were viewed by the advertising men as largely irrational, hence unresponsive to rational promotional tactics (Leiss *et al.*, 1990).

The leading practitioner of MR was the Austrian-trained psychologist Ernst Dichter, whose Institute for Motivational Research in New York carried out thousands of commercial research studies from the 1940s to the 1960s. His *Handbook of Consumer Motivations* is a racy compendium of interpretations of the meanings of hundreds of commodities. Some draw loosely on psychoanalysis, some are common-sensical. His understanding of why people behave as they do in relation to goods is close, at one level, to that of many of the academic critics of advertising (see Chapter 4): '[the consumer's] customs, motivations, desires and hopes are often not too far removed from the rituals and fetishes of the New Guineans. He buys his fetishes in the department store, and the New Guineans carve theirs out of the skulls of their enemies' (Dichter, 1964).

In mid-century Europe, psychoanalysis was a considerable influence within psychology, so although he was not himself an analyst (and would have scandalised the psychoanalytic community if he had been) Dichter's concerns were often with the unconscious and specifically sexual meanings of things. Asked to look at the problems of marketing ladies' gloves, he would first of all explore the general meanings of clothes. He would note the ambiguity of clothes as things which we wear both to conceal and to show off the body. He would then look at the ways in which gloves were used, the kinds of experiences which they involved, especially in the taking off of the glove to shake hands. He suggested that this disrobing evoked images of other garments being removed, and allowed a somewhat ostentatious moment of skin contact. He argued that such knowledge of how people experienced everyday things at deeper levels was essential to an effective marketing and advertising strategy. Glove marketing should play subtly on this sexual element, he concluded, though not too strongly in case anxiety about sexual display is evoked.

Most psychoanalysts would see Dichter's work as having little connection with psychoanalysis proper. It is unsystematic, selective and not at all sophisticated. In his often muddled writings, fragmentary psychoanalytic formulations are mixed up with much common-sense psychology, in which a vaguely-defined 'emotional security' often figures. Dichter saw himself as much an anthropologist as anything else, and one can certainly see the similarity as well as the differences between his work and that of academic anthropologists writing about consumption (e.g. Douglas, *The World of Goods*, 1979).

The same blend of anthropology, psychoanalysis and other kinds of psychology is to be found in the more sober and intellectually ordered work of Pierre Martineau, whose *Motivation in Advertising* (1957) was another text of motivation research. 'Advertising essentially is dealing with a primitive, pre-logical process of the mind—with the compulsion to action initiated by suggestion, by a long list of conscious and unconscious motive forces.' Despite statements of this sort, however, Martineau's book has much less of the ethnographic and interpretive flair that Dichter (albeit inconsistently) offered. He tends more towards a rationalistic social-psychological method, for example in his attempt to classify car owners by a personality typology derived from everyday observations rather than psychoanalytic categories.

Martineau did however stay firmly with the idea of the consumer as irrationally driven. In contrast, the gradual supplanting of a strongly psychoanalytic approach to market research by a model of the consumer as basically rational is closely traced by Miller and Rose (1997) in a detailed study of the work of the Tavistock Institute of Human Relations (TIHR) in London between 1950 and 1970. As they point out, the TIHR was only one organisation, and not a typical one, but through its close link with the Tavistock Clinic, which is one of the major centres for psychoanalytically-based work in the UK, it pioneered the application of psychoanalytic ideas in market research in the 1950s. For one example see the research undertaken by Menzies Lyth on ice-cream, reported in her *The Dynamics of the Social* (1989), one of many such studies detailed in the archival research by Miller and Rose. Avoiding a simple choice between marketing as manipulation and the consumer as autonomous agent, they observe how market research fed into advertising strategies and so helped to 'mobilise the consumer' in a variety of different ways in different contexts. Thus in the TIHR the Kleinian psychoanalytic approach of Menzies Lyth, e.g. in exploring the associative links between ice-cream, milk and the breast, eventually gave way to more quantitative studies based on a model of rational choice, e.g. in the construction of flavour profiles for beer and biscuits.

However, the notion that motivation research was powerfully and sinisterly dominant in market research, though never true, remained current long after the high point of its influence, due largely to the impact of Vance Packard's *The Hidden Persuaders*, published in 1957, and other writing on the uses of depth psychology in marketing (see Chapter 4). Some writers were more sceptical (e.g. Brown, *Techniques of Persuasion*, 1963; and Fox, who suggested that Packard's vision said more about American paranoia than about the advertising industry). But the brief publicity given to techniques of subliminal communication in the 1950s added to the inaccurate picture of advertising as a major apparatus for the use of psychology in social control.

After the 'heyday' of motivation research techniques in the 1940s and 1950s, the behaviourist, quantitative paradigm was widely reasserting itself, e.g. in the form of numeric data gathered weekly (now daily and hourly) to track television audiences. This quantitative turn was in keeping with turns to quantification and 'objectivist' approaches such as behaviourism in psychology and the social sciences generally at this time, and with the waning of psychodynamic influence, and was also stimulated by the early development of computing technologies. Moreover, more rationalistic approaches continued to be discovered afresh. For Rosser Reeves (1961), advertising effectiveness had less to do with 'liking', and much more to do with 'remembrance' and 'product purchase'. In the debate over whether advertising should be governed by scientific or artistic principles Reeves sided with science, and in his *Reality in Advertising* likens promotion to 'engineering' (Fox, 1984). In the increasingly competitive and promotion-saturated environments of the 1960s and 1970s, Reeves' idea of the 'unique selling position' (USP) made a lasting impression in marketing and advertising circles. USP drew attention to a singular claim or concept conveyed through a simple and clear message. 'The besieged consumer could only retain one strong claim or concept from a given ad; any elaboration simply cluttered the advertisement to no effect' (Fox, 1984). Symbolic clutter, though perhaps seductive, distracted readers or viewers from the product, and risked creating 'vampire ads', where the symbolic content sucks the blood out of the product. People remember the message, but fail to make the link to the product (Fowles, 1996). The consumer was not irrational, so much as plagued with information overload.

From the late 1970s, market research became more omnivorous in its academic interests, and began reaching beyond psychology and sociology to give linguists, anthropologists and cultural studies experts more of an ear (see Lury and Warde, 1997). Advertisers drew upon linguistics for 'semiotic analysis', which insisted upon the arbitrary nature of signification (see Chapter 4). As people who had lived by creative associations between products and words, advertisers were probably already quite familiar with this idea, though this intensive focus on language complicated a traditional sender/receiver model of communication, as it stressed that there was not necessarily a direct relationship between the intended message and how it was decoded by readers. Thus, instead of imposing their understanding of products on consumers, some researchers elicited from individuals the chains of associations they made to goods. These were gathered through qualitative research methods, synthesised, then incorporated into advertising campaigns (Leiss et al., 1990). From anthropology there now came an intensified influence from ethnographic studies, taking researchers out of the lab and directly into the consumer's home. In some recent developments this has extended to placing cameras in homes to record the minutiae of everyday life.

But perhaps the most powerful impact on market research in the 1980s came from more sociologically-oriented work on patterns of consumption. To identify and target consumption 'tribes' and to develop typologies of 'lifestyles', individuals were sized up on a comprehensive battery of variables. The old demographic and behaviour variables remained but were supplemented by regional and lifestage data, media and leisure usage and preferences, as well as a host of other more subjective variables such as personality traits, beliefs, attitudes and feelings. Faith in the predictive power of demographic variables had weakened as it was increasingly found that people could share similar demographic characteristics, yet display divergent tastes. Subjective variables and niche marketing simultaneously grew in importance (Leiss et al., 1990).

In the 1990s market research embodies a convergence of academic disciplines and methodologies. The old dichotomies of qualitative/quantitative and rational/irrational, and power struggles between creatives and researchers remain, but old 'purist' conceptions have been eclipsed by growing attempts to unite what was once passionately held apart. No phase now supplants the foregoing ones, but rather each complements the others, adding variations and new operations to the existing repertoire (Leiss *et al.*, 1990). 'Triangulation' between qualitative and quantitative methods has become common, and emotional and rational appeals linked (Leiss *et al.*, 1990). A recent commentator captured the eclectic spirit of the times in arguing that given the dynamic fluidity of the consumer environment, advertisers should stop looking for 'general theories' and undertake 'tailored research which looks at the marketing problem at this point in time' (Broadbent, 1997). Thus since the 1980s, though a full-blooded MR approach would be hard to find, psychodynamically-oriented techniques are well established in an expanded and differentiated research industry accommodating a diversity of approaches. That some draw on the semiotic work at the heart of academia's critique of advertising could be cited as another tension in advertising, between its (mainly practitioner) advocates and its academic critics, the latter sometimes fascinated by its apparent power and unable, it seems, to generate a critical language which cannot be absorbed back into the form itself.

Yet despite the dominant eclecticism, the old debates continue; the basic value of research is questioned, and the merits of one main approach or another are challenged. For example, a recent contributor to the Institute of Practitioners in Advertising *Marketing Appraisals* argues that despite the growing 'sophistication of advertising research techniques, research has not made advertising any more credible or easier to understand' (Hedge, 1998). He argues that there is a dangerous trend in British consumer research towards using simple numbers to validate advertising and to reassure management. Hedge argues that this quantitative trend creates a conservative bias which dampens innovation. Fowles concurs that scientific data can be problematic:

> The nuances, styles, and fluctuating symbolic codes of successful communication cannot be prescribed or even implied by data collections... The ideal balance occurs when the data are allowed to suggest an armature onto which an imaginative appeal—the creative, so called—is then fashioned. (Fowles, 1996)

In a more radically questioning mode, another commentator suggests that marketing has reached a 'third phase' within which it is 'business as "unusual"'. Cronk (1995) argues that advertisers had it easy in the first stage of marketing's history when goods basically sold themselves; promotion simply had to let the public know about products. In the second phase, with the growing sophistication of consumers' wants, advertisers had to find out what people wanted, make it, then sell it to them in the most appealing way. However, within the third period of market saturation, consumers 'don't necessarily know what they want' so 'companies will have to take the initiative and be inspirational in the context of the consumer understanding they already have.' Consumer research is still relevant, but only as 'one of many springboards for ideas'. The unknowability of the consumer extends here to the consumers themselves.

CONCLUSION

This sketch of aspects of the advertising industry's origins and development hopefully conveys that advertising is an integral part of a complex of activities which are widely regarded as being at the core of late modern cultures. The notion that we live in a 'mediatised' culture and an 'information' society rightly foregrounds the role of the mass media and of knowledge-based industries in defining our social world, and both exist in an interdependent relationship with advertising. As Nava (1997) has stressed, advertisements do not constitute a unique cultural form or a distinctive discourse (*pace* the structuralist commentators on advertising, discussed in Chapter 4). They are institutionally and semantically embedded in popular culture as a whole, and practically interlocked with a proliferating range of professional activities. So the space of advertising is not a strongly boundaried one. Yet it incorporates a distinctive mix of historical tensions.

We have focused here on conflicts and tensions around consumer research, including its place in relation to the advertising industry, debates about its efficacy and about the merits of quantitative and qualitative work. As communications researchers we are obviously predisposed to take the side of the advocates of research against its detractors in the industry, but there is a diversity of available approaches and not all will be equally useful. We have given particular attention to the place of psychodynamically-influenced research, since that is a major element in our own orientation. Arguably, the limited influence enjoyed by this approach can be attributed to the fact that it has never been applied in a rigorous way in commercial research. Later in the book we attempt to apply it to the content of advertisements, i.e. as a basis for communications research rather than as an approach to consumer research which, as we have described, has been its predominant use to date.

Chapter 3

THE HISTORY OF ADVERTISEMENTS

Our focal concern in this book is not with the advertising industry, but with its products and with the development of new techniques for analysing message content. In this chapter we describe other research which has, like ours, been concerned with the history of advertisements themselves, though the first two works we discuss—those of Fox and Jackson Lears—have framed their analysis of advertisement content with an analysis of the industry.

Stephen Fox (1984) offers a 'group biography' of the people who have worked in American advertising. Detailed attention is given to the careers of key industry individuals, agencies, research techniques, and consumer movements. It is therefore basically a study of the industry, but we describe it in this chapter as it presents different phases in the history of the industry as marked by differences in the nature of advertisements. In chronological order we are taken through a narrative from advertising's 'pre-history', around 1870, to the 1970s. However, the latest edition includes an introduction outlining the significant mergers of the 1980s which have seen the British agencies with their soft sell strategies and humorous copy breaking America's traditional hold on the industry.

According to Fox the industry oscillates between two orientations. One emphasises quantitative research, the hard sell, 'reason why' copy, and the product. The other emphasises qualitative or no research at all, a soft sell, image-based copy, and the advertisement over the product. While the industry has seen its highs and lows, its basic dynamics, in the tension between these two orientations, have not changed very much during the twentieth century. The industry is prone to historical forgetfulness and tends to label as innovations what are, in fact, recycled techniques.

> By its nature concerned with the present and future tenses, advertising has no historical memory. Cycles in art and copy styles reappear with new names to be greeted as innovations. Among observers of the American scene, discussions of advertising in our national life always lack a historical dimension. (Fox, 1984)

By the turn of the century the emergent skills of the advertising agency were beginning to influence marketing. Much more attention was being given to the 'look' of the ads, and to facilitate this emphasis artists and designers joined copywriters. The account executive was brought in to mediate between the client and the creative. During this period, jingles, humour and 'reason why' copy predominated.

> True 'reason why' copy is logic, plus persuasion, plus conviction, all woven into a certain simplicity of thought—predigested for the average mind, so that it is easier to understand than to misunderstand. (Fox, 1984)

The American industry began to mature in the 1920s, when postwar growth created new spaces for consumerism and more sophisticated soft sell approaches were developed. New goods and services, a new emphasis on marketing promotion, and less public disdain put advertising in a position of what Fox refers to as 'high tide and green grass' (1984). More artful construction competed with 'reason why'. This 'golden era' was cut short during the depression, when there was a swing back to hard sell and scientific legitimisation. In the 1930s new psychological research methods promoted by, amongst others, the leading behaviourist psychologist John B. Watson (who moved from academia to JWT), promised to put advertising on a more scientific footing. In the 1950s, a second period of post-war growth led to a second surge of more adventurous creative innovation.

> During the fifteen years after the end of the Second World War, American advertising parlayed an expansive cluster of circumstances—cars, highways, new patterns of suburban consumption, and the explosion of the ultimate advertisement medium—into its greatest prosperity since the 1920s. (Fox, 1984)

Motivational research (see Chapter 2) 'replaced the older statistical techniques of polling and counting with esoteric methods borrowed from the social sciences, especially depth psychology and psycho-analysis' (Fox, 1984). The 1960s brought what is referred to as the 'creative revolution' when Burnett, Ogilvy, and Bernbach invigorated the industry with their unique perspectives.

> From Burnett came a tradition of gentle manners, humour, credibility, and a disdain for research. From Ogilvy, a civilised intelligence, a classiness that spoke up instead of down to the audience and the visual style of Hathaway, Schweppes and Rolls-Royce. From Bernbach, a creative union of art and copy, candour, the reduction of the account executive, and a looser management style. (Fox, 1984)

By the late 1960s, however, in the face of increased consumer resistance movements and recessionary problems, the industry abandoned its creative phase and went back to the hard sell of 'reason why' copy. But by the 1980s, it faced the problem of increased clutter due to the proliferation of print media, and to developments in television: more use of shorter (fifteen second) spots, and an audience which, equipped with video and remote controls, had a greater ability to ignore advertisements. The success of the British agencies at this time, according to Fox, was based on the power of their artful and humorous copy to stand out amidst the clutter and hold the attention of the reader/ viewer.

Fox argues that social trends lead advertising, not the other way around. Advertising responds to economic and social change, and to technological developments in media, and so moves back and forth between its two basic alternatives in search of difference and impact. It is, moroever, in its value content essentially a mirror of society, and what upsets its critics is the reflection it provides of the more base forms of human behaviour such as greed and materialism.

> The people who have created modern advertising are not hidden persuaders pushing our buttons in the service of some malevolent purpose. They are just producing an especially visible manifestation, good and bad, of the American way of life. (Fox, 1984)

Advertising is 'an exquisitely sensitive barometer' of changes in the larger context of American society (Fox, 1984). However, Fox is less clear on how the oscillations of copy style are a 'mirror' of wider social dynamics, and on the relationships between these oscillations and 'external' events, than he is in his richly-documented account of the internal dynamic of the industry, by which audience saturation with one strategy apparently leads, every decade or so, to a shift to the other.

In an elegant study of the development of the advertising industry in the U.S. in the late nineteenth and early to mid-twentieth centuries, the cultural historian Jackson Lears (1994) argues against the widely-held belief that advertising facilitated the emergence of a more hedonistic culture. He suggests instead that it served to modernise Protestant disciplines. The rise of Protestantism brought a new sense of order and reason to market relations, which would inform and legitimate advertising practices. Lears points to the need of the first modern, professional advertisers to distance themselves from the deceptions of the patent medicine advertisements and other aspects of modern advertising's prehistory. These included the 'barkers' of the open-air fairs and carnivals who heckled passers-by to draw attention to the goods on sale on their tables, and the 'hustlers' of late eighteenth-century America who traversed the country in wagons selling primarily elixirs for health. These peddler-promoters invoked around their goods a discourse of traditional symbols and stories, an earthy and chaotic pre-modern domain of magical powers and enchantments.

The influence of the 'reason why' paradigm and its rationalistic approach to persuasion reflected the desire of the new professional advertising to break with this past. Science became the tool used by the industry to proclaim superiority over traditional practices, and magic lost its classical legitimacy. The old voice of the hustler was demonised and driven out of the business. Promotional tactics which had once been considered quite legitimate salesmanship were seen as 'swindles', as advertising took on the 'plain speech' of 'good', 'honest' business practices. Lears views the rationalisation of symbolic practices through the advertising industry with some suspicion, and celebrates the persistent cracks within the system which he believes continually thwart the industry's quest for total order. The old magical powers continue to bubble up through the contemporary advertising industry.

He finds an emphasis in much rationalised modern advertising on the creation of an 'efficient' individual and on a *performative* ideal of selfhood, according to which the consumer was instructed to reach certain standards in body and mind. Lears' thinking is quite strongly coloured by the work of the French historian Michel Foucault and his preoccupation with regulatory power, i.e. with the spread of controlling forms of regulation in modern society, especially through the development of the human sciences and their applications. In this spirit he suggests that a 'managerial' philosophy was at work in the development of advertising, i.e. a concern with regulation, rationalisation, and efficiency. He sees the history of advertisements primarily in terms of the tension between this (ultimately dominant) tendency towards discipline, rationality and objectives, and a pull in the opposite direction towards the carnivalesque—the unbridled play of fantasy, the preposterous claim, the domain of excess and flow. In the 1930s, there was on the one side the fusion of advertising with politics on the social-scientific terrain of 'public opinion', while at the same time the establishment of mass radio was a stimulus to the resurgence of the excessive claims of the pre-professional era and of colourful 'barking'.

As in Fox's account, there is here a notion that the development of advertising is driven by a tension and oscillation between two powerful strategic paradigms, one allied to rationalisation and the other to a complex of countervailing forces. In Lears' account the tension is given more cultural and historical depth, though his argument suffers from an arguably romantic vision of pre-modern discourse, and from the characteristic weakness of Foucauldian history: a lack of systematic evidence. Although Lears uses a number of powerful illustrations, he rightly eschews the use of individual examples as the basis of his argument—but he has no evidence of the more substantial kind which a scrutiny of a large number of advertisements might have yielded. However, the richness of the cultural history in which he locates advertising, and of the key conceptual distinction he makes, suffice to make his an important and suggestive study of the dynamics of advertising, which links major trends in the content of advertisements with the industry's struggle for legitimacy.

The notion of a tension between major social forces expressed in advertisement content is similar to our own, and we also try to understand the history of advertisements (though in a later period than Lears studied) in terms of an oscillating balance between those forces. Further, Lears' conception of the forces involved (the managerial/professional and the carnivalesque) is in some ways similar to the notions of containing and contained forces developed here in Chapter 6. There are important differences, however. In describing the structuring tendencies as 'managerial', Lears is implicitly posing them as oppressive and limiting, and is locating the forces of structure and order in a quite specific social milieu rather than seeing them as distributed across the social landscape.

Lears takes one cultural tension, albeit a profound one, and constructs an account of advertising around it. In the biggest and most important study of advertising to date, Leiss, Kline and Jhally (1990) construct an account of advertising around a large empirical study of advertisements, and relate their data to a number of cultural tensions and social issues. Their sample was taken from advertisements appearing between 1910 and 1980 in two Canadian popular magazines—one predominantly for men, one for women. The media and the product categories were selected because of their relative stability over time (in type of readership and frequency of advertisement respectively), so that any changes observed in advertisement content over time would be most likely to be due to shifts in the discourse of advertisements and not to different parts of that discourse coming into focus.

They begin with the notion of 'elemental codes', those simple types of content to which all advertisements can be reduced. The advertisement message must be about a product, but may also be about people and/or about setting(s), physical and/or social. Depending on the combination of product, person and setting codes, a number of different 'formats' or message structures are possible. They identify four such formats:

i)   product information, where only the product code is used;

ii) product image, where product and setting codes are used (with the aim of transferring values or meanings from the setting to the product, in the manner much discussed by semioticians in critical writing on advertising—see Chapter 4);

iii) personalised, where product and person codes are combined so that the product shares the qualities of a person or group of people, or is seen to have a powerful influence upon a person; and

iv) lifestyle, where all three codes are in use, with the person or setting codes pre-eminent.

These communicative formats correspond roughly to historical periods, characterised by the dominance of different approaches to advertising, which they describe in the following terms:

i)   product-oriented approach, 1890–1925: rationalistic advertising to the fore, with the written text at the heart of strategies;

ii) product-symbols approach, 1925–1945: more emphasis on non-rational choice, on the characteristics of the consumer and the social contexts of consumption. Advertising is more professional and research-oriented (as Lears points out), and makes use of the communicative possibilities given by radio, cinema and colour photography;

iii) personalisation, 1945–1965: a strengthened focus on the consumer's psyche, understood as accessible to research and manipulatable through the new medium of television; and

iv) market segmentation, 1965–present: the knowledge-base for advertising is now given by psychographics and demographics, i.e. by knowledge about lifestyles, subcultures and segmentation.

Finally, these four formats/phases are linked to their most fundamental typology, of 'cultural frames' for goods or, more precisely, for our relationship to goods. There are four frames, each conveyed by a different format. Leiss *et al.* argue that in a consumer society it is primarily advertising and other marketing communications which mediate our relationships with material objects, and therefore play an important role in the generation and reproduction of culture, since material goods are important carriers of cultural meanings. A cultural frame for goods sets broad parameters for the experience of goods, and defines a basic orientation towards them. The frames they describe are:

i)   idolatry, characterised by the veneration of goods—the early
     modern, rationalistic approach to goods, through which the
     individual might develop some practical expertise as a consumer
     but receives no symbolic or cultural preparation for the consumer
     society;

ii) iconology, in which the utilitarian aspects of goods are subordinated
     to symbolic qualities and values. Persons are involved here but not in
     a full-blooded 'personalised' way; they represent social values rather
     than the fact of their individual personhood;

iii) narcissism, when the individual person is the focus of attention and is
     not abstractly presented as in iconology. Emotion, interpersonal
     dynamics and (allegedly) ordinary human experience are the
     mainstays of this frame; and

iv) totemism, when a good stands for membership of a particular social
     group through association with a particular lifestyle.

This is the most comprehensive framework so far developed for
understanding the social meanings of advertising, and our own research
can be seen as building upon it. However, as we will discuss in Chapter
6, our attempt to develop an approach to advertisement content which
takes full account of its psychological dimensions, in a way that Leiss
et al. did not, led to the production of some data which significantly
modifies the historical scheme they propose for the later decades of the
twentieth century.

Though by far the largest empirical study of advertisements, Leiss
et al.'s research is not alone in having engaged in the systematic sampling
and coding of advertisements as a way of investigating their cultural
meanings. Jhally undertook a separate study of 1,000 U.S. television
advertisements in 1980–1981 (Jhally, 1987), using coding procedures
based on those developed by Leiss *et al.* for the magazine study. He
compared advertisements on prime-time TV with those on sports-time
TV. The former were predominantly for products aimed at a female
market (food, household, personal care), the latter for male-oriented
products (cars, alcohol, personal care). He found a number of differences
between the two groups of advertisements, some predictable and others
less so. The prime-time advertisements featured the 'ordinary' (i.e. not
famous) person more frequently than the sports-time. Romantic love
predominated over friendship on prime-time, the reverse on sports-time.
These and other differences enabled Jhally to find support for his
theoretical position (see Chapter 4) which stresses the trend towards
audience segmentation. His data also showed differences in the kind of

relationship to the product portrayed in the two groups of advertisements, with the sports-time advertisements making more use of the idea that the product can mediate relations with others (e.g. by being an occasion for or enhancement of a social scene) and the prime-time advertisements giving prominence to the direct impact of the product on the consumer. Jhally links the latter kind of difference to the concept of fetishism which is central to his approach, and which is also discussed extensively in Leiss *et al.* We discuss this concept in the next chapter, but an empirical observation related to it can be noted here. Jhally found that more 'magical' powers were attributed to the commodity in the 'female' advertising of prime-time television (e.g. the message that in some mysterious way the commodity could transform the consumer), and links this with the longitudinal finding of Leiss *et al.*'s magazine study that these attributions have increased fairly steadily since the 1920s. More 'rational' claims (e.g. that the commodity can fulfil a particular function, independently of any effect on the consumer's feelings or self) tended to be associated more with 'male' sports-time ads, and these were found in the magazine study to have been in overall decline.

In another major study of advertising content, Marchand (1985) immersed himself in 18,000 American advertisements from the 1920s and 1930s, as well as poring over industry records and contemporary marketing discourse. He sought to dispel some commonly held assumptions about advertising. He argued that promotional materials can, and should, be viewed as important historical documents, noting that 'ads actually surpass most other recorded communications as a basis for plausible inference about popular attitudes and values'. Advertising's power, he suggested, stems from its ability to resolve tensions, or bridge inconsistencies, and to remain flexible and eclectic. He also contested the view that advertising is a 'mirror' neutrally reflecting society, by showing how tensions within the industry, assumptions about the audience, and the class position, gender, and identity politics of advertising professionals shape the content of advertisements. Indeed, advertisers believed that if they did hold up a social 'mirror', their work would not be popular, since people did not want to see the reality in advertisements but life as it 'ought to be'.

Marchand charts the social distance between creatives and the 'common folk' whom they sought to address. Advertisers were predominantly male, white, urban dwellers, schooled in elite institutions and possessing the cultural tastes of the upper middle class. They saw their predominantly female audience as having low literacy levels and minds 'averse to effort', being prone to irrationality, and possessing bad taste, relishing as they did the melodramatic tales of *True Story* and the sensationalism of the *Daily News* tabloid. They were thought to value illusion and escape, and to be 'driven by inarticulate longings'. But advertisers were caught in a double bind. They had to create messages which spoke to the presumed characteristics of the audience, while they also had to defend their work before their peers, and before a national cultural elite. For the advertiser, therefore, the consumer was jointly 'the voice of god and a fool.' Marchand finds evidence for this dissonance in his sample. Repetitive use of emotional appeals, short personalised copy, and an emphasis on 'romance, glamour, and color' mingle with sophisticated urban environments, and depictions of upper middle class taste, and leisure pursuits. When the tactics of allurement threatened the advertiser's cultural standing, he justified his position by noting that he was simply reflecting the whimsical tendencies of his female readers. When his heavy use of elite symbolism brought the charge that he was 'out of touch' with the 'common folk', the advertiser argued that he was providing a redemptive 'civilising influence' for the masses.

Marchand breaks the 'living language' of advertising into what he takes to be its constituent aspects: social tableau, parable, visual cliché, and icon. As social tableaux, advertisements depict persons 'in such a way as to suggest their relationship to each other or to a larger social structure'. Advertising's tableaux formed 'living pictures' which offered instruction on social behaviour and guidance in identity patterning. Despite the distance advertisers felt from their female readers, they presented them in diverse roles. Women were variously presented as business associates, the executive managers of consumption, leisure seekers actively enjoying their modern free time, creatures of self-expression, and all-round super-women. Men were the steady foil next to the numerous incarnations of womanhood—generic and standardised models, filling the role of either businessmen or husbands. The characters in the tableaux displayed an openness to change, a required sentiment for the socially mobile. Advertising became the 'slang' through which one stayed up-to-date. The upper class were presented as particularly at ease with the increased tempo of modern life and in possession of the 'instinctive taste' which marked them as the 'best sorts of people'. Despite the drastic decline of domestic retinue during the period, servants were uniformly presented as happily accepting their subordinate position as the handmaidens of modernity, catering to the sophisticated characters within the tableaux.

The use of parable drew attention away from the advertiser as seller, for homilies anonymise authorship and are generally associated with the realm of folk wisdom. Parable enabled advertisers to impart, and audiences to receive, 'practical moral lessons from incidents of everyday life'. The parable of the 'first impression' educated readers on the need to open themselves up to judgement in a modern world which promised 'new roles and new opportunities'. The parable of the 'democracy of goods' let people know that the wonders of 'mass production and distribution enabled every person to enjoy society's most insignificant pleasure, convenience or beauty'. Although freedom might be receding in the realms of politics and production, the modern marketplace offered new and abundant freedom. The parable of 'civilisation redeemed' depicted products working with nature to enhance beauty and health. The cumulative effect of parables was to educate consumers into the modernity epitomised by the advertising agent. They served as 'guideposts to modern "logical living"'.

Visual clichés and icons allowed message designers to say what words could not, or what in written form would sound absurd. The visual cliché of the 'office window', for example, empowered the reader by providing a sense of control over the modern landscape and its social processes, while 'the family circle' remade the intimacy of the traditional family within a modern environment. Icons enabled religious connotations to be imparted in secular contexts. The use of 'heroic proportions', which exaggerated the size of forms, turned the everyday into the extraordinary. The 'adoring throngs' revelling ecstatically around the product, the evocation of a mystique of being 'in the presence' of the product, the use of 'holy days, poignant moments, festivals, and historical symbols', and the presentation of goods in 'radiant beams, halos of light' all served to appropriate traditional religious feelings for modern ends.

Through these four constituent elements, advertising contributed powerfully to a visual and verbal vocabulary through which people could be acculturated into modern, complex, urban life. Advertising's appeal came from its dramatisation of the everyday. The objective of selling goods, coupled with the development of market intelligence, encouraged advertisers to acknowledge their audiences in ways that other architects of modernity (e.g. scientists, engineers, and city planners) were not obliged to. In particular, 'advertisers paid close attention to the signs of consumer resistance to their messages and thus acquired particular sensitivity to certain consumer discontents with modernity'. These discontents became the common ground which the advertisers shared with their audiences. Advertisers, like 'ordinary folk', experienced 'the complex and impersonal modes of modernity' and understood its psychological cost. Dialogue between different social groups 'was most likely to take place in the area of basic cultural anxieties and dilemmas', and it is in this area that Marchand believes advertising presents its most accurate reflections of American life.

> If we focus on the cast of characters in the tableaux—the French maids and the office-window imperialist—we will certainly be impressed primarily by the advertisements' distortions of social circumstances. If we focus on their specific prescriptions and advice—their promises of equality and autonomy through acts of consumption—we will be most impressed by their manipulative evasions, their efforts to finesse the problems of modernity. But if we focus on the perceptions of social and cultural dilemmas revealed in the tableaux, we will discover accurate, expressive images of underlying 'realities' of American society in the 1920s and 1930s reflected in advertising's elusive mirror. (Marchand, 1985)

For Marchand, advertising constitutes a historically contingent 'living language', which arose within, and embodied attempts to mediate, particular modern psycho-social tensions. More than any other modern specialists advertisers understood the stress modernity posed for individuals. Advertisers became the 'mediators of modernity'—the 'helping professionals' who offered 'therapeutic advice'. They brought the complex and impersonal down to a friendly and human scale. 'Far from suggesting that people seek to avoid the modern pressures and urban milieus that fostered "jangled nerves", advertisements brought news of products that would keep nerves "focused", healthy, and under control to cope with such conditions.' Advertisers helped people cope with the enlargement of choice which was often felt as disorientating and overwhelming. The upheaval wrought by modernity left people hungry for advice on best ways to live, for endless reassurance and for sympathetic support in dealing with their anxieties, all of which advertisers were happy to provide. 'By the 1920s advertisers had come to recognise a public demand for broad guidance—not just about product attributes, but about taste, social correctness and psychological satisfactions.' Advertisers transformed themselves from barkers and hawkers into 'social therapists who offered, within the advertising tableaux themselves, balms for the discontents of modernity'.

There is some similarity here with Lears' analysis of the professionalisation of advertising and the parallel rationalisation of advertising strategies. Marchand's emphasis on anxiety and its management is in one way close to a central concern of our research, which we discuss in Chapter 6. His attention to how the social position of advertisers interacts with the more psychological dimensions of the modern experience to shape the production of advertisements is a psycho-social approach very much in keeping with our own. Like Lears and Leiss *et al.*, he uses analyses of advertisements, as we will, to elaborate a broad theory of cultural change.

Much earlier, in an isolated precursor of the growth of empirical work on advertising in the 1980s and 1990s, two American social psychologists, Dornbusch and Hickman (1959), had used advertisements to test rather than to develop a theory of social change. While on a relatively small scale, and reported only in a brief journal article, their investigation is worth a description here as it used a theory very relevant to our concerns, and also illustrates some of the difficulties in this kind of research. The theory they attempted to test was that of David Riesman, who defined and contrasted two types of character—the 'inner-directed' and 'other-directed'. The former were people guided in their actions and beliefs by a stable and coherent set of inner values. The latter were those who were influenced by what they thought others wanted of them, by the reactions of others. Riesman (1961) had suggested that the former type was becoming less common in twentieth-century America, and the latter more common. His theory was highly influential in 1950s social science, and remains so today, though indirectly, as an influence on more recent work. It was a forerunner of ideas about the development of a 'narcissistic' culture, and was a part of the wide body of work critical of 'mass' and popular culture which we review in the next chapter.

Dornbusch and Hickman assumed that the content of advertisements would reflect the relative predominance in society of these two character types and the values they embodied. They took two features of advertisements as evidence of 'other-directedness'—the use of endorsements (including testimonials from celebrities but also general assertions that, e.g. 'Housewives prefer...' or 'Mothers know...'), and the presence of suggestions that buying or using the commodity would improve the consumer's interpersonal relations. They then examined advertisements from one issue of the *Ladies' Home Journal* (a U.S. equivalent of *Woman's Own*) in each year from 1900 to the mid-1950s. They chose this publication as one which had been in print throughout the century, thereby enabling the comparison of like with like from different dates, and as one with a middle-class readership since they argued that changes in character-type would be most evident in that stratum. These questions of medium and readership are vital to any advertising research, and will be discussed later in relation to our own research.

Counting for each year the proportion of advertisements that included some 'other-directed' appeal, they found that the Riesman hypothesis was broadly confirmed. These appeals were much more common in the second half of the period they covered than in the first half. However, the trend was not steadily up: 'other-directedness' was measured as *decreasing* after 1936. Perhaps, as they suggest, appeals to 'other-directedness' had to become more subtle, as the growing self-consciousness of the consumer society made more open appeals to it seem crass and dated. Or perhaps the deception lay at a deeper level: not in the advertisements, but in the social character-type, as the emergent narcissistic personality (the more developed or sophisticated form of 'other-directedness') came to adopt postures of 'inner-directedness'.

This study was on a small scale but focused on a broad theoretical question about cultural change. Its findings illustrate well the difficulty of translating from a psycho-social theory of values to advertisement content, and back again. If things are not necessarily as they seem, this is a problem for any research using cultural texts as its data. It is obviously a very dubious procedure to claim that 'other-directedness', or any other trait, is there if we see it, *and* there if we don't, because it has become covert. One lesson to be drawn from this is that textual content analyses should be at as fine-grained a level as possible, so that they can identify value patterns which are less affected by the fashionableness of more gross features of style and strategy such as the use of endorsements.

A final work to mention in this chapter is one which has, like the above studies, analysed the value content of advertisements over a period of time, but has then attempted to use this analysis predictively. An unusual study by Fowles (1976) derived a set of content coding categories from the list of basic motives or needs given in the theory of the American psychologist Henry Murray. Fowles took his cue from a classic work in social psychology by David McClelland, who analysed children's stories popular in 1925 in a number of different national cultures for the presence of Murray's 'need for achievement' ('*n ach*'). He then found that measures of economic growth in those countries over the next twenty-five years showed a high degree of correlation with the 1925 *n ach* ratings, and argued that historical variations in the presence of *n ach* (as measured in cultural models of character, in the 'motivational lessons' present in children's literature) influenced the future economic activity of societies.

Fowles' approach was to take the full set of needs as defined by Murray (including, for example, needs for autonomy, affiliation, order, sex, nurturance) and to code samples of advertisements for the presence of these needs. He then grouped the needs into two broad categories—'benign' and 'assertive' motives—and totalled the presence of each category in advertisements taken (for various products, from *Life* magazine) at three sampling points—1950, 1960 and 1970. The finding was that 'benign' motives rose from 1950 to 1960, then fell back in 1970, while 'assertive' motives did the reverse. To this data Fowles brought the assumption that advertisements will express values around a decade before they become culturally predominant, and so predicted that American culture generally would show similar fluctuations a decade later. To test this he took front pages from the *New York Times* and coded them as either benign or assertive, according to the content of the lead story. The predictions were confirmed.

This study has a number of weaknesses. It distinguished between 'product-related' and 'associative' content, bracketing off the former in its mapping of values. It thus could not take account of the way in which products themselves and the advertisements' descriptions of them are embedded in associative matrices (see Chapter 6), in non-product-related ways of thinking and feeling. The coding of the newspaper stories was conceptually crude and open to question (e.g. stories about sport as well as about war were coded as 'assertive'). Indeed, taking a small number of front pages from one newspaper as a base from which to describe a whole national culture is not a defensible procedure. And the notion that advertisements as a whole are at the leading edge of changes in values is implausible. While some may pick up on and express incipient changes, others are surely late in registering changes. While the advertising industry as a whole may have moved more into a cultural vanguard in recent years, it seems more likely to us that advertisements themselves reflect the whole range of values at work in a culture at any one time, those waxing and (though perhaps to a lesser extent) those waning. Although they can be used (and this is a premise of our own research) to take the temperature of a culture, i.e. as a cultural thermometer, to adopt a somewhat limiting analogy, they cannot be used predictively, as a cultural barometer. (Fox's use of this metaphor seems inaccurate, since he is not ascribing a predictive role to advertisements.)

Nonetheless Fowles' study is instructive. It showed how a set of categories from a psychological theory can be used to derive a procedure for coding advertisement content, and then for coding other kinds of public text to compare with advertisements. It sought to implicate advertising in overall patterns of change in cultural values, and in particular in the possibility that there have been phases of a decade or so in length in the post-war period during which significant overall shifts have taken place. It also, *contra* Fox, raised the question of advertising's responsibility to the moral future of the society of which it is a part.

Chapter 4

THE ACADEMIC CRITIQUE OF ADVERTISING

Advertising can usefully be considered as one of the key signatures of modernity. As such it has attracted a great deal of attention from writers and researchers attempting to understand and explain some of the workings and experiences of modern, and lately so called 'postmodern', living. Repeatedly, a general fascination with the significance and the impact of advertising has been given intellectual expression as academics and other writers have conducted studies or made pronouncements on advertising. The large body of thought and writing on the subject of advertising offers an insight into almost every aspect of twentieth-century cultural analysis. The study of advertising has always been intermeshed with larger questions about culture and value, language and signification, technology and humanity, motivation and morality, identity, economy, politics and social organisation.

An exploration of the range of work on advertising is a prerequisite for a full understanding of current attitudes towards it. Such an exploration, which we offer in this chapter, can clarify the affiliations and assumptions which support the contemporary discourse about advertising including, of course, our own contribution. Though chronological in organisation it is worth saying that that chronology is not meant to give any sense of seriality or culmination. None of the positions outlined here is obsolete, in that they are continually being re-expressed in academic, journalistic and conversational discourse about advertising. They are relevant in the sense that they retain the power to help thinking about advertising and our responses to it. They also, perhaps, can obstruct that thinking by instituting ritual argumentation.

THE SCRUTINY OF ADVERTISING

'Society is all but rude
to this delicious solitude'
Andrew Marvell, 'The Garden'[1]

The first sustained response to advertising as a form of social and cultural communication was conceived amongst a group of writers associated with the journal *Scrutiny* and orchestrated by the influential critic F. R. Leavis. *Scrutiny* was launched in 1932. Its typical contributor at that time is characterised as a Cambridge University literature graduate in his mid-twenties (Mulhern, 1979). The journal aimed to extend the remit of literary criticism into new jurisdictions formally the preserve of sociology, anthropology and psychology. Ostensibly perhaps a precursor of more recent ambitions towards 'interdisciplinarity' in cultural studies, *Scrutiny* remained, fundamentally, a literature journal maintaining 'literary', 'humane' and 'disinterested' values at the centre of its agenda for socio-cultural critique (Mulhern, 1979; Williams, 1983). The intellectual roots of *Scrutiny* are far ranging and cosmopolitan (Mulhern, 1979). Notable in this context is the journal's ritual echoing of Matthew Arnold's famous opposition between 'Culture and Anarchy'. Arnold's critical strategy proposed that the restorative power of 'the best' cultural expression must be mobilised against the anarchic and 'philistine' elements of encroaching utilitarian modernity. In *Scrutiny* advertising was continually presented as harbinger and evidence of this dissolution.

The *Scrutiny* ethos can be summarised as a complex combination of 'moral seriousness' and some of the more conservative elements of Romanticism and Puritan Nonconformity (Rustin, 1991). This ethic sponsored a conviction that productive work was the proper goal of man (Leavis, 1964). There is a suppression of the more hedonistic currents in Romantic thought in favour of idealising nostalgia.

Scrutiny's manifesto declared the extent of its ambitions in the study of culture: 'a pervasive interest of the magazine will find expression in disinterested surveys of some departments of modern life in an attempt to increase understanding of the way in which civilisation is developing' (cited Mulhern, 1979).

Advertising was one such 'department' of modern life ripe for a stringent survey. The major scrutineer pre-occupied specifically with advertising was Leavis' co-editor Denys Thompson, a school teacher, and we can summarise the position of the *Scrutiny* authors on advertising as follows. It sprang from their rejection of 'industrialism', the system of mass, standardised production for a mass market, because of its 'levelling down' effects and its corrosive impact upon 'culture' (the finest values, necessarily embodied by a minority). Advertisements are part of the rise of industrialism, and can be held partially responsible for the corruption of language in two ways: in their own degraded use of words, and in their wider effect on the press, which in the pursuit of advertising revenues is forced into going for readability and maximum readership, and therefore in sweeping traditional standards away.

The first edition of *Scrutiny* included Thompson's essay 'Advertising God' (Thompson, 1932a) which sets out some of the recurrent themes of the *Scrutiny* account. A second essay by Thompson, 'A cure for amnesia' (1932b), develops the arguments in the context of a ruralist nostalgia motif which underpins much *Scrutiny* thinking and for which Thompson in particular is noted (Mulhern, 1979). These essays straddle the production of a more extensive work, *Culture and Environment: The Training of Critical Awareness* first published in 1933 (Leavis and Thompson, 1964). This book, a work of analysis and a school text, was designed to assist in the project of 'advertising defence' (Thompson, 1932a). This involved mobilising schools against an advertising and popular culture industry seeking to 'replace' education (Thompson, 1932a), and the project was sustained over several decades. Much later, selections from the 1960 National Union of Teachers conference proceedings were edited by Thompson in 1964 into a Penguin paperback *Discrimination and Popular Culture*. This book was influential well into the 1970s (Inglis, 1995). The first chapter, by Frank Whitehead, is the best researched and most comprehensive account of advertising in this critical tradition. Whitehead's language is revealing. He argues that advertising is the 'cultural kingpin' of twentieth-century Britain, in a basically bad way. Advertisements show a particularly distasteful form of 'contempt for human nature', they play on primitive fears and anxieties, and appeal to irrationality. They stereotype experiences in simplistic ways, and undermine the capacity for spontaneous emotional response. The strongly elitist nature of his critique is evident in other remarks: that advertisements are aimed at a 'self-deluding majority' with 'discreditable impulses', and that popular artefacts of any kind are of a necessarily 'low' level, and are characterised by 'conventional triviality'. The good life pictured in advertisements makes no mention of symphony concerts and art exhibitions, focusing entirely on the possession of mass consumer goods. That would not be true today, when some forms of high culture have become objects of cultural consumption by quite wide groups, and are accordingly represented in advertisements. But Whitehead's vision of the good life is still that of an elite group, the cultured middle-class intellectuals for whom the convenience of a washing machine or of having your own car is a mere vulgarity. Yet many of the goods featured in advertisements that drew his distaste were already considered essential for many people including the intellectual classes. So it was not so much the fact of possession which offended but the 'materialism' or preoccupation with material goods that was believed or imagined to lie behind the advertisements and to envelop their popular audience.

The *Scrutiny* critique of advertising has become routinised in much contemporary thinking and foreshadows much of the later work on advertising in other traditions. Thompson's essays are concerned to make a plea that readers take notice of advertisers' rapidly expanding influences on culture. With recourse to a metaphor of disease, characteristic of the vivid rhetoric favoured in *Scrutiny*, he writes: 'Advertising was once parasitic in dimensions as well as in function: but it has swollen so dropsically that its parent is dwarfed' (Thompson, 1932a).

Thompson is concerned that there is a lessening prospect of any widespread public criticism of advertising within the media because publishers are unlikely to 'bite the hand that feeds them' (Thompson, 1932a; see also Whitehead, 1964, and Orwell, 1982). Thompson goes on to highlight governments' reluctance to enforce measures likely to inconvenience advertisers and their failure to protect the natural landscape from the blots advertising makes upon it. In the face of an inert government, a ransomed press and a gullible public, advertising is free to grow unchecked. Advertisers are 'lords of creation' (Thompson, 1932a) presiding over an Americanising cultural economy whose inexorable law was one of standardisation, 'levelling down' and decay. Advertisers are 'gangsters plotting one's murder' and, perhaps worse, 'uniformly illiterate' (Thompson, 1932a).

Advertising is charged with 'cheating' the consumer by 'lowering the quality of...goods' by deflecting the traditional priority of the manufacturer away from the tenet that 'quality production' be the first and only consideration (Thompson, 1932a). This criticism is an elaboration of the Leavisite suspicion that modern mass production, mass distribution and standardisation can only operate according to a logic of levelling down. Thompson feels a particular regret at the decay of a traditional unalienated craft economy of localised production and consumption which was imagined to have existed before the mass era (Thompson, 1932b). This nostalgic feeling can be found in much of the other advertising criticism examined in this chapter. But while it is asserted here with passion, the major thrust of the *Scrutiny* critique is primarily a story about language.

Thompson's (and Leavis') main point regarding advertising is that it causes the corruption of cultural and consequently moral life. It is worth asking why they did not work from a base in moral philosophy or religion. It is their sense of the relations between language and art which provides an answer. Hence, aesthetics and not ethics became the ground for the fight.

Advertising was such a prominent target because it is a linguistic and an aesthetic medium seen as directly competing with literature and the arts. For the Leavisite movement 'Literature' represents a gold standard. There was a felt need that connection to this standard be re-established in order to bolster the symbolic economy of the age against further decay. Advertising was 'debasing the currency of living' (Thompson, 1932a) and the currency of living was, ultimately, language. 'Largely conveyed in language, there is our spiritual, moral and emotional tradition, which preserves the "picked experience of ages" regarding the finer issues of life' (Leavis and Thompson, 1964).

The motivation for *Scrutiny* to extend its critical judgements and methods beyond the literary and to apply them to such practices as advertising lies in their conviction that it was only in 'Literature' that any connection to an authentic language and culture could be apprehended. Their own confident possession of this apprehension was felt to authenticate judgements about other modes of utterance and practice. A cultivated literary sensibility and a stringent training coloured and shaped their responses. Advertising provided them with suitable linguistic evidence upon which to found their broader social analysis.

The *Scrutiny* writing on advertising routes its dissatisfaction with the modern world through a comprehensive dissection of the way it speaks. Linguistic forms are felt to reflect directly forms of life. Every instance of aesthetically suspect advertising expresses the depth of the modern crisis. Thompson, and critics like him, heard the jingle jangle of deficient language everywhere. *Scrutiny*'s most cited influence Matthew Arnold had heard a 'melancholy long withdrawing roar' in his poetic analysis of the recession of Faith from Victorian society. (For a discussion of the 'poignancy' of Arnold's poem in the 1960s and 1970s, see Booker, 1980.) Less than one hundred years later Frank Whitehead listened despairingly to language which had been 'processed to the uniform consistency of a cheese spread' (Whitehead, 1964).

RESPONSES TO THE *SCRUTINY* CRITIQUE

The claim to be engaged in 'disinterested surveys of...modern life' and to allow the 'play of free intelligence' (Mulhern, 1979) in the study of advertising was a flimsy alibi for a very 'interested' energetic and radical argument which, as Mulhern observes with reference to the whole *Scrutiny* enterprise, 'was social and political in character and purpose' (Mulhern, 1979). Elaborations and emphases of this general point have been made often by later writers on advertising and popular culture. Nava points to Leavis' 'elitism' and 'contempt' for mass culture (Nava, 1991). Fowles (1996), singling out Arnold and T. S. Eliot (Eliot, along with Pound, was a key influence in the Leavisite project) makes a similar point. Celia Lury, following Bourdieu, develops the point in the observation that the critical sensibility or 'habitus' upon which the *Scrutiny* movement was based 'represents the judgements not simply of a particular class but also a particular gender and a particular ethnicity' (Lury, 1996). Turner cites Bennett's accusation that Leavis and his followers produced a 'remote' and 'patronising' critique, 'a discourse of the "cultured" about the culture of those without "culture"' (Bennett cited Turner, 1992).

Another important reservation about this work on advertising is that it tended to assume that the process of reading advertisements was inactive. While the reading of good literature was infused with 'activity' and 'life', bad literature (e.g. advertising) was received by a process of absorption.

There are good reasons to be dissatisfied with the account of advertising set out in *Scrutiny*. In passing it should be noted that there were significant modifications and additions to the agenda set by Thompson's initial essays even within *Scrutiny* itself. These go a little way towards tempering the elitist tone and the limiting culturalism, i.e. the belief that the most meaningful perspective from which to examine advertising was as bad language. For instance, an article by Gifford, amongst predictable lamentations about 'slovenly prose', sets out a Marxist critique of advertising as economic waste (Gifford, 1935). In a generally uncritical book review Churchill takes Thompson to task for his invocation of 'shabby schoolboys', his failure to acknowledge the limited success of certain advertising campaigns and, relatedly, his assumption that any capacity for resistance to advertising's power is confined to 'upper class' readerships (Churchill, 1944/5). One contributor even allows, half seriously, that advertising increases significance by means of techniques of verbal rhythm reminiscent of those employed in the poetry of D. H. Lawrence.

To some extent *Scrutiny*'s complaints, fuddyduddy as they may now seem, can be read as a refreshing dialogue with some contemporary celebrations of advertising's artistic brilliance, and as a counterweight to excessive enthusiasm. Importantly *Scrutiny* expanded the remit of literary studies to include 'genres' such as advertising. This in turn has broadened the capacity of 'cultural' analysis to capture the imaginations of new constituencies of teachers and students. This consequence has been largely tangential to the initial aims of the journal since 'the literary' and 'culture' in their Leavisite conception are not at the heart of any subsequent academic studies of advertising. That said, Mulhern was correct when he noted that *Scrutiny* 'directly legitimated the expansion of criticism into new territories of study (*journalism and advertising above all*)' (Mulhern, 1979, our italics).

This expansion was undoubtedly hampered by a too-narrow sense of method and an opaque set of values too closely identified with an unhelpfully traditional rendering of 'the good'. However it is a legacy which it is ultimately more useful simply to acknowledge than to subject to a repetitious rebuke. The intellectual space from which to scrutinise advertising at once opened and colonised by writers like Thompson has been re-colonised and extended in its turn by analysts utilising more effective and explicit theoretical tools and methods. Raymond Williams saw the deficiency in Leavisism in its limited definition of culture and in its methodological reliance on a particular kind of 'criticism'. This left the work unable to examine social institutions such as advertising convincingly. In 1958 Williams stated

> It is obvious...that the ways of feeling and thinking embodied in such institutions as the popular press, advertising and the cinema cannot finally be criticised without reference to a way of life. (Williams, 1987)

This statement seen in the context of Williams' considerable work on the definition of 'culture' set the agenda for a new departure in academic approaches to advertising.

'OBJECTS ARE NOT ENOUGH'

The approach to culture and communication inspired and developed by Raymond Williams can be distinguished from the *Scrutiny* critique conceptually and sociologically. Leavisism was resoundingly a discourse of the academy, its centre the English faculty of Cambridge University. Williams' account of the genesis of his innovative media studies text book *Communications* indictates its attenuated relation to the academic centre of 'Culture'. The book, published just as Williams was beginning his career at Cambridge, had its substantial origins in lecture notes written for adult education college courses outside the 'cultural atmosphere of a university' (Williams, 1968; Turner, 1992). This trajectory is similar to those of other key figures in this group, notably Stuart Hall and Richard Hoggart (Turner, 1992). It is no coincidence that the maturation of this critique is best associated with a centre of its own—the Birmingham Centre for Contemporary Cultural Studies founded by Hoggart in 1964. The work of this centre has had a considerable influence on the scope and form of subsequent cultural studies. C.C.C.S. cannot be easily represented with reference to work from any one phase in its four-decade history. The early output on advertising, in a sense rather unrepresentative of the C.C.C.S project,[2] is of interest here. The arguments are best represented by two key texts: Williams' essay of 1960, 'Advertising: the magic system' (1980) first published in *New Left Review*, and Hall and Whannel's chapter 'The big bazaar' from *The Popular Arts* (1964).

Both pieces revolve around the proposition that advertising is 'the official art of modern capitalist society' (Williams, 1980; Hall and Whannel, 1964) and a 'true part of the culture of a confused society' (Williams, 1980). Williams' essay is a powerful argument exploring this claim and proposing the benefits of a socialist alternative. Hall and Whannel provide a more investigative illustration of Williams' ideas and attempt to expose the tricks of the 'magic system'.

Williams points to the dependence of media on advertising revenues, the incursion of advertising into political discourse and the transition in advertising from an informational to an 'educational' and 'values' based appeal. He castigates the co-option by advertising of academic knowledge from the arts and social sciences in the service of manipulation rather than emancipation (Williams, 1980). In a key change of focus from that afforded by Leavisite criticism, he proposes that advertising can only be understood in a context where the economic, social and cultural facts about advertising are visibly related. Advertising is a pervasive form of public communication with a great cultural impact. Its function is to stimulate and regularise consumption. Its responsibility is to private interests and not to the community. Its aim is to convert 'audiences' into 'markets' and its rhetoric is one of persuasion not information. Its private agenda has unhappy consequences for the quality of public communication.

The distinctive point of the critique is based in the idea that in capitalist culture 'objects are not enough'. He observes

> It is often said that our society is too materialist, and that advertising reflects this...But it seems to me that in this respect our society is quite evidently not materialist enough, and that this, paradoxically, is the result of a failure in social meanings, values and ideals. (Williams, 1980)

The 'magic system' of modern advertising operates by distorting relationships to material reality—hence its position as a 'problem of materialism and culture'. Advertising, by means of its rhetorical and imagistic formats, which are peculiar to the modern capitalist cultural pattern, systematically misdirects consciousness. The advertising form encourages distortions because its associative style is one which promotes interference between two discrete spheres—the material sphere of usage and the cultural and personal realms of values and ideals. In a better world 'beer would be enough for us, without the additional promise that in drinking it we show ourselves to be manly' (Williams, 1980). Feelings of 'manliness' would be more directly available—presumably in productive, unalienated labour.

The essay hinges upon a distinction between man as a consumer and as a user of things. Williams discerns a society overwhelmingly predicated upon the 'consumer'. The market constitutes him as an impersonal 'channel along which the product flows and disappears', a 'belly' and a 'furnace' (Williams, 1980). The idea of the 'user' of goods is meant to imply the conscious rational pursuit of realistic ends where choice is more than a matter of 'sales resistance'. But advertising interrupts rational usage. Instead it encourages fantasy and consumption. This point provides the basis for Hall and Whannel's application of some psychoanalytic observations. In modern advertising

> psychological feelings are being explored, subtle associations are made, strange, dream-like transformations enacted. 'Dream' colours are used (pinks and blues) or the photographs are deliberately blurred to recreate a trance-like state in the reader. Frequently...there is an appeal to feelings which are deeply subconscious. They would not normally escape the censor of social custom had they been more directly treated. Such advertisements depend upon sexual moods; the use of recognisably Freudian symbolism...violence and aggression...self indulgence...exhibitionism...masochism'. (Hall and Whannel, 1964; *gaps in original*)

Advertising represents a problem because it privileges an individuating ethic of consumption over a collectivist and responsible programme for the social use of things. It maintains a cultural pattern where important values are only indirectly available and inauthentically realised. While Williams discerns that advertising does address 'real human tensions... which involve deep feelings of a personal and social kind' (Williams, 1980), he perceives, in the execution of that address, no valid resolution or clarification. Instead there is a 'displacement' which inexorably defers and re-routes any criticism of the society which produces such tensions and anxieties leaving 'the whole area of human need unsatisfied'. This is a picture of an anxious population privatised and manipulated into the perpetual pursuit of imagined solace at the expense of the true individual and social needs and freedoms.

The Williams argument is, like that of Thompson, ultimately a critique of language and referentiality. The magic of advertising lies in its capacity to associate goods to values where there is 'no real reference' (Williams, 1980). Hall and Whannel underline this basic point. In advertising we tend to find 'a line of argument, though no reasoning or facts in the accepted sense' and 'a rush of language to the head, loose bastardised poeticising' because

> The language of much advertising cannot be understood except as a kind of verbal invocation. The 'slogan' is itself a distilled and compressed form of speech...So are the mood phrases which frequently recur—the newly minted adjectival compounds, or the coupling of adjective-and-noun or adjective with adjective. These work in the same way as the compounded nouns in Anglo Saxon poetry (e.g. king-sword) or the ideogram in Japanese poetry. They are modern 'kennings': 'foot-fabulous'...'Wash-white'...'The born-beautiful look'...'Tomatoful'...'Youthliness Long legs'...'Teenfresh', etc. (Hall and Whannel, 1964)

Hall and Whannel develop Williams' critique in direct and engaging analyses of a selection of advertisements. This is a useful departure for a number of reasons. The presentation of the object of study within the pages of the critique is a helpful counter to charges of remoteness and unfamiliarity. It also allows for greater consideration of the visual aspects of the genre, largely ignored by more literary critics, and consequently for a more convincing attempt to engage with the workings of advertisements. This focus and specification enhances presentation and substance. It facilitates an account of differentiation between advertisements as opposed to the tendency elsewhere to lump all advertisements into an homogeneous mire of disdain. It guides the account towards an exposition of different modes and styles of appeal. The critique begins to reflect on the actuality of advertising practice which varied its appeals to suit different audiences. This marks an implicit deconstruction of the unhelpful notion of 'the mass' audience and prefigures Hall's later recognition of the need to consider reception within different audience fractions.

These extensions of method, coupled with refreshing empirical attention to the frequency and distribution of advertisements in the press and on television and a heightened sensitivity to the differences between media, lead to a more comprehensive and balanced account. Potentially at least the critique allows for the practice of 'discrimination among' rather than 'against' advertisements (Turner, 1992). In practice however the conclusions are uniformly suspicious of the systematic manipulative distortions of the advertising system. The critics' role remains one of equipping students against technocratic witchcraft. Hoggart, in a journalistic attack on the industry, sums up the position:

> The overriding fact is that much of the work of this profession, as it is at present practised, consists of exploiting human weakness through language. Anyone who thinks that it is better to try to understand one's weaknesses than to indulge them, anyone who thinks that language (the articulation of our thoughts and feelings in communicable form) can help that better grasp, anyone with these two premises must regard most modern advertising as, at the best, a stupid waste of good human resources and at the worst, a wicked misuse of other people. (Hoggart in Wilson, 1968: 54)

Despite its plausibility there are a number of major question marks hanging over the notion of advertising as a 'wicked', 'magic system'. These are linked to more general problems in the totalising explanatory paradigm of Marxism which was a dominant influence in the early development of cultural studies in Britain. Firstly there is the charge of untheorised organicism in the pervasive evocation of 'use' (authentic, natural and rational)—leading to a too-sharp distinction from 'consumption' (fake, fabricated and 'insane'). An essential, truly human way of relating to objects is assumed to exist, and to be different from the ways of consumer society.

Secondly there is a lack of attention paid to the subjectivity of the reader of advertisements (Nava *et al.*, 1997). The theory focuses on the production and distribution, the form and the content and finally the intent of advertising. It has little to say about how readers might actually, or even notionally, respond—except repeatedly to render them as compliant.

Thirdly there is a questioning of the assumption that productive rational action is necessarily the privileged arena of satisfactory identity formation. This has led some critics on to assert the pleasures afforded by advertising messages and to highlight the vivacity and validity of identity forged in an aestheticised economy of goods. Additionally there have been reservations about a critical methodology still, in parts, grounded in Leavisite literary impressionism (Turner, 1992) and preserving an implicit judgemental distinction between the languages of art and the languages of the everyday. This last point underwrites the emergence of the next phase of advertising criticism which turns to a more 'scientific' theory of language and signification in the attempt to provide a more objective account of the way advertising orders reality. An English tradition of humanist and socialist critical sensibility was to give way in academia to a Marxist structuralism and a psychoanalytic semiotics being developed on the continent. Before turning to these later developments, however, we will discuss some American and early European work which, like the *Scrutiny* tradition, exerts a continuing influence outside of academia.

THE AMERICAN CRITIQUE

Vance Packard's *The Hidden Persuaders*, *The Status Seekers* and *The Waste Makers* constitute an important and influential part of the American critique of consumer society, advertising and the market research industries in the 1950s and 1960s. The books had enormous commercial success; each was a No. 1 best seller and in 1963 Packard was one of America's most widely read non-fiction writers (Horowitz, 1994). The most famous and relevant of the three texts is the first, *The Hidden Persuaders*. It was published in the UK in 1957 and is a source for part of Whitehead's critique of British advertising in 1960 (Whitehead, 1964) discussed above. We devote considerable space to it here because of its continuing influence on popular ideas about advertising, and its formulation of themes important in the academic literature. In general there is a difference as well as similarities between the British moral criticism and Packard's approach. This is ultimately as much to do with differences in institutional and cultural locations of the producers of the critiques as it is to do with any difference in the plight of American as opposed to English culture. Indeed the Leavisites seem to feel that English culture is beyond salvation. Packard has some hope for the future (Packard, 1960). In Packard there is less of the highbrow culturalism of the Leavisites. While the English critique was a defence of culture as language and then as literature and *then* as 'a way of life', Packard offers a more straightforward defence of a lifestyle. The tone of Packard's writing is far more sensationalist. While the relation of the Cambridge University *Scrutiny* group and the world of advertising can best be characterised as one of disdain and detachment, Packard, as a magazine journalist, is immersed in and fascinated by the people and the practices of the industry he is writing about. Horowitz notes one anonymous critic who wrote to Packard: 'It seems to me as if you yourself are a little fascinated among all the vast million dollar figures, just like most of the gangster-movies in spite of the gangster's violent death provide most youngsters with a feeling that gangsterism is a hell of an exciting way to live' (cited Horowitz, 1994). Davidson describes *The Hidden Persuaders* as 'that psychological thriller of the 1950s' (Davidson, 1992). This is not an accusation one could level at the *Scrutiny* writers of any decade.

The Hidden Persuaders arose out of a journalistic assignment suggested by the editors of the *Reader's Digest* for whom Packard was working in 1954. Packard was asked to look into the emerging industry of 'motivational research'. The resulting article was not printed because, Packard suspected, the magazine feared alienating advertising clients. *Reader's Digest* was about to revoke a prior ban on carrying advertisements (Horowitz, 1994). This perceived moment of censorship within a commercial press spurred him to pursue independence and write a book.

Packard had chosen a felicitous cultural moment for the publication of his critique. The advertising industry was growing apace—there was a 600% increase in expenditure between 1939 and the late 1950s (Horowitz, 1994). Awareness of new motivational techniques was growing amongst the public along with an attendant suspiciousness of 'a strange and rather exotic new area of modern life' (Packard, 1957). There was a growing cultural unease which regularly found expression in critical portraits of the advertising industry. In the dozen years before *The Hidden Persuaders* appeared, a series of novels, some of them turned into movies, paved the way for Packard's non-fiction, by depicting advertising executives as materialistic, status-conscious, immoral people who cynically manipulated the consumers' desires (Horowitz, 1994).

The intellectual climate also seemed to be moving in a direction akin to Packard's. American intellectuals in a number of spheres were beginning to count some of the costs of the affluent corporate consumer culture of the 1950s (Whyte, 1956; Riesman, 1961; Friedan, 1982). In many ways Packard's books point to a revaluation of the optimism attached to the 'American Dream'. It was perhaps most appropriate of all then that Packard examined the practices of those he felt to be the manufacturers of the dreams and desires of the American public.

The simple expansion of advertising was not Packard's major object of critique. Packard was more concerned about the evolution of advertising from a discourse of simple information provision and recommendation to a sophisticated art of commercial communication. He reports how 'advertisement men' had 'become depth men'. The tone of the book is one of someone surveying a lamentable and sinister process of social decay. 'We move', Packard tells us, 'from the genial world of James Thurber into the chilling world of George Orwell and his Big Brother.' He is interested in the 'hidden' persuaders; the back-room 'depth boys' who used an array of psychological techniques to get to the heart of desire or 'the triggers of action'. Packard reveals the diversification of research methods in the post-war industry. This is summed up as the rejection of 'nose counting' in favour of new techniques. Based on the premise that 'in very few instances do people really know what they want, even when they say they do' (advertising executive cited by Packard, 1957), it is important to go beyond rational and conscious expressions of needs and wants, and do more than simply ask people what they want.

This is where Packard finds the target for his anxieties. The advertising industry was beginning to draw upon an array of new sources of information, techniques and personnel in its quest for better information about what consumers wanted. He is worried about an emerging unholy alliance between academics and the industry. For instance Packard lists the academics on the staff of Ernst Dichter's Institute for Motivation Research, finding 'twenty-five resident specialists, including psychologists, sociologists, anthropologists'.

Related to this influx of academic expertise is the array of novel research methods employed. Hypnosis, Rorschach, Szodi, TAT and lie detector tests (Packard, 1957) are all outlined. Packard's aim seems to be to depict the immensity of the armoury at the advertisers' disposal, assuming this proves their mastery of a science of motivations rather than pointing to the difficulty, if not unmanageability, of the task of enumerating desires in a complex modernising society. The book piles up a series of revelatory case studies, each one pointing to the application of MR techniques to the selling of goods to the unsuspecting public.

The three books share assumptions and their argument follows some of the routines found in other critiques. In particular *The Hidden Persuaders* has much in common with other critiques in that it insists on the power and expertise of the industry and upon the docility and malleability of the consumer. 'The lone consumer of ordinary intelligence and impulsiveness is usually no match for the subtle and massive onslaughts aimed at him' (Packard, 1960).

The book also depends upon an implicit theory that there are real needs to be met and that advertising deflects individuals and society from the fulfilment of these needs. Like other critiques the implicit narrative is one of disintegration from a state of relative authenticity to one of bewildered searching after specious satisfaction. The state of grace from which the society has been led is in this case one characterised by 'producer values' (Horowitz) of work, simplicity and restraint rather than a consumer ethic with its overvaluation of possessions and pleasure. Underlying all this is an idealisation of rural life and a deep discomfort with modern urban living. As with other critiques Packard is especially concerned to protect women and children from the seductions of advertising and from their own undisciplined floating desires. For instance he reports that women consumers are often overtaken with what is called 'hypnoidal trance'.

> ...many of these women are in such a trance that they passed by neighbours and old friends without noticing or greeting them. They had a sort of glassy stare. They were so entranced as they wandered about the store plucking things off the shelves at random that they would bump into boxes without seeing them. (Packard, 1957)

Packard's critique requires that the reading of advertisements is an automatic and depersonalised process. There is never any sense that the motivations discovered, unconscious or not, might be 'real', or that the reader of the advertisement may be applying his or her own agenda to the persuasive process. The reader is seen as subject to rather than subject of the reading transaction. In short, there is no conception of the process of reading. As we will discuss below more recent critics have questioned these assumptions. Spontaneity is equated with the irrational impulse and that impulse has nothing to do with the subject acting or the audience looking at the advertisement. The following sets out his assumption about what happens when people read:

> ...astute persuaders always use word triggers and picture triggers to evoke desired responses. Once a response pattern is established in terms of persuasion, then you can persuade people in wholesale lots, because all of us...are creatures of 'conditioned reflex'. [T]he crux of all persuasion jobs, whether selling soft drinks or a political philosophy, is to develop these conditioned reflexes by flashing on trigger words, symbols or acts. (Packard, 1957)

Thus the reader of an advertisement simply and unwittingly extracts a message able to undo his or her intelligence or will, and complies with its suggestion. The theoretical gap where the reader's response might be is evident in his depiction of the work of MR. Though he does not believe the activities of the MR people to be 'right' in a moral sense, he seems to accept that they are 'right' intellectually, however diverse and conflicting their approaches. He offers a sensationalist recounting of anecdotes and claims about the aspirations and power of the motivationists rather than any serious scrutiny of what they actually did or believed. While privately Packard found some of their methods ludicrous (Horowitz, 1994, reports that 'He almost fell off his chair laughing when typing material for the book') in his text he is largely unreflective on the question of the power of their contribution. This led Dichter, for instance, to thank Packard for writing, in *The Hidden Persuaders*, an excellent advertisement for the industry (Horowitz, 1994).

Packard is an important nodal point in the literature on advertising. While his populist approach is not academically respectable, his work brought advertising squarely on to the agenda as a worthwhile object for analysis, and showed that there was a market for popular criticism of advertising. His work was recommended to students by Marcuse (Horowitz, 1994) and remains an important reference point in thinking about advertising in society, despite its fundamental flaws.

Some of these were magnified in later work by other writers. *Subliminal Seduction*, by Wilson Bryan Key, is an exposé of 'media rape'. The corruption of advertising culture is highlighted by his unfailing capacity to find the word 'SEX' inscribed, subliminally, across the texts of American advertising—from ice cubes to Ritz crackers, the offending syllable is 'there'. As he 'demonstrates' in Chapter 6, 'sex is alive and embedded in practically everything' (Key, 1974). His thesis depends upon the assertion that 'media has the proven, completely established ability to programme human behaviour much in the same way as hypnosis' (Key, 1974). In a moment of near-lucidity, Key says of his own work, 'the author has frequently believed, while researching this book, that he might be off on a paranoic delusion of some sort. There appears to be a subliminal dimension in everything...' (Key, 1974). As William Leiss *et al.* note of Key's contribution, 'no commentator, either within the advertising industry or outside it, has ever corroborated Key's assertions about advertising practices, nor is there any evidence that motivational effects result from subliminal stimuli' (Leiss *et al.*, 1990).

Packard however needs to be taken more seriously than his imitators. Like Leavis and the English critics, he wrote out of a passion rooted in a thinly disguised romantic nostalgia, coloured by Puritanism and not a little paranoia, as opposed to any overt political programme, though there was a timely critique of capitalist overproduction. The work of the 1950s was to do with a principled if obsolete humanism. Packard explains his purpose:

> All this probing and manipulation has its constructive and its amusing aspects; but also, I think it is fair to say, it has seriously anti-humanistic implications. Much of it seems to represent regress rather than progress for man in his long struggle to become a rational and self guiding being. (Packard, 1957)

The work of the 1950s, on both sides of the Atlantic, found its ultimate motivation in a stalwart defence of tradition against the commercial manifestations of modernity. For this reason it is ultimately conservative social criticism. The limits and preoccupations underlying Packard's critique can be seen in the naivety of the concluding vignette of *The Waste Makers* (which was in part an influential early statement of some environmentalist concerns).

> Actress Siobhan McKenna makes a trip every summer to the bleak Aran Islands of Ireland to live a while with the fishermen and sheep clippers there. They are a joyful, hospitable people who always have a welcome pot of tea ready for a visitor. She says that she makes this annual trip in order to renew her faith in the essential pride and nobility of human beings who still come to grips with the cosmos instead of with artificial problems people invent for themselves. (Packard, 1960)

It is interesting that Packard finds this inspiring (and writes of it in the manner of a tourism advertisement!). We can see strong similarities to Leavisite organicism. Further, the passage highlights an important underlying theme in the critique of modernity, in its juxtaposition of authentic masculine humanity and the figure of the feminine actress. There is also an appeal to the existence of an ordered cosmos—presumably an organic one—as opposed to the 'artificial' problems of everyday life. Packard holds an important and ambiguous position in the broader literature on advertising and consumption. He provided texts which focused some of the general discontent at 1950s materialism more directly upon advertising. Nevertheless his recognition that there are important unconscious processes at work in the production and reception of advertising fails to be developed in a systematic way. He does not differentiate attempts to colonise the unconscious from other approaches in the growing array of market research techniques. He does not consider the possible value of attaching unconscious gratifications to the process of consumption, and sticks rigidly to a producer ethic of utility and purposiveness in his sense of cultural value. Nor does he consider that the reading of advertisements can afford the reader with any real and meaningful experience. Like Adorno whom we discuss below, Packard was convinced that big business had untrammelled power to take up residence in the minds of a de-natured populace. Unlike Adorno this perception was not couched in a broader philosophic account of the processes of modernisation and the attendant transitions in the sphere of the symbolic. Packard shares the intensity of Adorno's lament but lacks the rigour and depth of analysis necessary to make a plausible defence of such far-reaching pessimism.

Wilson Bryan Key's *Subliminal Seduction* is prefaced with a comment about advertising from a key figure in what came to be known as the Frankfurt school. Marcuse proclaims that 'the real catastrophe is the prospect of total moronisation, de-humanisation, and manipulation of man' (Marcuse cited Key, 1974).

This assertion sets the tone for an important and influential critique of advertising whose sophistication nevertheless goes way beyond the apparent sensationalism exploited by Key. That said, the work of the Frankfurt school retains something of the disgust we have seen elsewhere at the banality of the products of mass culture and despair at the masses' plight within such a culture. In many ways the Frankfurt school theorists prefigure the contributions of Williamson and her successors in the Althusserian analysis of advertising though they are less interested in highlighting the ideological contents of advertising messages. They also echo Leavisite fears about the impact of advertising on the quality of language and expression within culture.

In the Frankfurt school writers' few direct allusions to advertising (which for them was an epitomisation of the 'culture industries' as a whole) there is a tendency to decry the dynamics of the system of commodity circulation on the basis that in its very nature capitalist modernity is sick to its core. They share an affinity with the Leavisite critique on the basis that advertising, as the highest (or lowest) form of capitalistic linguistic expression, offers the prototypical form of language for a society destined to be cut off from any knowledge of the real and authentic goodness of culture. The Frankfurt school offer a philosophical account of the erosion of man's ability to know the world by any means other than those afforded by a de-naturing and de-humanising rationality. This is nowhere more true than in the writing of Adorno and Horkheimer whose *The Dialectic of Enlightenment* (1944/ 1973) sets out a critique of modern consciousness.

Here we will restrict ourselves to the specific critiques of advertising which they formulated. What distinguishes Adorno and Horkheimer's work from that of the Althusserian-based Marxists is that the concept of 'false consciousness' ceases to dictate the argument. This is so because, for Adorno and Horkheimer, the very fabric of thought in the twentieth century is in some sense false. They find in advertising the exemplary state of this thoughtlessness. Somehow language 'is lost in the announcement'.

> This affects language and object alike. Instead of making the object experiential, the purified word treats it as an abstract instance, and everything

else (now excluded by the demand for ruthless clarity from expression—itself now banished) fades away in reality. A left half at football, a black shirt, a member of the Hitler Youth, and so on, are no more than names. If before its rationalisation the word had given rise to lies as well as to longing, now, after its rationalisation, it is a straitjacket for longing more even than for lies. (Adorno and Horkheimer, 1972)

The language of advertising is one which leaves the object it describes devoid of real qualities. Advertising does not refer to a thing or to an experience—to any good. It stands in for that good, rather than introducing us to it. Adorno and Horkheimer are concerned that the language of advertising de-humanises object relations. The advertising sign is, for them, in every respect 'empty'.

This emptying out of the sign—a common complaint in analyses of modern advertising—is a result of the specious objectification of the object, the reification of the thing. Things, under such a regime of knowledge, become mere 'matter' (Adorno and Horkheimer, 1972). This objectification of the object effected by the language of advertising implies that there is a negation of the subjective moment in reception of the message. Reading is once again eradicated from and subsumed by the proposed dynamic of advertising. Indeed the character of the subject is to be 'without qualities' in just the manner that the language read is without qualities. Yet we can see that there is a general claim about the atrophy of the mental apparatus of the receiver of messages. Thus Adorno describes the consumer or 'man with leisure':

> The man with leisure has to accept what the culture manufacturers offer him. Kant's formalism still accepted a contribution from the individual, who was thought to relate the varied experiences of the senses to fundamental concepts; but industry robs the individual of his function. Its prime service to the customer is to do his schematising for him. Kant said that there was a secret mechanism in the soul which prepared direct intuitions in such a way that they could be fitted into the system of pure reason. But today that secret has been deciphered. (Adorno and Horkheimer, 1972)

This position is reiterated in the following claim:

> The blind and rapidly spreading repetition of words with special designations links advertising with the totalitarian watchword. The layer of experience which created the words for their speakers has been removed; in this swift appropriation language acquires the coldness which until now it had only on billboards and in the advertisement columns of newspapers. Innumerable people use words and expressions which they have either ceased to understand or employ only because they trigger off conditioned reflexes. (ibid.)

So we see how for Adorno the thought takes on the quality of the manufactured environment of the culture industries. He found no evidence to dissuade him from the conclusion that, alongside other cultural activities, advertising colonises the mind, without resistance and compromise. A further less subtle rendering of this point comes in the observation that 'the might of industrial society is lodged in men's minds' (Adorno and Horkheimer, 1972).

It is less a case of what advertisements do to society or the individual or to culture, and more a situation in which in our minds and in our lives we *are* advertisements.

The Frankfurt school thesis is often accused of being elitist and damning of mass culture. For instance Bennett Berger speaks of their 'furtively elitist understanding of mass culture and technology as de-humanisation' (Berger, 1995). The elitism of the Frankfurt school is related to their failure to consider the reader and the question of reception, which renders their critique of mass culture conceptually weak. Thompson makes the following observations about the work of Horkheimer and Adorno:

> Today it is clear, however, that [their] argument exaggerates the passivity of individuals and takes far too much for granted concerning the process of reception. Assumptions of this kind have to be replaced by a more contextualised and hermeneutically sensitive account of the ways in which individuals receive media products, use them and incorporate them into their lives. (Thompson, 1995)

This point is echoed by Lee. He sees the need to

> ...address more precisely some of the ways in which commodities function symbolically at the moment they have passed through the market and have entered into the realm of everyday life; that is, at the moment when they are transformed *from commodities for consumption to objects of consumption*. (Lee, 1993)

The intellectual insufficiency of the Frankfurt school critique of advertising lies in its despairing pessimism, which is linked to the historical genesis of the critique. Although written in the U.S., *The Dialectic of Enlightenment* (1944) was the work of writers who had witnessed the rise of Nazism at first hand in the pre-war period. There is often an elision in the analysis between Nazi propaganda on the one hand and American culture, and implicitly western European culture or the 'culture industries', on the other.

ADVERTISING AND THE LANGUAGE OF STRUCTURALISM

Following developments in a number of academic disciplines, the traditions of academic hostility to advertising began in the 1970s to foreground language. They paraded impressive new terminologies originating in Saussurean structuralist linguistics. These terminologies were being extrapolated into cultural analysis on many fronts, notably by Roland Barthes and Claude Levi-Strauss, with the former especially identified with a new method called semiology—the science of signs. The sociology which underwrote this semiology was Marxist, and most often it was Althusserian (structuralist) in its particular inflection. One important theoretical addition, often via Althusser, came in the form of Lacanian psychoanalysis—itself a structuralist elaboration of Freud. The Lacanian influence is already present in Barthes' semiological account of advertising. For instance he writes that today it is thought that 'the psyche itself is articulated like a language' (Barthes, 1964). We can usefully distinguish two strands of structuralist analysis of advertising. One strand, represented by Williamson and later Goldman and Papson, is based in a critique of political economy. The other strand, in general more anthropological than sociological in its register, is represented in the work of Langholz Leymore and later by O'Barr. We will review the work of these writers, and so outline and evaluate what 'structuralism' has meant in the context of advertising research.

The first sustained application of structuralist ideas to advertising is Langholz Leymore's *Hidden Myth* (1975). While picking up on the structuralist fascination with mythologies as essentially conservative in nature the book is generally less motivated than later interventions by any specific political agenda. Leymore employs a very full application of Levi-Strauss' structural approach to the study of advertising in what was one of the earliest empirical studies of British advertisements. She closely examined magazine advertisements in five product areas during one year, and TV advertisements for three brands (in different product sectors) over four years.

She described advertisements as being at the intersection of the exchange of signs and of commercial exchange. Her basic approach was to see advertisements as a sign-system, and to assume the universality of the symbolic function of the mind. On this basis modern advertisements can be seen to be constructed like tribal or Greek myths, using the same sign-system to have the same function in society, of reinforcing accepted modes of behaviour. Also advertising reduces anxiety, by re-stating the essential problems of life and solving them with simple answers. In

Leymore's structuralist terms, this means posing the essential binary dichotomies of life (good *vs* evil, life *vs* death, happiness *vs* misery, etc.) and resolving them, through the triumph of the 'positive' pole. For structuralism, the universality of binary oppositions reflects the innate, structuring, essentially classificatory activity of the mind.

By listing the product attributes described in her sample of advertisements, Leymore developed a list of binary oppositions, which she then reduced to a list of core binaries called Exhaustive Common Denominators (ECDs), which, she argued, constituted the deep structure of the advertising sign-system. Thus an analysis of butter advertisements revealed the following oppositions (defined not just by the stated characteristics of butter but by its alleged differences from margarine):

    butter:marg. // dear:cheap
        concord:protest
        content:discontent
        care:negligence
        love:hate

From these she derived a basic pair which she claimed is at the root of the above:

    peace:war // butter:marg

Peace:war is an ECD, the most fundamental type of binary theme to be found beneath the surface of advertisements. These themes express the basic dilemmas or tensions of life with which we all have to grapple. They constitute the underlying structure of advertising messages. Other ECDs emerged in other product sectors: from an analysis of baby food advertisements she derived the pair life:death, and from those for cheeses, endogenous:exogenous (the crucial issue here was where the cheese came from).

Overall the major ECDs which she found were war:peace, new:old, life:death, in:out, body:soul, good:evil, eternal time:profane time, happiness:misery, knowledge:ignorance, culture:nature, and hot:cold. She then proceeded to link these together into a system on the basis of conceptual links between them. The resulting schema was claimed to be a fairly full description of the overall advertising system—i.e. that from which all advertisements must draw their meanings.

It is impossible either to replicate or to criticise the procedures used by Leymore to code advertising content and to generate the binaries, because she gave no information as to how this was done, or about some key aspects of her sampling method. The impression is however that considerable use was made of intuitive techniques, and that the influence, *a priori*, of the axioms of structuralism might therefore have been strong.

While working ourselves from a different theoretical orientation, we can identify some features of this work which link it with our own research. In its method, the (apparently) systematic study of advertisement content, and the hypothesis that all advertisements in a product sector within a given period comprise a signification system of some sort (i.e. draw upon common meanings), are features consistent with our approach. And in its theory, the notion that advertisements deal in anxieties and their reduction is very close to the theory we advance in Chapter 6, with the important difference that we conceptualise anxieties in a psychoanalytic way rather than using an ethnographic typology based on the structuralist theory of mind. We can also support the idea that advertisements, like myths, prescribe behaviour, though Leymore's formulations are open to the usual interpretation of this prescription as necessarily being an oppressive normalisation rather than a guide to or model for action which the reading subject may reject or modify.

The anthropological-structuralist approach sees advertising as a highly *organised* force, which presents us with a unified, coherent set of images or value statements, as if advertisements spoke to us in a single language or with a single voice. In the more general language of the social sciences and social criticism, two terms are often used to express this sort of organisation. One is 'ideology': it may be said that advertisements all contribute to an 'ideology' (of capitalism, materialism, consumerism, sexism, etc.). The other, of more recent origin but already a well-worn term in social and cultural theory, is 'discourse'. The Concise Oxford Dictionary tells us that 'discourse' has two meanings—a loose one, when it can refer to a conversation or a piece of writing, and a more precise one which originated in linguistics, where it means a 'connected series of utterances'.

This second sense is the one in which it has been taken up in cultural and social theory, though there may often have been some slippage such that the apparent precision of the second meaning is attached to the flexible use of the first. Discourse in the second sense means a set or series of statements which are linked in some way—they share the same assumptions, or they are about the same thing, however broad. The 'statements' involved may be written or spoken; they may be official documents or casual remarks, or may even be visual images. In this sense one can speak of the discourse of contemporary sociology, British

Conservatism, pop music lyrics, or holiday brochures. A discourse in this sense is quite likely to be ongoing, i.e. it is constantly being 'spoken', or added to.

In some more recent work the idea of advertising discourse is the main legacy of the structuralist-anthropological approach. In *Culture and the Advertisement*, the American anthropologist William O'Barr says:

> The discourse of advertising is roughly connected in that any advertisement is actively part of a larger flow of such messages...New advertisements do not exist in a vacuum. They are part of a larger flow, a discourse of advertising. (O'Barr, 1994)

Now a discourse in this sense need not be unified by all its statements having the same ideological values, or by the same assumptions lying behind all the utterances in the discourse. The statements just quoted from O'Barr are in themselves saying no more than that advertising is a kind of language, and of course within a language it is possible to express all sorts of different ideologies or different discourses in the sense of statements sharing some values or assumptions. But there is often a slippage in writings about advertising, such that the term 'discourse' comes to mean an ideologically coherent system, as happens in O'Barr's work.

He distinguishes between the 'primary' discourse of advertising, what advertisements say about goods and services, and the 'secondary' discourse, which comprises ideas about society and culture (a distinction close to that of Barthes between denotation and connotation). His book is an exploration of one portion of that secondary discourse, namely the ideas that American print advertising, primarily in the earlier years of this century, offered to its readers about 'foreigners', i.e. non-Americans, with some attention also paid to representations of non-white Americans. As he puts it, in anthropological language, it is a study of how 'otherness' is construed in advertisements. It is implied in the book that this discourse is fairly unified, i.e. that advertisements speak with one voice. Apart from the interesting idea of comparing these representations of 'the other' in images of national and ethnic others with the images found in holiday travel photos (and a study of where the two met in early advertisements for cameras), O'Barr's argument follows a predictable path.

As we might expect, the representation of 'others' and 'otherness' found here is not a positive one. Foreigners are patronised, marginalised and denigrated, and the discourse of advertising is a fairly uniformly oppressive one. O'Barr does note some changes in representations of Afro-Americans since the Civil Rights movement, and since the growth of large markets amongst blacks for a widening range of goods, but otherwise presents advertising as a grossly repetitive and prejudiced discourse, one that would well merit the earlier and more evaluative term of 'ideology'. There can be no suggestion that this is not an accurate portrayal of advertising discourse in the materials he studied, but the structuralist assumption that advertising is a unified and ideological discourse is not adequate for the study of more recent developments.

The political economy strand of structuralist analysis has been more durable. It has drawn heavily on the work of Althusser and Lacan to formulate a critique of advertising as ideology. In advertising studies Lacan was used with special attention being paid to his theory of 'the mirror phase', a translation of which had been published in *New Left Review* (in 1971). His assertion that the unconscious was structured 'like a language' also attracted semiotic theorists as it provided legitimation for their belief that the study of cultural signification was, in a direct way, a study of social subjection.

The illustrative texts in this tradition are Barthes' essays 'The rhetoric of the image' (1964/1977) and 'The advertising message' (1988), John Berger's book *Ways of Seeing* (1973) and Judith Williamson's *Decoding Advertisements* first published in 1978. These works heralded an extensive re-drafting of the tradition of cultural analysis. Most of them were composed outside the UK and were marked with the persuasive glamour of imported theory. While Leavisites pursued a vocation marked by a passionate commitment to the values of the elect, the structuralist critic was a professional, marked by an initiation into the language of an intellectual technocracy.

Barthes' 'The rhetoric of the image' (Barthes, 1964/1977) outlined a strategy for analysing visual texts. Images denoted the product but at the same time a quality such as Italianicity or freshness. It is Barthes' first attempt to apply the structuralist methodology directly to a single advertisement text. In a variety of ways it anticipates the much more extensive study provided by Williamson and discussed below.

The principal question the essay explores is the relationship between denotation and connotation, i.e. the relation between an artificially conceived literalness, what's 'there' on the page, and the cultural associations which are likely to underlie it for any culturally competent reader. For instance, in looking at a simple advertisement for *Panzani Pasta* Barthes identifies denotative elements (a tomato, a string bag, etc.)

and elaborates the connotative elements associated with these signifying elements (market day freshness, Italianicity, etc.). This is by no means in itself a profound operation. What is important about the essay is what it says about the advertising image's mode of producing and managing connotation.

Barthes asserts the need to elaborate the various 'lexicons' from which connotative meanings are drawn by the reader. He proposes two distinct 'locations' for these lexicons. One is the psyche which, following Lacan perhaps, he says is 'articulated like a language' (Barthes, 1964/1977). The other is culture and, more particularly, 'ideology'.

Barthes' critique of advertisements shares with his famous work on 'Mythologies' the aim of showing how the cultural constructedness of their meanings is concealed in the production of signs. That is, he wants to reveal how signification of any kind is used in order to turn culture into nature. He claims that advertisements use tricks of imagistic arrangement in order to claim for their products meanings which they have no right to attach to them. Advertising rhetoric facilities the myth making which, as a denial of history and a cloak for its own constructed operationalisation of meaning, is a barrier to a true apprehension of the world. The aim of Barthes' essay is to perfect the applicability of semiotic analysis to imagistic modes of information such as advertising in order to offer tools that might denaturalise the specious naturalisation performed by the rhetoric of the advertising image. This is an invitation which has been taken up with relish by countless semiotic decoders since. Williamson in particular has utilised Barthesian approaches in her attempt to implicate advertising as the major mode utilised by capitalist and patriarchal power to secure its ideological domination.

However a second essay by Barthes, this time looking at an ice cream advertisement, offers the sense that advertising provides readers with something else along with the production of serial mystification. In this essay, which nods to an anthropological conception of our symbolic use of goods, and which disaffiliates itself from the Marxist commitment to a unitary conception of the truth underlying representation, Barthes offers a more sympathetic view of the mobilisation of connotative associations.

> By its double message, the connoted language of advertising reintroduces the dream into the humanity of the purchaser: the dream: i.e. no doubt, a certain alienation (that of competitive society), but also a certain truth (that of poetry). (Barthes, 1988)

He even goes so far as to suggest that advertising, when it is done well, can be in some manner therapeutic. It is placed by him 'among those great aliments of psychic nutrition...which for us include literature, performances, sports, the press, fashion' (Barthes, 1988).

We discuss later the plausibility of linking Barthes' second and more positive account of advertising connotation to our psycho-social approach, in which we, too, are concerned with the possibility that by swathing the product in advertising language, we give it meaning and thereby 'transform its simple use into an experience of the mind' (Barthes, 1988).

Barthes' two essays represent a basic polarity which has divided academic accounts of advertising since the 1960s. On the one hand we see a pessimistic structuralism unpicking the ideological deceptions concealed in advertising imagery. On the other we see a positive valuation of some advertising, which is justified in terms of its capacity to link readers to symbolic resources within the self and within the culture.

Now we will consider in detail the argument put forward by Williamson. Her *Decoding Advertisements* fuses many of the ideas which mark this phase of the critique. Published in 1978 and reprinted for the eleventh time in 1995, it remains central to any understanding of the academic discourse about advertising. It is given an extended exploration here because its psychoanalytic approach places it very close to some of our concerns. Also because Williamson's argument leads her to some conclusions which we are interested in contesting, it is important to look at them closely. The complexity of her formulations and the wide range of theory she attempts to introduce into the debate make her argument resistant to the kind of summary approach used elsewhere in this chapter. For these reasons her contribution requires a more extended analysis than those given to other theorists' work.

In *Decoding Advertisements* a selection of advertising texts were studied in the belief that the application of a science of signification would assist in the work of emancipating a society fixed in unequal social relations by means of the powerful ideological systems of capitalism and patriarchy. By alerting audiences to the mechanisms which held them in place it was hoped that truer and better 'ways of seeing' could be fostered, i.e. ways which might be able to see right through advertisements as opposed to seeing blinkeredly through them (*Ways of Seeing* is the title of Berger's classic account of representational strategies which concludes with an extended critique of advertising). Structuralism provided her with a crucial extra dimension to the established critique of false consciousness by providing an account of the representational mechanisms of advertising in a language which hoped to articulate how signs work.

Williamson attempts to demonstrate how particular arrangements at the level of 'the signifier' helped advertising in its task of making the reader transfer desirable cultural meanings onto the product at the level of the 'signified'. The result of this transfer of meaning is the reader's reproduction of the product as a 'commodity sign'. Advertisements provide a matrix for the transliteration of objects from an inert world of things into a realm of cultural meanings. This establishes functional objects in a 'currency' of meanings—an economy of signs. The advertising matrix simultaneously secures the individual into an ideologically constructed identification with that commodity sign. For Williamson these cultural associations were dangerous and unnatural. The attendant personal identification was a betrayal of authentic selfhood. Discussing a notional car advertisement, Williamson writes:

> Suppose that the car did a high mpg: this could be translated into terms of thriftiness, the user being a 'clever' saver, in other words, being a certain kind of person. Or, if the mpg was low, the advertisement could appeal to the 'above money pettiness', daredevil kind of person who is too 'trendy' to be economising. Both the statements in question could be made on the purely factual level of 'use value' by simple figures of '50 mpg' and '20 mpg'. (Williamson, 1995)

This is very much in line with Williams' account set out fifteen years previously. What makes Williamson distinctive is her way of describing the way this transition from use value to exchange value is brought about. The transfer of meaning is achieved by the extensive repertoire of sleights of hand through which advertising presents the product. She is interested in advertising as a 'form' of communication which system-atically misdirects human feeling—just as a bent croupier misdirects the eye of the hapless gambler. In Williamson's preferred terms the 'signifier' creates specious meanings by allowing for a correlation to be made between depicted elements of the advertisement (product representation and value representation—e.g. mpg and 'thriftiness'). This correlation or association is importantly 'non sequential', i.e. 'the two things are linked not by the line of an argument or a narrative but by their place in a picture' (Williamson, 1995).

Williamson, unlike previous advertising critics, has an explicit theory of the role of the reader. The postulated transfer of meaning is explicitly not performed by the advertisement. Instead readers are required to 'complete the transfer'. In Williamson's model the transfer is made between a depicted component of the advertisement, which is full of meaning, onto the product representation which is basically devoid of meaning. The full elements are selected from the shared stock of established cultural concepts which Williamson calls 'referent systems'. These are 'mythological' and 'ideological' reservoirs where the individual subject sinks or swims. The advertiser is free to draw upon this reservoir of meaning. With every wave of advertising the individual confronts, its waters become more choppy. For Williamson the subject is always already at sea, not waving but drowning.

In Williamson's model the reading of the advertisement is seen to proceed as follows. The reader peruses the advertisement ('the signifier' which is itself the conjunction of many signifiers) isolating the depicted elements (e.g. an antiques market, a film star's face, a jetty) which are accepted mythological representation of an (apparently non-negotiable) ideological concept or mytheme (e.g. bohemian trendiness, femininity, strength). This is the signified. At the same time the reader finds in the advertisement (at the level of the signifier) a representation of the product. By means of a variety of techniques—colour co-ordination, juxtaposition, rhetorical patterning—this representation of the product is 'correlated' with the mythological representation of the signified quality. By (mis)association at the level of the signifier the product comes to inherit, by proxy, the signified proposed alongside it. It is the reader who performs this associative work, the reader who permits this misconstruction.

Williamson is careful to note that advertising's significations 'depend for their signifying process on the existence of specific, concrete receivers' for the process of meaning transfer to unfold. All this finding and correlating meanings demands that real audiences co-operate, each and every individual in compliance with the illogic of the advertising signifier.

For the meaning transfer to take place the advertisement must 'enter the space of the receiver' (Williamson, 1995). Williamson's account of the form of this entrance is key to a full understanding of her theory. The mechanism which allows the reader and the advertisement to interact is called 'interpellation', a process first articulated by Althusser. Williamson cites his description:

> All ideology hails or interpellates concrete individuals as concrete subjects, by the functioning of the category of the subject...ideology 'acts' or 'functions' in such a way that it 'recruits' subjects among the individuals (it recruits them all) or 'transforms' the individuals into subjects (it transforms them all) by that

very precise operation which I have called interpellation or hailing, and which can be imagined along the lines of the most commonplace everyday police (or other) hailing: 'Hey, you there!'...Assuming that the theoretical scene I have imagined takes place in the street, the hailed individual will turn round. By this mere one hundred and eighty degree physical conversion, he becomes a subject. Why? because he had recognised that the hail was 'really' addressed to him, and that it was really him who was hailed (and not someone else). (Althusser cited Williamson, 1995)

It is not just the police who hail us. Hailing is done by advertisements too. According to Williamson the reader of an advertisement is 'hailed' and 'positioned' in just this way. For Thompson, advertisers are imagined as 'gangsters plotting ones' murder' (see above). For Williamson the prototypical authors of advertising are like secret police. Advertising producers, faceless in both species of critique, are figured according to opposed political fantasies. While obviously addressing a larger number of people the advertiser in practice addresses an imaginary individual, a 'you'. This 'you' is an aggregated identity composed of the signifying elements of the advertisement. It is an individuating call which corresponds not to any real individual but to an imaginary individuality. Each advertisement

> ...projects into the space out in front of it an imaginary person composed in terms of the relationship between the elements within the advertisement. You move into this space as you look at the advertisement, and in doing so 'become' the spectator, you feel that the 'hey you' 'really did' apply to you in particular. (Williamson, 1995)

As well as becoming the imaginary spectator, constructed and positioned by the advertisement, by stepping into the imaginary position afforded by the advertisement, or being 'sucked into the centre of the screen' (Williamson, 1995), the reader 'becomes' the person depicted in the advertisement or one implicit in its scene. Worryingly perhaps 'we become the person at the head of the table whose friends' drink Cockburn's port, the person who is like the No. 6 smokers in the picture' (Williamson, 1995). And we are 'nothing but that subject' (Williamson, 1995). Any sense of self and any sense of relations to objects and people other than those being proposed by the advertise-ment are, according to Williamson, banished.

Since someone shouting 'hey you' does not constitute a persuasive model of communication (for a critique of the notion of hailing, see Eagleton in Zizek, 1994) upon which to graft the intricate set of processes proposed by Williamson, she provides a further theoretical formulation which is intended to secure the account of how we end up being positioned by advertisements.

Williamson's account hinges upon an explanation of how it is that, despite our differences as individuals, we are susceptible to a form of address, advertising, which replaces our variously constituted and unique selfhood with a false selfhood which has nothing to do with us and everything to do with the images laid before us by advertisers. To explain this Williamson, following Althusser, turns to certain 'tools' from psychoanalytic theorist Jaques Lacan. In particular she is interested in Lacan's account of the 'mirror phase'. Lacanian theory posits a model of subjectivity based on an account of early child development (although Williamson supports the idea that the formulation of 'the mirror phase' model is based on empirical observation of children and mirrors, she herself prefers to see the model as a metaphor). The young child, unintegrated and lacking boundaries between its (non)self and the (non)external world, lacks identity. The infant is simply a blob of life, congenitally premature, an unwritten character in search of an author. Suddenly however, 'When the child is confronted by his image in a mirror, there is a process in which he recognises himself—it really is him' (Williamson, 1995).

This is something of a crisis for the child as he knows that this imaged 'other' person both is and is not himself. To cope with this discrepant sense of self 'the child is required to place his identity in separation' (Williamson, 1995). That separation is between an unintegrated self, constituted out of subjective experiences of non-identity and an 'Imaged-I', a fictitious, totalised, mirror image which has the status of an object. Williamson writes of this situation as follows:

> That the image of this totality has this status [i.e. the status of an object (eds)], provides the subject with the permanent capacity to place himself in a similar relation to an object; this capacity is exploited by ideology. (Williamson, 1995)

This capacity is, for Williamson, one which advertising is perfectly designed to turn to its advantage. For in offering up images of idealised mythological wholeness and 'hailing' spectators, advertisements provoke a reiteration of regressive aspects of the prototypical and irreversible split in the subject. Williamson's advertising audience is like the infant in front of a mirror. It is compelled to step into the image by a desire for identity and completeness and by dread in the face of the absence of these things. The viewer of an advertisement unfailingly answers its call. Accepting this call offers a certain gratification (that of wholeness) but this is by necessity an alienation—a sacrifice of real relations in the name of fake ones. In this neo-Faustian contract we exchange our uncertain and ragged self for identity as misrepresentation. Williamson writes:

> Lacan says that the ego is constituted, in its forms and energy, when the subject 'fastens himself to an image which alienates himself from himself' so that the ego is 'forever irreducible to his lived identity'. (Williamson, 1995)

This explains why the Lacanian subject is perennially 'split' and alienated. However an important question remains. Why is advertising the exemplary discourse of such exploitation?

The answer lies in its capacity to disrupt the 'proper' boundaries marking social identity and ordering the referential boundaries of language. In Lacanian terms this principle is called the 'Symbolic' order. 'The symbolic' governs the infant's emerging capacity for signification. The symbolic oversees and is constitutive of the infant's apprenticeship into language, society and identity. Assuring the differentiation, first between self and other, the two genders and consequently, between signifiers, 'the symbolic' allows language to operate structurally as a relatively ordered signifying system. In Lacanian terms the entry into language and society through the symbolic necessitates and is necessitated by alienation. For Williamson advertising, as a special signifying system, has properties which exacerbate this alienating effect.

In Williamson's argument advertising's special power lies in a peculiar hybridity. Advertising performs a potent mutation of the symbolic order. Like any representation, it works by signification. It is therefore governed by the symbolic. Yet, because of its use of duplicitous and seductive images to enhance its emphatic solicitations of identification, it invites, into the ordered processes of differentiated symbolic signification, a disruptive tendency towards regressive and imaginary sameness. The sign is collapsed 'into unity with its referent'. Consequently distinctions are effaced and social identity is given over to perverse and regressive identification with fictive objects of desire, i.e. commodities.

So, in answer to the question 'why are advertisements especially damaging to society and personal identity?', Williamson's answer is that it is because advertisements form a symbolic system which appropriates and apparently represents the imaginary, therefore embodying the inherent contradictions of the mirror phase. An advertisement dangles before us an image of an other, but invites us to become the same. It thus capitalises on our regressive tendency towards the imaginary unity of the ego ideal. In offering us symbols as the objects of unity they ensnare us in a quest for the impossible (Williamson, 1995).

So in Williamson's reading of Lacan, advertising is harmful, as it were, twice. Once because like all language and signification it fosters alienation. Secondly (and this is distinctive to advertising) it disrupts the symbolic structure of referentiality implicating readers in a regressive and narcissistic playing out of desire and meaning.

Advertising serves only to bolster ideological orthodoxy. Advertising implicates us in the concretion of connotative associations which are based on referent systems existing anterior to the advertisement. They are 'always already' in place within the 'position' created by the advertisement for the reading subject.

There is a cognitive outline in which the product is inserted: we exchange because we know. The assumption of pre-existing bodies of knowledge allows reference to take the place of description, and connotation that of denotation: this reference must inevitably take place on the formal level, by pointing to another structure, since the 'content' or substance of the reference is the product itself. So the referent system is always a connotation because what is denoted is the product. However here a circular process is involved because having introduced the referent system by means of connotation, it is then made to denote the product—to 'place' it in a system of meaning (Williamson, 1995).

The collapse of the 'symbolic' into the 'imaginary' leads to narcissistic identification with the object. This description of psychological processes has its correlate at the level of linguistic and rhetorical processes. The correlative moment, at the level of the signifier, is the collapse of denotation into connotation leading to the ideological constitution of the product as commodity sign.

Actually, according to Williamson's theory, the readers, avowedly central to the process and billed as 'active receivers' (Williamson, 1995), seem less to perform the transfers of meaning than to affirm them. We merely rubber stamp the ideological associations made for us by advertisers. Anything distinctive about the reader is absent from the process. 'Active' reading is 'synonymous and simultaneous' (Williamson, 1995) with the advertisement's power of appellation. In so far as we respond to an advertisement we give ourselves over to it entirely. We lose ourselves in the advertisement and its ideological and mythological world.

Williamson, in common with previous critics, feels an anxiety about referentiality in the language of advertising. Her conceptual tools allow her to recognise, more explicitly than they had done, the 'arbitrariness of the signifier'. Williamson is concerned that this arbitrariness, which opens up each and every sign to a minor labour of interpretative integration, is solely and exclusively arbitrated by the dictates of capitalism and patriarchy on the one hand and narcissism and perversion on the other. This proceeds at the expense of more personal or more rational ways of seeing and knowing objects. In the face of advertising, history, thought and the self are foreclosed, and personal development, already a fraught task, is further sacrificed to a logic of development which substitutes the inhuman logic of profit for any potential growth.

There are a number of objections to Williamson's vision. Her account of the reading process and the production, by advertisements, of subjectivities, through interpellation and positioning, rests upon the assumption that this is an irresistible, complete and inevitable process towards ideological control. What Bourdieu writing of Althusser calls the 'iron cage of pessimistic functionalism' is evident in Willliamson's work. There are two ways to overcome this objection. One is to actually look at readers and see if they behave in the way Williamson suggests. This approach will be considered later. The other way is to refine the account of 'hailing' in order to see what happens to readerly resistance. This second approach is relevant here.

THE EMPIRE OF SIGNS

Most important in the development of Williamson's position is the work of Robert Goldman (Goldman, 1992; Goldman and Papson, 1996). Goldman begins where Williamson left off, with an account of how spectators are 'hailed' by advertisements. Advertisements position viewers to participate in an interpretive process based on

> ...false assumptions (Williamson, 1978), positioning viewers to presume a line of equivalence between the product and the glamorised traits of the model. Advertisements tend to invite us to step into the 'space' of an advertisement to try on the social self we might become if we wore the product image. (Goldman, 1992)

What is distinctive about Goldman's work is a partial historicisation of both producers and the readers of advertisements. Williamson, by her invocation of the interpellation and 'the mirror phase' as the sole articulation of the way in which advertisements are framed and received, gave insufficient attention to the fact that real readers are often reluctant to perform the 'advertising work' the advertisement sets out for them. Williamson identified 'advertising' in terms of a collection of

1970s examples. Goldman records the exhaustion of this 1970s 'commodity self' format and its attendant strategies of simple meaning transfer.

Goldman is not a critic of Williamson. Rather he perpetuates her basic assumptions by means of imaginative extensions and elaborations of her basic position. Goldman attempts to fuse two strands of cultural theory which, in the 1970s, provided the ground for an important division in the study of the reception of popular cultural forms. Goldman maintains the Lacanian and Althusserian perspective of Williamson—though in a manner more tacit and compromising. But Goldman also considers more seriously the possibility of an audience refusing the 'hailing' performed by advertising language. This is theorised initially in terms developed by Stuart Hall in his famous conceptualisations of processes of textual 'encoding and decoding' (Hall, 1980). Goldman combines this with Williamson's model of interpellation. The product of this theoretical hybrid is a notional reader of advertisements who both is and is not subject to the interpellative procedures described by Williamson. This is the 'alienated spectator'.

The 'alienated spectator' is not bound to take up the positions offered by the advertisement. These newly-conceived readers are capable of rejecting the preferred reading encoded into the advertisement and offering up their own attitudes to the proposed product image. Goldman's readers can, and do, refuse to perform the 'advertising work' set them by the text.

Advertisers have not abolished non-preferred meanings or misinterpretations. Try as they might advertisers have been unable to produce perfectly transparent communications (Hall, 1980) which guarantee mirrored decodings. Furthermore viewers tend to be neither static nor unmotivated in their encounters with advertisements (Goldman, 1992).

This is an important acknowledgement of the agency of the reader. Goldman's primary interest however is not in proposing this as evidence of the falsity of Williamson's basic assumption that advertising has an inexorable power to subject. Instead it is for him the ground upon which to build an account of changes in advertising formats which were developed to outsmart the restiveness of the refusing audience. Advertising now routinely incorporates messages which contradict the dictates of patriarchal and capitalistic ideology, such as the messages of 'commodity feminism' and 'green consumerism'. Advertising also engages in a number of aesthetic deconstructions of the prototypical advertising format. Goldman acutely observes how the critique of advertising communications has spilled out of the pages of academic texts and journalistic polemics and into the gloss of advertisements themselves. The imagistic clichés which were advertising's staple, become, in the 'new' advertising, the object of parodic play. Goldman depicts a world in which advertisers, audiences and academics seem in some sense united in consensual derision of the traditional consumer and his/her petty, sentimental, materialistic gullibility.

But, for Goldman, it is the advertiser who is laughing last. Various audiences' critiques of advertising, expressed in terms of boredom, apathy and scorn as much as in any overtly political formulations, are incorporated into advertising. This does not happen, according to Goldman, in any genuinely dialectical way. Instead the critiques, formal and explicit, remain subjected to the logic of the commodity form. Advertisers simply do what they have always done. They mine a seam of meaning to exploit its semiotic power in the service of the production of the product as commodity sign. Critical and popular distaste at advertising provides a meaning system which is as ripe a candidate for appropriation as any of the other referent systems advertisers use. Indeed it is more useful, for it allows the commodity sign to ratify its authenticity not simply by association but in the postmodern modality of reflexivity. In one of his many impressive textual analyses Goldman discusses a Levi's advertisement which deliberately rejects and transgresses advertising formalities by showing a character refusing the interpellating gaze of the camera:

> ...playfully transgressing the camera's boundary rules initiates a reflexive awareness about the nature of this text as advertising, and a momentary refusal to participate in the society of the spectacle. The scene ostensibly exposes the cult of the image and the role of the advertiser. But instead of unmasking the ideological construction of commodity signs, this advertisement fashions the self reflexive hipster into the newest—'most authentic'—sign yet. (Goldman, 1992)

Going beyond Williamson's conception of the audience Goldman introduces the idea of a 'savvy' audience able to assert some kind of autonomy in the face of a 'hailing' text. However he insists that the lineaments of that autonomy are always, ultimately, drawn by the advertiser, expropriating from us desire, in the form of cynicism, and selling it back to us as authenticity. The alienated spectator is re-duped into a pseudo-individuality in the end just as fake as that described by Williamson.

Goldman has another, related concern developed with Stephen Papson in their 1996 text *Sign Wars* (Goldman and Papson, 1996). Confronted with a cynical audience, advertisers are forced into devising an ever-expanding array of signifying strategies to improvise the authenticity the postmodern audience craves. At the same time increasing similarity between competitor products makes 'image' the ground of the differentiation and choice. Advertisers work increasingly hard to maintain and augment the 'sign value' attaching to their products and brands. 'Sign value' is a concept akin to the more familiar term 'exchange value'—it describes the 'value' of the commodity signs produced through advertising (see below). As in Williamson's theorisation, advertising works to transform objects into a 'currency'. This currency, as with any other currency, is subject to inflation and devaluation. As the 'economy of sign values' becomes saturated more signifiers need to be mobilised to represent the same amount of commodity. Corporate strivings for distinctive brand marketing lead them to plunder new seams in the 'giant mine' of meaning (Goldman and Papson, 1996). There is a spiralling escalation of signification driven by competitive capitalism's ever growing appetite for more and more signs ravenously to exploit and discard. In Goldman and Papson's view meaning will be depleted by the expropriative logic of a signifying culture which, in confronting meaning, commodifies it. In this world 'no meaning system is sacred' (Goldman and Papson, 1996).

To keep advertising's commodity sign machine purring requires continuously scouring the landscape for new signifying materials. Indeed advertising now chews up signs from other discourses so rapidly that it has begun to cannibalise its own system (Goldman and Papson, 1996). Again we see the concern about the 'advertising machine'; 'unpolluted meaning systems' are 'sacrificed' to it. Language is once again perverted.

Advertising's own unremitting efforts to reproduce and sustain a system of sign values contributes to breakdowns in the signifier-signified circuit. Signifiers trade places so readily with signifieds that it grows impossible to tell which end is which. But with the relationship between signifier and signified reduced to a state of equivalent indifference, the fixing of differential meaning becomes ever more difficult (Goldman and Papson, 1996). The whole system is pushed into deeper crisis.

This is largely the same point Williamson had made twenty years earlier employing a Lacanian terminology to describe the disruption of 'the symbolic' order by 'the imaginary', though the reader in Goldman's view has a certain robustness in the face of advertising dominance.

However he cites simultaneously a competing picture of a much less robust figure. He is attracted to a startling image of the reader as vealcalf.

> Veal, that's what we've become, especially the young 'uns'. That's what anyone raised by corporations, fed their version of 'fun,' 'excitement,' and above all, 'hip,' becomes—pale, docile, and unmuscled, a creature finely tuned to the aesthetics of its own flesh but incapable of standing on its own legs. Your movement beyond the TV box may be restricted, your opportunity to frolic in uncommercialised fields may be nil, but it's OK, being veal: All your life, the corporate stock feeders bring you sugar food and hormone entertainment. Raised to consume, kept soft in head and belly—the modern spirit is slaughtered early. (cited Goldman and Papson, 1996)

Goldman does not seem to resolve the tension he skilfully articulates between resistance and docility, perhaps because his interest in actual readers is limited. He prefers, like Williamson, to concentrate on imagining what is being done to readers by the creatives in the advertising agencies. Next, we will consider some different approaches to advertising which are more interested in readers, either as a theoretical category or an empirical object of study.

THE ALIENATED READER

One of these is based on a use of Marxism which is more theoretically elaborate than that found in the work of Williamson and Goldman; this is to be found in Sut Jhally's study (Jhally, 1987), the more empirical aspect of which we reported on in Chapter 3. In the theoretical framework for that study, Jhally advances a Marxist analysis of television advertising. He argues, as he does with colleagues in Leiss *et al.*, that advertisements must be seen in the context of our relationship to objects, since that is what most of them are about. And our relationship to goods is typically a fetishistic one. Marx used the concept of fetishism to refer to the way in which the operation of the capitalist market seems to be beyond human control. The term was and still is used by anthropologists to refer to the worship of some inanimate object as if it had magical powers. In Marxist theory, the fetishism of commodities refers to the way that the social origins of goods are typically concealed from the consumer. How much do we know about the social context in which our clothes were produced, or about the relations of production of our hi-fi systems or PCs? Goods are thus stripped of their social meanings, in the sense of their social origins, and the powers they have to satisfy or please us cannot be traced to the skill or effort of those who produced them. They are denuded of their rightful meaningfulness.

Jhally argues that it was Marx's central insight to see how goods are emptied of their meaning when they appear in the capitalist market. Capitalist production and distribution obscure from the consumer the social relations of production. All commodities in the market are measured by their abstract exchange value, and are not known by their specific origins. We do not know where things come from or how they come to be as they are. (By the same token we are likely to be involved in making things without knowing where they are going or how they are used—sometimes, in components manufacture, without even knowing what they are a part of.) This is an aspect of the general Marxist theory of alienation: we are alienated from the products of our own and others' labour.

The role of advertisements, says Jhally, is then to fill this emptiness—to rush into the void and endow goods with meanings. These will be fetishised meanings, because it will seem as if the products themselves have the powers attributed to them, and a worship of the commodities for what they can do is generated. What is obscured is the origins of the commodities in specific relations of production, and their creation by human labour and skill, and also the fact that our use and appreciation of them also depends on social relations. The value which we place on a particular brand, for example, must depend on the reputation of that brand, i.e. on its place in a cultural scale of values. The mystique of, say, BMW, or Armani, or Haagen-Dasz, derives from the image of the brand, which is a social construction.

As evidence for this line of argument Jhally discusses some research (Easterlin, 1984) which sought to compare levels of reported happiness in different societies. Happiness was found *not* to increase over time, or with the overall wealth of a society relative to another or to an earlier period in its own history, but was found to be greater amongst richer people within the same society—i.e. goods do not in themselves bring happiness, but *relative* wealth, i.e. goods measured against what others have, does bring happiness (at least as far as that can be apprehended through the techniques of social research).

Advertising, however, seeks to persuade us that it is the product itself in some intrinsic way which possesses this mystique, as if the metal of the car or the material of the jeans is somehow empowered and empowering. It encourages us to see the good as if it has an existence independent of human effort. Fetishism is then the tendency to endow things with human or superhuman powers.

We must note the differences between this anthropologically-based notion of fetishism, and the meaning of the term in psychoanalytic theory. In the latter, it refers to an object which is taken as the focus of sexual interest, or which is necessary for sexual pleasure, as a defence against castration anxiety. By investing libidinal energy in the fetish object, the fetishist can avoid confronting the question of the phallus, its absence in women and the phantasy of its loss. Most fetishists are men, and the fetish is, in a sense, the woman's phallus. There is a common theme between this and an anthropological/sociological conception, in the idea of the fetish as a stand-in, but the sexual element is not present in the Marxist concept.

The concept of fetishism as originated by Marx is also important in the approach of Leiss *et al.*, for whom advertising is 'a lush and entertaining realm of fetishes' (Leiss *et al.*, 1990). However, they argue that these fetishes are not all 'harmful or manipulative in general'. The distortions of communication which ensue are intrinsic components of the world of goods, i.e. in any social context goods will be called upon to tell particular stories and not others. Their analysis of 'cultural frames' for goods (see Chapter 3) shows how the broad parameters of communication through goods have changed during the period of modern advertising, how different general kinds of story have been added to the 'fetishistic' repertoire of marketing.

In addition to this use of the theory of alienation and fetishism, Jhally's more Marxist approach also tries—in keeping with the assumption in Marxism that economic processes are fundamental—to focus on the economic relations of advertising. One economically-oriented approach is to focus on advertising revenue and see it as a form of rent. This focuses on the hiring of the space (in print or broadcast medium, poster space or web space), so advertising is a form of property business. This, while it is a basic dimension of the industry, and especially of its relations with the media, gives no starting-point for understanding why the *content* of advertisements is what it is. It also omits the role of the audience from consideration.

Jhally tries instead to construct an analogy between the consumption of advertisements and the capitalist labour process, i.e. to see advertisements in the context of the theory of production as well as of consumption. His approach is based on the idea that watching television advertisements is a form of work. He hypothesises that there is a parallel between labour power, the capacity of the worker to labour and so to generate value, and 'watching power'. The industrialist buys the labour power of workers, and pays them enough to reproduce their labour power (to feed and clothe themselves, etc). During the hours of wage labour, though, the workers produce much more value than is required to maintain them. This 'surplus value' is the capitalist's profit.

Similarly in television advertising, argues Jhally (and the argument can be extended to print media, though not easily to poster sites). The television network buys our watching power, paying for it with programming. In other words, programmes we want to watch bring us back the next evening or week and so 'reproduce' our watching power. It is as if we work for the television networks, by labouring away in front of the screen. What we 'produce' from watching advertisements is knowledge about products, and meanings. These products of our 'watching power' are sold to the advertisers. To get us to continue watching, the networks have to provide us with programmes as well as advertisements. But since advertising revenue is greater than the costs of programming, there is surplus value which accrues to the networks.

Since there is more value to advertisers in a targeted, selected audience, the networks are driven towards 'narrowcasting', i.e. to aiming programmes at segments of the population. The move to diversity in TV is driven by the need to maximise advertising revenue.

So rather than taking the path of Baudrillard and developing a critique of Marxist political economy, Jhally tries to find a way of applying it to the world of images. Marx had described objects as having two kinds of value: use-value, based on their practical function (the use-value of food is that it dispels hunger, gives nutrition, etc.), and exchange-value, their market value (this depends on scarcity, demand, transport and packing costs, etc.). Commodity fetishism is in a sense the triumph of exchange-value over use-value. To this analysis of value, Baudrillard—under the influence of structuralist linguistics—added sign-value, which is based on the difference of the object from others and on the social meanings marked by or attached to that difference. In a full consumer society, sign-value is the dominant kind—hence objects are 'commodity-signs'.

Baudrillard therefore supplied a concept which Jhally's analysis—of advertisements coming into fill a void—requires: why would there be a void unless objects always had, and we needed them to have, a meaning-dimension? Jhally recognises this in answering the charge that his analysis of television viewing as work is flawed because people don't have to watch in the way they do have to work for a material living. His reply is that watching is driven by another kind of need: we have a need for meaning, and because traditional institutions no longer satisfy this need we are driven into engagement with media and with the information and images they offer.

Overall therefore Jhally builds in to an analysis of advertising a strong model of the subject/reader, as having certain deep and active needs. However, there appears to be no tension between this subject and the commercial and ideological imperatives of advertising; the subject's needs for entertainment and for meaning simply mesh with the operation of the advertising industry, indeed provide the space within which it can work.

WORDS AND FEELINGS

While it is the structuralist theories of language, as appropriated by sociologists and cultural critics, which feature most in the better-known critical writings, there is a body of work in which linguists have examined the verbal language of advertising in some detail. In the small number of studies by linguists of the verbal language of advertisements, it is language *in* advertising which is under scrutiny, rather than the language *of* advertising. The earliest and most detailed of these is the study by Leech (1966) of language in a sample of 617 television advertisements from 1960–1961. Studiously non-judgemental, Leech was concerned to describe advertising language in terms primarily of its grammatical structure and vocabulary. Assuming that language is shaped by its context, he argued that advertising had earlier in the century developed a distinctive, colloquial style, which embodied 'universal principles of salesmanship' and which he called 'standard advertising English'. It had remained within this style and, Leech predicted, would continue to do so despite the production of novel and unorthodox forms. It is unlikely, though, that this prediction would hold against the profusion of styles and appropriations of non-commercial idioms that Goldman and others have discussed.

The most recent and readable is by Greg Myers (*Words in Ads*, 1994), who discusses features such as sentence construction, punning, the use of pronouns, metaphors, and the construction of slogans. He argues that while advertisements do constitute a distinct genre, they can only be understood with reference to discourses with which their readers will be familiar. In their characteristically 'intertextual' messages, which draw on many other cultural materials, they both 'position' readers (i.e. imply that the reader is a certain sort of person or has certain needs or wishes) *and* provide opportunities for diverse reconstructions of their meaning by their audiences. Myers also offers an outline of stages in the history of advertising, seeing the 1920s and 1960s as moments of substantial change. In the 1920s attention shifted

from relatively simple brand identification based on product characteristics to a semiologically richer approach in which positive
meanings of various kinds were associated with the product. In the
1960s, he suggests, came the beginnings of more oblique or self-
conscious approaches to communicating with consumers who were
now wise to marketing stratagems, and bombarded with advertising
messages.[3]

Cook's 1992 text *The Discourse of Advertising* is a sophisticated
attempt to mobilise literary and linguistic theory in the study of
advertising. Taking the term 'discourse' to distinguish his work from the
textual semiotics of structuralists, Cook highlights his understanding of
the complex and embedded nature of advertising's linguistic and
communicative function. This leads to an emphasis on the difficulties in
isolating advertising as a special discourse type. The book demonstrates
at the level of technical linguistic description something which, for
instance, Fowles (1996), Willis (1990) and Nava (1997) propose in
broader terms: the permeability, in form and in function, between
advertising and other kinds of popular communication.

Rather like Stern (see below), Cook covertly attributes some cultural
merit to advertising simply by demonstrating that it is susceptible to
analytic modes formerly reserved for more highly valued forms of
expression. For instance, of a slogan for vodka he writes:

> The particular form of words mimes and reinforces the meaning, it represents
> it, indeed it *is* it. This is a kind of language associated with poetry, and it seems
> reasonable to me, in a general sense, to call this advertisement 'poetic'.

Cook does not develop his sense of why the kinds of linguistic play he
identifies demand a re-evaluation of advertising's cultural role. He
suggests that play and the pleasure derived from it might afford
unspecified 'cognitive benefits of which we are only vaguely aware', but
goes no further in any attempt to justify what such play might mean or
what its value might be.

Ultimately Cook's major contribution is to alert readers to the
untenable nature of critiques of advertising grounded in the dismissal of
its formal bankruptcy. He successfully shows that as an unstable but
identifiable discourse type advertising displays innovation and imagination quite as much as other cultural forms. Cook does not commit
himself to any final adjudication on the question of advertising's
cultural value and is ambivalent about the significance of the verbal
richness his detailed readings articulate. At times wanting to celebrate

advertising virtuosity, Cook fights shy of specifying its virtues. In the end he restricts himself to finding advertisements 'interesting'.

DISSONANT VOICES

The culture industry thesis and Althusserian structuralism, which together underpin so much important academic writing about media culture, have been questioned by writers unconvinced by the implicit negation of the experiences of media audiences in the cultural processes in which they are supposed to be taking part. In different ways the works of the *Scrutiny* critics, the Frankfurt school theorists and more lately semiotic analysts such as Williamson and Goldman all employ a model of a subjectivity which seems to capitulate too readily in the face of any media input, especially that in an advertising format. Some writers have striven to test the assumption that the self is so rigidly bound to this kind of compliance. Thompson expresses the basis of the dissatisfaction with this critical tradition:

> One of the less fortunate legacies of much critical social theory in recent decades—especially those forms of social theory which have had most impact in critical media studies—has been an impoverished conception of the self. (Thompson, 1995)

Buttle draws a similar conclusion specifically from an examination of academic writing about advertising. Her broad-ranging survey of academic literature on advertising in the 1970s and 1980s finds a majority of theorists bound to

> ...an indefensible ontological and epistemological position, producing not knowledge, but something else (perhaps politics) and betraying, for the sake of theoretical elegance and parsimony, the complexity of the human condition. (Buttle, 1991)

Few of the critics we have looked at would feel particularly wounded by the accusation that their projects are political in intent. But it is the case that the kind of analysis which has been dominant in advertising studies, i.e. the close reading of individual advertisements in search of evidence (unfailingly found) of corrupt and corrupting semiotic arrangements, has sometimes been negligent of the complex lineaments of response. The suggestion that there has been an occlusion of the moment of *reading* in debates about advertising's cultural impact has opened an interesting new space of enquiry which demanded new approaches.

These challenge the assumption that advertising has the power to control and deform the social and semiotic agenda of everyday lives. Often interdisciplinary, these approaches range across ideas from literary theory to life history and ethnographic methods. They share a plea for acknowledgement of the robustness of human agency in the face of advertising communications. It is not without irony that the methods of literary studies, which owe their institutional power, if not all their current forms, to the work and energies of F. R. Leavis and Raymond Williams should have been deployed as part of a rebuttal against claims about the power and maleficence of advertising. Yet this seems to be the case. Stern (1989) sets out a comprehensive account of the possible interfaces between literary studies and advertising research. In a sentence which would have horrified previous generations of literary critics Stern proposes the following analogy, apparently unconscious of the value distortions and elisions implicit in her proposal.

> Literary criticism, as a mode of enquiry can be applied to any document read as a text, since a triangular dynamic generally interrelates the author, the text, and the reader (Quilligan, 1979). If we substitute 'company persona' for 'author', 'advertisement' for 'text' and 'consumer' for 'reader', an analogy to consumer research can be seen. (Stern, 1989)

Whatever mischief this formulation performs it nevertheless demonstrates how a variety of perspectives have something to say about advertising which had previously been unsaid in academic writing in that topic. The desire to look more closely at the 'authorship' or production of advertisements, at different aspects of their textuality and ways and experiences of reading advertisements provides a challenging supplement to the orthodox model of the diffusion of commercial power and meaning in society and culture.

Even when writers like Goldman have given full accounts of reception and subjectivity in the advertising process, for instance in the acknowledgement and characterisation of readers' knowingness and boredom or in the use of Williamson's Lacanian formulations, there remains an evident blind spot. It is possible to perceive in this critical strategy a desire to locate, unify and totalise symbolic power in the hands of the advertising industry. The upshot of this is a critical approach which tends to locate this power in advertising texts themselves. The text becomes the sovereign source of consumer knowledge. The consumer has no meaningful input into the way that objects around him or her are known. This assumption provides grounds for the further claims that texts are potent and irresistible conduits of both commercial and ideological coercion.

In this connection Nava has observed that advertising has been 'framed' by academic critics, which is to say advertisements have been set apart and 'incriminated' as '*the* iconographic signifier of multi-national capitalism' (Nava, 1997). She considers three works as exemplars of this incrimination: Thomas Richards' study of the development of consumer culture in *Victorian England* (Richards, 1991), Armand Mattelart's critique of the international advertising industry (Mattelart, 1991), and Robert Goldman's work. Following Lee (1993), she notes the 'Fordist' conception of culture on which these works are based, by which advertising is seen as mediating the power of the economic 'base' of society in a monolithic and inevitable way. She suggests two things: firstly that a less deterministic account of advertising signification is more appropriate, and secondly, that alongside such an account can come a more balanced and more complex view of advertising's social and cultural impact. In Nava's account advertising images should not so readily be treated as simply the various reiterations and encryptions of a singular and overarching proposition of commercial power. Between advertising as the rendering of a commercial intention and advertising as an aesthetic activity, Nava suggests there lies the space of a creative disjunction. By turning attention towards the reader of advertisements and away from textual analysis a richer description of this space becomes possible. Such a description is provided in Nava and Nava (1992) in which the question 'discriminating or duped?' is proposed and explored.

A useful bridge between the broadly semiotic approaches and the ethnographic or reader-interview based approaches comes in the work of Trevor Pateman. His position, coming from pragmatic linguistics, counters some of the structuralist assumptions of semiotic readings of advertising. Without recourse to ethnographic interviews with actual readers he nevertheless asserts the importance of the context of reception in the advertising transaction. In particular he questions the descriptions of the process whereby a reader 'gets' the connotative messages associated with an advertisement. Pateman astutely counters Williamson's 'semiotic' readings of the connotations operative in advertisements (Pateman, 1980). He sees a misconception in critics' use of the term connotation.

>...quite often connotation is taken to be a straightforward semantic function or operation in which connotations figure as properties or entailments of texts

or images, rather than as the result of structured operations performed upon texts or images by knowledgeable readers. (Pateman, 1980)

Pateman's analysis raises two key issues which ethnographic analysts were to pursue later. Firstly he asks how the textual analysts know that there will be a predictable operation of connotative meanings in the shaping of reader responses (Pateman, 1980). The work of connotation is more mysterious and hazardous than some critics seem to imply. Secondly, by asserting a sense of the reader as a social actor exercising competencies he raises the question of pleasure. Since advertisements are a discourse calling upon a range of 'sophisticated linguistic and cognitive competencies' (Pateman, 1980) it follows that there is, at least in theory, some enjoyment to be had in our everyday reading of them. So we see in Pateman's critique of semiotic analyses of advertisements the emergence of three key themes: readers' sophistication, readers' specificity and readers' pleasure. These themes were explored empirically in the next phase of academic advertising critique.

WHAT READERS DO WITH TEXTS

Writing from an anthropological perspective, Daniel Miller offers an account of consumer culture in line with that recommended by Schudson.

> It is time for a study that will not be a reflex-like intellectual revulsion at the world of goods but an effort to understand what place material culture might hold in a good world. (Schudson, 1984)

> The problem with reducing the analysis of specific material domains to their place in social differentiation and the reproduction of dominance is that...this approach may tend to ignore all the other projects in the development of which goods are employed. (Miller, 1995)

Miller's interest in social materiality enables him to question the pervasive assumption that advertisers have the upper hand in all transactions with the consumer. He proposes, instead, that in the case of a great many everyday material goods analysts must examine 'the complex articulation between producer and consumer' (Miller, 1995).

Using examples of the actual consumption and use of goods he provides evidence that the concerns of consumers can play a role in subverting and re-shaping marketers' strategies, the material forms available in the market place and the symbolic associations these material forms come to enshrine. Miller does not write as a simple champion of consumer sovereignty. Instead he charts examples of the modes and situations in which consumption can serve as the space for a renegotiation of dominant ideologies according to the interests of dominated groups, and as the primary and sometimes anticipatory mode of materialisation and self-objectification for new social groups, lifestyles and subjectivities (Miller, 1995).

Miller's argument about the reciprocity between the spheres of production and consumption is illustrated by his account of the power of the consumer in relation to material form in various categories of goods. Miller suggests that for instance in the case of small, low cost everyday objects 'ranging from saucepans to skirts' which are the subject of 'mass marketing and advertising' it is the dictates of demand which inform the market.

> ...little research and investment is likely to be put into the active promotion of new forms determined by production, and the producer may be reduced to a more or less passive respondent to apparent shifts in demand. (Miller, 1995)

With specific regard to advertising this 'articulation' of the reciprocity between production and consumption allows him to question the claim that advertising serves only to guide consumers to adopt producer interests and ideologies.

> The critic who points out that the advertisement appears to have nothing to do with the material and functional nature of the product is merely reproducing the general illusion of vulgar functionalism enshrined in modernism. It is the secondary, often social, but possibly also humorous, moral or sexual connotations which represent the actual value of the aestheticised commodity (Haug, 1986) to the purchaser. (Miller, 1995)

Though Miller's primary interest is in material culture, his acknowledgement here of the role of advertising in the idiosyncratic work of connotatively endowing the object with meaning offers a powerful critique of the Marxist paradigm in advertising studies. This critique was to be developed further by the writers discussed below.

The question of connotation is taken up by Mick and Politi (1989) where they describe the problems associated with researching idiosyncratic consumer response as the 'hell of connotation'. In a later work Mick draws on literary and psychological models of reading and aims to explore this variability further. He identifies two broad orientations in how advertising comprehension has been approached. The first, 'objective' orientation describes 'the grasping or extracting of pre-specified meanings from the message' (Mick, 1992). The second, 'subjective' orientation is described as 'the generation of meanings by a particular individual through the activation of mental concepts related to the message and the processing context' (Mick, 1992). Mick develops this subjectivist definition drawing on the psychoanalytic reader response theories of literary theorist Norman Holland to suggest that the way of understanding an advertising message is a function of both the social and psychological specificities of the reader.

> In essence this orientation maintains that the subjective experience of a message takes precedence over intended meanings or objective features as the individual attempts to generate meanings that fulfil psycho-social needs. (Mick, 1992)

Mick's interest in this 'subjective' orientation has prompted him to explore it within a different number of research paradigms ranging from quantitative psychological analysis of varying response (Mick, 1992) to qualitative 'life history' based analyses (Mick and Buhl, 1992). The latter is a particularly interesting analysis which carefully explores the relationships between three brothers' differing responses to advertisements and relates them to the respondents' life themes, relevance structures and psycho-social experiences.

This paper is one of a number of interesting studies which have directly confronted readers in an attempt to study what it is that they actually make of the advertisements they encounter. The general failure of academic analysts to confront readers as an object of study, so clear from Leavisism through to Goldman's critique, is countered by changing the research question asked by analysts. Buttle, echoing the central axiom of the ethnographic approach to the media developed by Katz, sets the change out clearly (see also, for instance, Katz, 1959; O'Donohoe, 1997).

> I am not interested in the question of what advertising does to people, but because advertising can be conceived of as a social resource, I am more interested in the reverse—what do people do to or with advertising. (Buttle, 1991)

The substantial consequence of this re-orientation is methodological. One way of attempting to do justice to the complexity of audience responses is to explore them directly rather than deduce them from the texts to which audiences are presumed to be simply subject. An important attempt to do this is reported in part of Willis' 1990 survey of youth culture, *Common Culture*.

In part of a wide-ranging exploration Willis pursued ethnographic methods in analysis of the media, drawing on research conducted by Nava and Nava (written up elsewhere as Nava, 1992). His analysis of the 'common culture' of advertising found evidence to counteract the 'blunderbuss' critique of mass manipulation proposed by most previous critics.

Willis reports that the advertising industry, in its attempts to confront a critical and televisually literate audience, had turned away from traditional 'hard sell' approaches in favour of more creative executions which fused advertising with other expressive forms. Advertising had been forced to change by the tastes of resistant audiences who had 'developed very complex interpretative and creative capacities' (Willis, 1990) and who, as a consequence, were selective in the distribution of their attention. This marries up well with Goldman's analysis which was being developed at the same time in America. But whereas Goldman illustrated his argument by serially reading advertisements to demonstrate the power and subtlety of their semiotic grip, Willis tries to identify a new settlement between reader and advertiser. The research attempts to evaluate responses to the question 'What's your favourite advertisement?' (Willis, 1990). The respondents seemed to have no difficulty in relating to this question. Advertising is easily discussed in ways appropriate to any other cultural form. Respondents subjected examples to their own keen critical criteria and took 'symbolic pleasure' in their creative responses. This approach to advertising is different to that of say Williamson or Goldman because what we see in Willis' text are verbatim responses from advertising readers as opposed to advertising texts interpreted for us by academic critics. This strategy transforms the conception of advertising in culture by relocating the interpretative and creative agendas into the life of the reader and connecting these with their everyday concerns. The consumer of advertisements is given responsibility for his or her response.

The advertisements discussed were seen to be consumed independently of the products they were representing. Young readers were able to inhabit the disjunction between creative aspects of advertising messages and their intended commercial persuasiveness. Advertising seemed to take on the quality of a 'free lunch'. Respondents, exempting themselves from the coercive economy of advertising, plundered commercial signs for use in their own individual semiotic economies and in minor acts of interpretive pleasure and social exchange. It was proposed that ostensibly banal elements of commercial imagery might be appropriated by consumers in acts effectively signifying important personal resonances and identities (Willis, 1990).

O'Donohoe in a later study finds evidence for a similar set of conclusions. Discussing advertising with groups of Scottish adolescents O'Donohoe develops her analysis noting the variability and ambivalence of respondents' accounts of advertisements. As 'sophisticated' and 'active' consumers of advertisements her respondents were able to articulate their enjoyments, their suspicions and their boredom with advertising. The study highlights audience awareness of the intertextual nature of advertising which is found to be a potential source of some kinds of pleasure as well as a source of 'postmodern panic' about the breakdown of boundaries between the formerly distinct discourses of popular culture. O'Donohoe tentatively concludes that heightened awareness of intertextuality in advertising lends it a firmer association with other popular cultural communications. This offers the consequence of advertisements being consumed independently of their commercial intentions, a conclusion proposed by Nava and Nava in their study. In an earlier paper O'Donohoe attempts to codify responses to advertising in terms of the uses and gratifications which they afford audiences (O'Donohoe, 1994).

ADVERTISEMENTS AS REALISM

Amidst the insistent fundamental critique of advertising as an institution, and of advertisements as cultural forms, there have been some other examples of writing which have pursued a more ambivalent or open-ended analysis. One of the first British books to step outside the dominant framing of advertising was *Understains* by Kathy Myers, published in 1986. Though writing from a Left/feminist and political activist perspective, Myers sought to move away from the simplistic models of human nature (distinguishing natural from false needs) and of communication (starkly contrasting information with propaganda) implied in much of the traditional critique of advertising, towards a recognition that the needs addressed in readers by advertisements were in some sense real and valid. Though her analysis remained rooted in a basically Marxist critique of commodity advertising, she argued against the puritanical fear of consumption, and for the merits of radical political advertising (inspired by the example of the Labour-led Greater London Council which had ventured into the field of advertising to defend itself against the threat of abolition by the Conservative government).

Some earlier American work, however, had also contributed to laying a basis for a more complex view of advertising, though one of these works—Erving Goffman's *Gender Advertisements* (1979)—is easily assimilated into the advertising-as-dominant-ideology critique because of its mapping of gender stereotyping in advertisements. However

Goffman's general suggestion was that advertisements basically do what all social interaction involves, namely using ritual signs to help orient people to one another. On this view (which derives from Goffman's 'dramaturgical' perspective on social behaviour) all social behaviour is in a sense ritualistic, and depends on ceremonial displays, on 'approved typifications' as he put it. Like the theatre and unlike most everyday life, advertisements are self-consciously posed, but Goffman believed that such 'artificial' images may be to spontaneous behaviour what written language is to spoken. They are more formal and consistent, but are saying the same things in the same language.

If advertisements differ from everyday life, it is because they are 'hyper-ritualised', i.e. the poses in them are pure or extreme versions of the ones we strike in other situations, and the images or narratives are 'edited'. In 'real life' we often bungle the ceremonies or vary them, while in advertisements these unscripted variations are edited out, leaving a distilled version of social processes and relationships. Nothing irrelevant to the characterisation, narrative or setting is included, producing a smooth, stylised rendition of a person, relationship, or episode. So Goffman is opposed to the view that advertisements present an unreal world, divorced from social realities. He sees them instead as embodying what he calls 'commercial realism'. This account may not differentiate advertisements from other forms of drama, such as film (and there are of course many connections between the two worlds, with the same people involved in making both), but the 'realism' is commercial because of the communicative use to which it is put. Also, given the very short exposure or time they have, advertisements are under greater pressure than any other narrative art form to use every word and millisecond, and thus to make the most stylised portrayals of reality.

Thus when for example he describes women shown in positions of 'ritual subordination' in advertisements (as when sheltered by a man, or reclining), or in states of 'licensed withdrawal' (as when dreamily drifting, or snuggling into a man) his argument is that this is an exaggerated version of how women do actually behave. Rather than berating advertisements for promoting sexism, he sees them as accurate if intensified portrayals of the real state of gender roles.

It may be thought that Goffman's analysis lets advertising off the hook by narrowing the moral gap between advertisements and real life in a way that demeans real life. Certainly his dramaturgical social psychology conveys a somewhat cynical picture of social behaviour, in which surface is all and the real is a fabrication. His research was also, as he admits, based on an unsystematic sample of advertisements, chosen to illustrate the points he wanted to make. Nonetheless, his book was an early challenge to simplistic critiques, backed up by subtle micro-analyses of posture and gesture in print advertising imagery.

Sharing a characterisation of advertisements as offering a kind of 'realism', though different in most other respects from Goffman's work, is Michael Schudson's *Advertising: The Uneasy Persuasion* (1984). Based partly on field work in the advertising industry, Schudson's analysis is of advertising as a complex and ambiguous field of practice. He suggests its characteristic style is one of 'capitalist realism', by analogy with socialist realism and its highly stylised, simplified, de-individualised depictions of the benefits of life under state socialism. Similarly the realism of advertisements celebrates a way of life, though it is one based on private consumption and not some social, public achievement. It presents a social order based on the consumption of goods, with an implicit message that this is the only desirable or available way of life.

The meaning of the term 'realism' here is perhaps less robust than in Goffman, as there is a tendency to propose that advertisements represent an *ideal* world, of goods and goodness allegedly obtainable through commodity consumption but in practice not available to all, and perhaps anyway an illusion. Schudson recognises that many readers of advertisements see them in this way. He does not believe that advertisements are necessarily effective in leading us to buy the specific goods they advertise. We do not even have to take them seriously; there is a widespread scepticism about their claims. For some readers, a detachment from most advertisements is possible, or a disinterested enjoyment of them as aesthetic experiences. But Schudson inclines to the pessimistic view that this detachment is illusory, because at a deeper level the reader is taking in a meta-message about the way of life being promoted.

Despite its ultimately negative note, Schudson's work was perhaps the first to take a scholarly, rounded look at the advertising industry and its products, and to offer an analysis of it that was not shackled by the full set of preconceptions that we have described above in so much other work.

CONCLUSION: HEROIC LIFE AND EVERYDAY LIFE

For most academic critics of advertising the advertising text has woven the subject into a capitalist tapestry of falsehood and inauthenticity. But studies of actual reading experiences show respondents to have an active capacity to untie advertising texts and re-articulate connections in ways relevant to personal desires, knowledges and meaning. This conception is also close to the sense of the reader we are proposing, i.e. one whose associative work in relation to advertising has more to say to personal concerns than to commercial intentions.

So while we do not advocate an *a priori* celebration of creative consumers, we do reject the epistemological heroism of critiques based in the grand narratives of Marxism or the enduring cultural values espoused by Leavis. Such narratives are sacrificed in favour of a more diffuse and particularistic set of accounts of advertising practices and experiences which while open to critique ought not to be homogenised and 'framed' as modernity's curse. Instead advertisements need to be explored judiciously as part of the significant materiality of late modern culture. This is more fruitful than an approach in which they are pessimistically dismissed as a bombardment of nails falling squarely into the coffin of the hapless human subject.

The difficulty of defending a more optimistic view of advertising lies in the very modest scale of the benefits which it is proposed that advertising offers. Ethnographic records of adolescents measuring out their lives in coffee advertisements or enhancing their televisual literacy do nothing to console cultural analysts committed to the heroic narratives of the master/slave dialectic. The optimistic critiques of advertising deliver up no vision of a collective salvation. Instead they confirm the picture of a culture dominated by the individual pursuit of small pleasures, the unpredictable distribution of meanings, values and intensities of feeling across arrays of trivial objects. They leave us, that is, with everyday life. We believe however that this is both a more realistic estimation of what is there to be seen and part of a more significant achievement—the assertion of individual desire and the accommodation of new freedoms in a context which remains hospitable to enduring, if re-figured, human values.

Notes

1. Marvell's complex religious poem 'The Garden' is the subject of a close reading by William Empson in *Scrutiny* 1. By coincidence it appears on the facing page to Thompson's essay 'Advertising God'. These lines dramatise *Scrutiny*'s rejection of 'rude' society, their distrust of 'mass' hedonism and, in particular, Thompson's Romantic regression into ruralism and nostalgia.

2. Hall's influential work of the 1970s on 'encoding and decoding' forms an important part of the theoretical position of some later theorists, as this chapter goes on to describe in relation to Goldman.

3. In contrast to Myers' broad introductory text, another study of language in advertisements, by Tanaka (1994), is within a very specific paradigm taken from philosophical pragmatism, a linguistic philosophy called 'relevance theory'. She uses this to discuss a convenience sample of Japanese and British print advertisements, focusing on a logical analysis of the assumptions and inferences which the reader must make if the communication is to have the effect desired by the advertiser.

Chapter 5

THE DYNAMICS OF CULTURAL CHANGE: COMMERCIAL CULTURE IN THE AGE OF IDENTITY

POSTMODERNITY AND THE PLACE OF ADVERTISING

It is commonplace to note that the term 'postmodern' has become a cliché, or buzzword, or catch-all. It has reached beyond academic discourses and has become a new theme in the discourse of some professional practices as in 'postmodern psychology' and 'postmodern marketing'. This multiplicity and diffusion of the term 'postmodern' may suggest that it is better avoided in any effort to be theoretically rigorous, as it is not likely to be a conceptually precise term. Yet it is increasingly common currency, with many writers apparently finding that it has some utility in denoting a phenomenon of importance (or perhaps more often in connoting something, in evoking an elusive but important set of qualities). While aware of the many possibilities for obfuscation and confusion which the use of the term presents, we also find it to be a terminological convenience, as a way of referring to a complex area of debate about the nature of contemporary society.

There is a cluster of related themes within that large debate with which we are particularly concerned in this study. They concern the nature of self-identity, and the relationship of self to cultural change. In the context of a widely de-traditionalised world, the parameters of the self are no longer given by traditional authority, inheritance and continuity. Whether the consequence of this is basically a degradation of the self, or an overall gain in the autonomy of the self, is one of the deepest issues in the psycho-social debates about the postmodern. Our aim in this study is to use advertisements as a way of exploring this issue. We assume that advertisement texts and images bear some relationship to current qualities of self-experience, and indeed to deeper determinants of identity. In them we can, therefore, seek evidence concerning the range and balance of the values which predominate in the everyday negotiation of identities, the qualities and strengths of social ties, and the nature of tensions within the self.

There is much support in the literature on postmodernity for the assumption that advertisements are likely to speak of these things, because their general place and importance in contemporary culture is such that they would be implicated in the vicissitudes of the self. A dominant theme in the classical writing on the postmodern, for example in the works of Baudrillard and Jameson, is the primacy of the symbolic and of the image, and the key role that the new cultural industries such as advertising play in the production of the symbols and images which now dominate social life. We do not subscribe to the overall cultural diagnoses offered by these authors, and we also recognise the danger of being seduced by the immediacy and sensual impact of advertisements into attributing to them a disproportionate social importance. However we do take the view that an essential part of understanding contemporary experience is the exploration of the dense environment of 'signs' in which we all now live, and that advertising is a particularly important source of these signs.

For Wernick (1991), the profusion of meaning in contemporary society stems centrally from market relations and the 'promotional' imperative which increasingly comes to inform communicative strategies in the marketplace. Capitalism still exists, but in a fundamentally altered way. The promotion and marketing of goods has become as essential as any of the other four factors of profit generation—labour, capital, technology, resources. The 'zone of production' is subsumed into the superstructure, via the growing attention to the aesthetic design of mass-market products, and so 'has itself become a major cultural apparatus'. Likewise the zone of culture becomes a major infrastructure, as marketing and advertising become more important economically. Under this fusion of promotion and design, 'the very distinction between the symbolic and the material economies, between the regime of accumulation and the regime of signification, cannot be clearly drawn'.

Wernick goes on to note the problems which the evolution of the 'commodity sign' (as Baudrillard called the symbolically-charged good) presents for the individual. In contemporary society it is not just advertising creatives who reproduce promotional culture, but all of us. We are all promotional subjects—'from dating and clothes shopping to attending a job interview, virtually everyone is involved in the self-promotionalism which overlays such practices in the micro sphere of everyday life.' We self-advertise, and in doing so we both produce and reproduce promotional culture. We construct ourselves as objects for circulation, donning a self-style which we hope will possess a symbolic appeal of advantage in the competitive economy of signs and desire. Given the continual dynamism of the symbolic field we may have continually to alter our self-style throughout our life, as our success and even social survival are now dependent upon self-promotion. As the paradigmatic form of promotional communication, advertisements can therefore speak with a particular authority to the individual in search of a self, as we discuss later.

Other ways of characterising the 'postmodern' also see advertising at the centre of social change. For example Lash (1990) describes changes in the 'regimes of signification' which have occurred in the post-World War II period. One of the central features of modernity (as seen by Weber and Habermas) was the demarcation of aesthetics from the real world. In postmodernity, this demarcation breaks down. 'De-differentiation' becomes the ordering principle of the contemporary world. Modernity was rooted in a regime of signification which was didactic and book-based, and which was based on a distanced study and appreciation of aesthetics. Postmodernism is rooted in the 'figural' regime of signification. The image takes precedence, spectators become immersed in objects, investing them with desire, and revelling in the immediacy of the experience. Lash notes that figuration obliterates the older maintenance of distance, and engages the perceptual memories of the unconscious, rather than the systematic rules of language and consciousness. Images directly signal through resemblance, whereas writing is a second order form of communication, a symbol about another symbol. This view would see advertising as an especially potent form of communication, given its development based on the use of visual imagery and on the condensed, figurative, allusive, and feeling-laden use of words.

If promotional communications now pervade most areas of social life, and if the figural mode which advertisements deploy is also now dominant, it must be asked whether advertising has any distinctive qualities which would justify studying it separately. The specificity of commodity advertising cannot stem from the communicative strategies it employs since these are now in wide use in a variety of settings. However consumer goods advertising does retain a distinctive and major social function, which can be seen as a corollary of its obvious commercial function, and that is to mediate our relationships with material objects. Here we follow Leiss *et al.* and Jhally (see Chapters 3 and 4) in their analyses of adverts as providing a discourse within which objects can become meaningful. This not only regulates our relationship to the material world, but is also a central means by which the experience of society as a whole is built up and sustained. As Douglas (1979) argued in her anthropological analysis of consumption, goods are essential vehicles for social communication, for marking social differences and for generating a picture of the social world within which the individual can then find his or her place. Similarly, perhaps even more directly, advertising for services (such as financial, information or professional services) contributes to the pictures and maps we have of the social world and our places within it.

This mediating role of advertisements will have become more powerful as they have become richer in symbolic content and less narrowly focused on the product, a process which has arguably been underway since the 1920s, possibly earlier (see Chapter 2). Current sociological theories suggest a number of key dimensions of contemporary society which advertisements could be expected to address, if they have this function of representing society, of conveying a meaningful picture of society and its possibilities for us. We will outline two of these, which we hypothesised are of particular relevance to the study of advertisement content.

RISK AND REFLEXIVITY

The postmodern individual is subject to a new set of responsibilities, related but not reducible to the now-familiar uncertainties consequent upon de-traditionalisation. According to Beck (1992) we live in a 'risk society'. What characterised industrial society was the production and distribution of 'goods'; whereas the risk society is structured by the distribution of 'bads'. In the risk society 'bads' are superimposed on 'goods' with fateful consequences. For example, we no longer unambivalently celebrate a new chemical plant for the employment and economic benefit it might bring. Rather, possible gains are weighed up against potential hazards—the impact on the community, on local economies, on the environment, on tourism. Beck argues that 'bads' are now factored into decisions, and so many areas of life become infiltrated with risk calculation, as the 'whole of society becomes a risk group in insurer's terms' (Beck, 1992).

However, as risk increases so does responsibility. What happens to individuals and their loved ones is 'understood as a product not of impersonal social and natural forces, but of earlier decisions he or she has taken' (Beck-Gernsheim, 1996). The lifeworld is permeated with calculation, which enters all of our thoughts. Planning, control and optimisation are increasingly dominant principles.

Insurance and the 'colonisation of the future' (as Giddens, 1991, terms the risk-oriented trajectories we try to plan) are however limited in their efficacy. While attempts might be made to minimise some risks, there are many hazards which cannot be insured. Beck notes that nuclear, chemical, and biological 'goods' create hazards so vast in their reach, and so deep in their potential impact, that no one can calculate their risks—they are un-insurable (e.g. global warming, nuclear accidents). These hazards have undermined the older modernist systems of authority. The nation state and its army, scientists, and industrialists are all unable to control them, hence they become everyone's problem. The hazards of risk society are so great that they fragment and diffuse authority.

Giddens (1991) adds the phenomenon of globalisation to this analysis. Globalised economies, communication, travel, industrial processes and their by-products have brought people into increased 'interconnectivity'. Nowhere on the earth is insulated; distance no longer shelters us from one another. Changes in one part of society have profound consequences for others. Globalisation is not something 'out there', for it reaches into the intimate recesses of subjectivity. Increased interconnectivity and global ecological threat, argues Beck, have brought epistemic and authority structures to their breaking point, as the hazards they produce turn back to haunt industrial society. Society is forced to confront itself, to become 'reflexive'.

Critics of this thesis argue that if increased awareness was a product of contemporary society then more social problems would be solved. However 'reflexivity', though involving some kind of self-confrontation, does not necessarily mean thoughtfulness or effectiveness. It does not necessarily foster reflection, critique, or positive change. Beck points to many instances where 'incalculable threats...are constantly euphemised and trivialised into calculable risks'. In a similar vein, Giddens (op. cit.) illustrates that 'reflexivity' can as easily foster fundamentalist or instrumentalist responses as progressive and creative ones.

There are other elaborations of the concept of 'reflexivity', of which Giddens' is particularly influential. His concept captures a crucial quality of postmodern experience; it refers to the wide variety of ways in which individuals, social institutions and bodies of knowledge can observe, analyse, modify or negotiate their identities and relationships. Despite the constraints still set by structurally-determined life chances in education and employment, life paths are now increasingly seen as subject to at least some degree of negotiated determination by the individual, exemplified by the 'transformation of intimacy' (Giddens, 1992). Women especially, argues Giddens, are seeing intimate relationships as a sphere in which individuals can articulate their needs and seek to contract parameters for the relationship which will recognise those needs and generally support or facilitate the self-development of each partner.

He refers to the term 'lifestyle' as an important organising principle for the 'late modern' subject. Here the term has a meaning much deeper than its marketing definition, in which it refers to the gravitation of a consumer group towards a particular ensemble of goods and services. For Giddens the idea of choice which the term conveys has a profound social meaning:

> ...we all not only follow lifestyles, but in an important sense are forced to do so—we have no choice but to choose. A lifestyle can be defined as a more or less integrated set of practices which an individual embraces, not only because such practices fulfil utilitarian needs, but because they give material form to a particular narrative of self-identity. (Giddens, 1991)

In a related vein, Beck notes that the risk society is permeated by 'individuation', which releases individuals from the social bonds— family, class, fraternity, state—which had tied them to the structure. Release from traditional ties introduces new perils. 'Reflexivity' fosters 'states of heightened uncertainty and anxiety, as decisions proliferate and the cultural codes used to negotiate those decisions become more and more complex and variegated' (Lash *et al.*, 1996).

PSYCHOLOGICAL DIMENSIONS OF CULTURAL CHANGE

We will return later in the book to the themes of risk and reflexivity. We will shortly move on in the rest of this chapter to link the general uncertainty and anxiety of the postmodern subject to the theme of identity, and so to outline an important part of our framework for understanding advertising. Firstly, however, we add a psychoanalytic dimension to the debates about the cultural and psychological gains and losses which the transition to the post- or late modern can be seen to involve.

From the viewpoint of classical Freudian psychoanalysis and its structural theory of mind, the advent of the postmodern is a crisis in superego functioning, or at least in how the superego is thought of. The postmodern condition can be seen as the collapse of the superego: the restraining boundaries and the commitments to social institutions which the superego embodied are dissolved or weakened. In his influential dissection of contemporary culture as 'narcissistic', Christopher Lasch (though writing in 1978, before the term postmodern gained currency) defined many postmodern features as pathological. In the absence of confident parental authority, he argued, the superego as a strong, benign psychic agency cannot develop. A rigid, defensive, brittle superego may develop instead, and be unable to contain the aggressive and regressively hedonistic forces now given greater or more direct cultural expression—and yet these forces are ever further from being stably integrated with ego and superego functioning. Only false organisations of self can develop, and personal identity is increasingly inauthentic, reflecting the degradation of public life. Lacking an inner core of authority and self-confidence, which comes only from the experience of benign and reliable authority in the external world, the narcissistic subject is easily manipulated by the media and especially by the seductions of advertising.

Earlier, as we noted in Chapter 3, Riesman (1961) had argued—not in a psychoanalytic mode but in the same tradition of moral critique—that the internal set of values underpinning the behaviour and judgement of the traditional subject had given way in the contemporary period to subjects who increasingly have to look outside of themselves for guidance on how to live. Riesman notes the dilemmas posed for the 'other directed' subject, whom he does not comprehensively condemn for not measuring up to the past.

A more optimistic psychoanalytic approach to cultural change (linked to the more positive conceptions of contemporary society as 'reflexive') sees superego functioning as undergoing radical changes rather than weakening. A more flexible, reality-oriented superego can be seen as emerging, with the external models and supports for this capacity being increasingly located in the institutions and content of popular culture and less in the traditionally authoritative social institutions—law, police, other aspects of the state, educational institutions and even the family, though this is a complex and controversial issue. Personal identity is increasingly reflexive and negotiated, and is strengthened by the range and depth of opportunities for self-development presented by the de-traditionalising of culture and by the profusion of new experiences and choices for the consumer (many though not all of these emanating from technological developments). Elliott (1995) develops a broadly 'positive' position of this sort, drawing on both British and French traditions in psychoanalysis.

This second, more optimistic view is close to that of Fowles (1996), who observes that individuals are increasingly responsible for their own emotional management, and that popular culture is a major resource for them in this task. He distinguishes however between popular culture and advertising, seeing the latter as consisting of 'intentional' artefacts paid for by the advertiser, while popular culture is essentially entertainment paid for by the audience. This underplays the close connections between the content of the two (see, e.g. Jhally, 1990), and the fact that both can play the same role in the psychic economy, in offering 'disciplines of delight'. Fowles in fact claims (though over-simplifying somewhat, it could be said) that the symbol domains of advertising and popular culture emerged in the same period (the 1920s) as part of an overall shift away from traditional mythologies and belief systems. He also argues that popular culture is popular because it richly addresses both the interior world of emotions, and the norm-governed social world. It is about pleasure and gratification yet also provides the 'elixir of emotional management', which is the role which we ascribe below to advertising.

The wider issues about de-traditionalisation and superego development are discussed more fully in Richards (1994, 1997). We can note here in relation to Fowles' categories that advertising is best considered as a domain within popular culture, as a form of communication not sharply set off from many others. They may be superficially distinct, being—as Fowles describes—typically brief, exceptionally polished and anonymously created artefacts. But this does not set them apart in terms of their basic, broad psychic impact and cultural presence.

The debate between the two polarised assessments of the 'post-modern' condition—narcissism and regression, or autonomy and creativity—can then be posed as an empirical question, or rather as a set of interlocking questions about the dynamic of cultural change. Is the uncertainty and the flux of contemporary culture, the postmodern configuration, matched by a persistence or regeneration of modern boundaries and order, so that new settlements can be negotiated? Is the increasing flow matched by a resilience of structure—not the old structures, perforce, but reconstitutions and replacements? Or are the refusals, indulgences and transgressions of the postmodern overwhelming the integrity of the culture and of the psyche, and the capacity for stable reality-orientation? Has the spontaneous flow of impulse swamped the structures of mature social obligation, leaving only brittle fragments of idealised relationships in their place?

While these are empirical questions, they are clearly of such scope and complexity that there will not be simple empirical answers to them. It might also be suspected that the actual situation is contradictory and not amenable to a consistent answer. Nonetheless the more systematic evidence from a variety of sources that could be brought to bear on it, the more confidently or precisely some answers might be offered, and later in the book we submit one body of evidence from the particular field of advertisements.

DE-CLASSIFICATION AND SYMBOLISATION

Against the background of the sociological and psychological theories outlined above, we will now develop a psycho-social account of the predicament of the contemporary subject within which we think advertising can be usefully considered.

Beck has observed that 'the notion of class society remains useful only as an image of the past' (Beck, 1992). Social inequality still exists, but is increasingly hard to grasp in terms of categories of class stratification which 'no longer correspond to reality' (Beck, 1992). Sociology has turned to the study of the emerging forms of cultural and social life, and the tensions around their emergence. We focus here on the dislocation and de-centring produced in the re-organisation of class-based narratives, and we are interested in the generation of 'anxiety' attendant upon such dislocations, though the transition from 'class' identity to 'lifestyle identities' is part of the more general processes of the development of a consumer culture, the 'aestheticisation of everyday life', the emergence of a 'promotional culture', reflexivity, individuation and the establishment of 'risk society', and what we want to call an 'identity work' culture (Fornas, 1995).

A perceptive rendering of the relationship between anxiety and the interruption of class trajectory can be found in the earliest texts of cultural studies. Hoggart identified at the end of the 1950s a cohort of people made 'anxious' by the experience of a discrepancy between cultural aspirations and socio-cultural location. These were identified as 'unbent springs' and 'the uprooted and the anxious' (Hoggart, 1957). The perception of a pervasive cultural anxiety has been developed, with various emphases, in other writing. Anxiety, historically the characteristic of bohemian poets and existential philosophers, was becoming demo-cratised. A detailed account is found in Booker's description of 'neophiliacs' in the 1960s (Booker, 1969). Booker presents an analysis of the establishment of new cultural groupings, bound not so much by commonalities of social origin, but more by a certain adeptness in symbolic expression and innovation. The 'neophiliacs' were characterised by a 'tense', 'crazy' and 'nervous' energy (Booker, 1969). 'Stylish' and 'dynamic', they made their mark in the expanding '"young" and "classless" world of "communications"', which included journalism, television, pop music and of course advertising (Booker, 1969).

More conventional sociological analyses describe the emergence and character of the 'new middle classes' in the period from the 1960s through to the present. These accounts often make use of Bourdieu's 'socio-analytic' framework and vocabulary. They note some of the consequences of broad structural changes in the organisation of society and economy, especially the post-war expansion of educational opportunity, including the recent expansion of the university sector. They articulate, in terms of 'anomie', 'anxiety' and 'unease', the experiential tensions attaching to the structural disruptions of individual and class trajectories (Bourdieu, 1989; Lash and Urry, 1994; Mort, 1996).

One crucial contribution these analysts make is the foregrounding of consumption, which has come to be seen by some as nothing less than 'the vanguard of history' (Miller, 1995). The 'new cultural intermediaries' (Featherstone, 1995) settle into this world as an anxious and expanding 'avant garde' of the consumer 'revolution'.

What is the quality of their anxiety? What is the constitution of these anxious subjectivities? We turn to the work of Pierre Bourdieu for a productive approach to these questions. The new 'classes' are described by him in the following terms.

> Classified, déclassé, aspiring to a higher class, they see themselves as unclassifiable, 'excluded', 'dropped out', 'marginal' anything rather than categorised, assigned to a class, a determinate place in social space. (Bourdieu, 1989)

In this context, strategies of 'distinction' (Bourdieu, 1989) and patterns of taste come more strongly into play, as aesthetic practices—leisure and pleasure—become a more intense site of social struggles for status and legitimation. But 'status' and 'legitimation' are not the only stakes in play. A sociological view tempered by psychoanalytic understandings finds a richer conception of the quest for 'identity' than is conveyed by the sense of status-seeking. We would want to include a sense of a legitimate search for 'well-being', even 'happiness', along with the competitive strivings undoubtedly present in the anxious dynamics of the cultural field.

A key theme in the emergence of the new classes or lifestyle cultures is the increasing exchange between activities hitherto seen as discrete, for instance expressive play and serious work and between intellectual and administrative vocations. The analysis of 'new' classes identifies the birth of a new type of social actor who generates new forms of communication and consumption. This leads to the manifestation of a new 'therapeutic morality' or 'fun' ethic which

> produces consumers who are isolated (despite all their associations, which are purely statistical groupings) and therefore free (or forced) to confront in

extended order the separate markets ('juniors', 'teenagers' 'senior citizens' etc.) of the new economic order untrammelled by the constraints and brakes imposed by collective memories and expectations—in short, freed from the temporal structures imposed by domestic units, with their own lifecycle, their long term 'planning', sometimes over several generations, and their collective defences against the immediate impact of the market. (Bourdieu, 1989)

The 'unbent spring' of the 'uprooted' anxious subject identified by Hoggart in the 1950s is redescribed by Bourdieu in his analyses of 'new' classes. Giddens develops the account as part of his theory of reflexivity, in terms of confrontations with 'dis-embedding mechanisms' and 'ontological insecurity'. In this context we want to highlight a key motif common to the understanding of these 'new' subjectivities: the increased importance of consumption. The turn to consumption is part of a quest for ways to express and manage tensions in new forms of life, and advertising plays a key role in this.

Some time previously Williams had seen advertising as dealing in the management of emotional tensions. He felt, however, that this was an obstacle to the creation of a society where resolution of these tensions could be achieved more directly and in a collective class culture (Williams, 1980). Hoggart saw his 'uprooted and anxious' characters as likely to seek out a particular kind of advertised product. The advertising he had in mind was for the self-improvement books designed for the 'TONGUE TIED' offering the mastery of 'WORDS—WORDS—WORDS' (Hoggart, 1957). Hoggart's intuition points to the use of advertising and consumption in the search for ways of symbolising the self which extends far beyond products explicitly to do with self-worth. Hoggart is identifying something which Giddens and Bourdieu highlight in greater detail—an anxious quest for self-improvement, performative assurance and legitimation as an antidote to uncertainty born out of sociological dislocation. Giddens notes the increased interest in self-help books to advise on emotional issues. Bourdieu finds anxious traces of social dislocation written into the bodily regimes of the 'new petit bourgeois' cultivated ethic of 'fun':

Aiming to substitute relaxation for tension, pleasure for effort, 'creativity' and freedom for discipline, communication for solitude, it treats the body as the psychoanalyst treats the soul, bending its ear to 'listen' to a body which has to be 'unknotted', liberated or, more simply, rediscovered and accepted ('feeling at home'). This psychologisation of the relation to the body is inseparable from an exaltation of the self, but a self which truly fulfils itself ('growth', 'awareness', 'responsiveness') only through the intermediary of the body treated as a sign not an instrument. (Bourdieu, 1989)

Increasingly, advertising for all kinds of goods implicitly offers new modes of self-expression. The quest for an untying of anxious tongues and awkward bodies extends across a number of personal registers and product sectors. The turn to a consumer culture which is in some manner 'therapeutic' is heralded in different ways in each of these accounts. The increasing significance of consumption and the consuming body/self can be seen to be the direct consequence of the emergence of psycho-social tensions emanating from changes in forms of social life.

This can be seen in the continual refrain that goods offer 'languages' of the self. Campbell (1987) cautions against the use of this metaphor, and we may ask exactly what kind of languages are constituted in consumer products. If, as we suggest later, advertising is about the evocation of a variety of associative modes, it is a moot point whether any of these 'languages' of goods are strictly speaking 'linguistic'. What is clear however is that goods, especially advertised goods, participate culturally in meaningful symbolic activity—in a 'passional economy' (N. Rose, 1991) of meanings.

In a related way, Warde (1994) also argues that there has been an over-estimation of the extent to which consumption is a major mode of identity-formation, and whether it is as laden with anxiety as some theorists, especially Bauman, have consequently taken it to be. He argues that many social norms and conventions still operate to guide or constrain consumer choice, which is not as anomic as often implied, though this is a point with which the theorists he takes to task—Beck, Giddens and Bauman—could at one level agree. The presence of supports and guidance does not mean that the 'reflexive project of the self' is not therefore a reality. From a psychoanalytic viewpoint, moreover, it is quite possible to agree with Warde that consumption can at different times be both highly pleasurable and casual, while still holding to the view that on these occasions—as on others when it might be an occasion for manifest doubt and anxiety—it is also shadowed by unconscious anxiety and by a deep struggle to reproduce a self.

Another psychoanalytic dimension to the debate about the relationship to identity of goods, and of the advertisements through which we partly know them, can be found in the work of Falk (see Chapter 6). Discussing the question of what it is that consumer goods mean, Falk acknowledges the instrumental use of goods as signs acquired in order to achieve social status. This is the model of goods as symbols sometimes apparent in Bourdieu's account of distinction strategies, and at the heart of Veblen's (1899) influential account of consumer behaviour. However Falk asserts that modern consumption is importantly also an 'imaginary' practice which does not lead to the realisation of a pre-defined social identity but to an imaginary realisation of a general and otherwise unrepresentable 'good' (Falk, 1994). Falk here articulates an important theoretical distinction, between the social and instrumental use of goods as signs and the psychological use of goods as symbolisation of internal feelings. Our approach embodies this doubling of the perspective.

We can link this to Bourdieu's statement that

> Social reality exists, so to speak, twice, in things and in minds, in fields and in habitus, outside and inside of agents. (Bourdieu and Wacquant, 1992)

He also speaks of a 'double and obscure relation' and an 'ontological correspondence between habitus and field' (Bourdieu and Wacquant, 1992). Our intention is to establish a psychoanalytic reading of this correspondence. Bourdieu himself refers explicitly to psychoanalysis in his work; the very first line of *Distinction* declares 'Sociology is rarely more akin to social psychoanalysis than when it confronts an object like taste' (Bourdieu, 1989). Speaking of detailed analysis of lifestyle choices he proposes that they should be 'the material of a social psychoanalysis' (Bourdieu, 1989). Despite this, Bourdieu's account pays insufficient attention to the psychological elements in social activity. It is not a sustained and explicit part of his analytic approach. We will therefore set out a double account of cultural change which examines it in two registers. One is a sociological account of the transmission of identity and symbolic power, the other explores the correlative intergenerational psychodynamics.

INHERITANCE AND GRATITUDE

New lifestyles are not handed down any more than the items of fashion that are often their hallmarks. The process of 'handing over' or 'handing down' (Giddens, 1992) at the root of all forms of 'tradition' (Williams, 1983) is jeopardised in postmodern social formations. Beck writes that 'The place of hereditary estates is no longer taken by social classes', as it was in industrial modernity, but by the individual who becomes the 'reproduction unit of the social in the lifeworld' (Beck, 1992). Bourdieu, in his account of the new *petit bourgeoisie*, describes a 'class' identity formed not in the 'hand-me-down' mode of reproduction characteristic of the strategies of lineage but instead, more often than not, in a repeated refusal of the traditional class trajectory.

> Their lifestyle and ethical and political positions are based on a rejection of everything in themselves that is finite, definite, final, in a word *petit bourgeois*, that is a refusal to be pinned down to any site in social space. (Bourdieu, 1989)

In a similar vein Ross describes a new 'streamlined' middle class 'disencumbered' of the pressures of 'lineage, inheritance and transmission' (Ross, 1995). Thus 'streamlining' not only describes a new style of product design characteristic of the 1960s, but also captures the quality of new lifestyles and modes of selfhood better equipped to pursue upward mobility in a 'dream of social flying' (Bourdieu, 1989).

One of the key axes in this dynamic is subjects' relation to the weight of inheritance or, as Bourdieu puts it, their relation to the 'gravity' of the social field (Bourdieu, 1989, 1996). Inheritance is never solely an economic consideration. Instead it is a kind of portfolio constituted out of the various forms of capital described by Bourdieu: economic, cultural and symbolic. We could say in this context that one of the characteristics of contemporary culture is that it is inhabited by subjects 'without portfolio'. The subject's identity is no longer determined by class origins in a concerted way. Instead he or she is consigned to an indeterminate existence at once free and directionless, liberated and anxious, powerless and empowered.

' "Heirlooms? Don't make me laugh" ' (respondent, Bourdieu, 1989).

Inheritance is at the root of Bourdieu's account of culture and practice. He says that 'the different inherited asset structures, together with social trajectory, command the habitus and the systematic choices it produces in all areas of practice' (Bourdieu, 1989). There is a range of possible relationships to inheritance, from perfect reproduction, to the complete 'refusal' of inheritance.

In a world where simple reproduction is the exceptional, almost impossible, destiny of the subject, some element of refusal of inheritance is becoming increasingly the rule. Obviously the breakdown of the process of reproduction is never experienced as complete refusal in the common sense of the word. Nevertheless some 'break' in the cycle is implicit in the idea of cultural change. The 'break' is not just a change in the content of activities but it is a qualitative break in the experience of life. The ambivalent relation to inheritance can find, in symbolic work in all fields of culture, 'real' pleasurable and creative narratives of selfhood.

In a discussion of Flaubert's *Sentimental Education*, Bourdieu shows how in contrast to the dislocated, narcissistic Frederic character he creates, Flaubert himself is able through his writing to embark on an 'enterprise of objectification', a transformative project of symbolising his own self and identifying a new trajectory for himself. This does not mean that the postmodern subject has to be an artist—only that he or she has an intensified imaginative life and a pressing need to symbolise internal anxieties in a distinctive idiom of his or her own. There are viable modes of cultural action and identity 'outside' the narrative of collective class identity, which are symbolic and imaginative modes but not necessarily delusional ones.

In a traditional culture of unmediated hierarchical power relations, where each is sure of their place and where boundaries and separations are firm, power is maintained by a sense of 'indebtedness' and practised in a mode of simple deference to the enshrined good of the society in shared social ritual. Lash describes Bourdieu's account of exchange in traditional societies as follows.

> Relationships of power are effectively 'exchange relationships', based on the indebtedness of subordinate agent to his/her superordinate...for Bourdieu this relation of debt also determines status and cultural valuations and classifications. (Lash, 1990)

This sense of indebtedness is not simply a matter of social observance, but has a psychological correlate; it is a feeling as well as a mode of conduct. Psychoanalytic language describes, in the primary relationship between mother and child, a similar 'exchange' going on. In normal development, from dependence towards separation a 'gift' is given.

> If the undisturbed enjoyment in being fed is frequently experienced, the introjection of the good breast comes about with relative security. A full gratification at the breast means the infant feels he has received from his loved object a unique gift which he wants to keep. This is the basis of gratitude. Gratitude is closely linked with trust in good figures. (Klein, 1988)

The child develops a sense of 'debt' which Melanie Klein terms 'gratitude'. Part of this sense of gratitude manifests itself in a strong sense of self, an inner confidence, and a trust in the authority of the outside world. This provides part of the basis for what we call elsewhere the 'moral unconscious' (Brown and Richards, 1998; see Chapter 6). In a traditional culture this will predispose many people to a conservative relation to its dominant values and ideals. The subject has internalised the resources necessary for the 'containment' (see Chapter 6) of anxiety which leads him to dispose of libido in extant and legitimate symbols, forms and meaning.

Previously we have described a state of affairs which, on the surface at least, is rather different. This state of affairs is evident in a modernist *avant garde* and in the 'mass' *avant garde* of postmodern cultures. In a culture where the relations of power are diffuse and mediated and where the relation to tradition and lineage is one of crisis and/or ambivalence, the sense of debt and gratitude to the foundations of tradition is disturbed. How can someone feel gratitude for that which he or she has, in part at least, refused, or for what was insufficient? An important question is what happens to the feelings of gratitude which in a traditional culture would be directed at traditional cultural materials. We want to argue that, predominantly, they are made latent, and that, given appropriate cultural conditions, they are re-routed.

This re-routing of anxiety occurs through the activity of the associative unconscious (Brown and Richards, 1998). Such activity may lead either towards engulfment in chaotic association, or towards a more disciplined reflexive project involving the grateful institution of containment.

In a late modern culture the development of identity takes place in a qualitatively different manner from traditional and early modern societies. Psychically and socially anxiety becomes a more prevalent characteristic. The social rituals which assisted in the management of anxiety and which reaffirmed the original separations from the mother are no longer available to the individual, or at least they are no longer implicitly trusted. The internal good object and the social orders which were formerly its correlates become a less sure resource for the containment of anxiety and the strengthening of the ego. Instead the subject defends him or herself against that anxiety by retreat into regressive illusion. This picture is not unmitigatedly bleak. Between stifling conformity and anomic narcissism there is a third way. There is a turn to 'style' implicit in the transition to lifestyle culture as the subject attempts to bring to life new containing forms for thought. Aspects of good inheritance, socially uncorroborated and psychically latent, are resurrected by acts of creativity and are expressed as 'style'.

We now need to link the sociological account of the disruption of inheritance with the psychoanalytic account of 'ingratitude', to help understand the move to a culture of stylistic innovation and intensified symbolic production and use. This can be done by looking at the object relations theory of symbol formation. Miller for one supports the idea that some degree of synthesis between object relations psychoanalysis and Bourdieu's work is convincing. He observes that Klein's theories of projection and introjection, symbolisation and ego formation, and the theory of self and subjectivity arising from them provide an account of the dialectical relationship between structure and agency which is unusually subtle. He notes that the account of the self 'as highly integral and largely intractable' and providing 'attitudes and perspectives which are taken for granted in relations with the external world, by virtue of the extent that they are models into which the world must be assimilated' ought to remind us of Bourdieu's concept of habitus. 'The parallel with Bourdieu's notion of habitus ...may be noted' (Miller, 1995).

ANXIETY AND STYLE

We are drawing upon the theory of symbol formation offered by Segal (1991) which develops earlier formulations by Klein (e.g. 1930). As with much psychoanalytic theory these accounts refer to extremes of clinical pathology which are not general to the culture. However the extremes of pathology can help in understanding aspects of 'normal' experience. Segal describes the process of symbol formation in the following terms. 'Symbol formation is an activity of the ego attempting to deal with the anxieties stirred by its relation to the object and is generated primarily by the fear of bad objects and the fear of loss or inaccessibility of good objects' (Segal, 1991). This statement is grounded in a Kleinian understanding of human development and the 'internal world of objects', the inner life out of which external actions are given form and meaning. The kinds of anxieties that the subject may have in relation to the 'internal' object are residues from early experiences of separation from the mother.

Segal identifies two kinds of symbol formation, termed 'symbol' and 'symbolic equation'. Segal distinguishes between them as follows:

> I should like at this point to summarise what I mean by the terms symbolic equation and 'symbol' respectively, and the conditions under which they arise. In the symbolic equation, the symbol substitute is felt to be the original object. The substitute's own properties are not recognised or admitted. The symbolic equation is used to deny the absence of the ideal object, or to control a persecuting one. It belongs to the earliest stages of development. The symbol proper, available for sublimation and furthering the development of the ego, is felt to represent the object; its own characteristics are recognised, respected, and used. [...] The symbol is used not to deny but to overcome loss...Symbol formation governs the capacity to communicate, since all communication is made by means of symbols. (Segal, 1991)

What Segal found in patients suffering extreme disturbances in their infancy has, in broad terms, a correspondence with the kinds of cultural trend we are exploring. When gratitude to an internal object can be projected onto a stable and viable set of cultural resources, then the culture of that society will remain traditional. Even the deviance characteristic of adolescence will be in the mode of rebellion and not revolution. It will take place in the space of an established 'psycho-social moratorium'—an apprenticeship or a grand tour. The logic of this culture will be the multiplication of sameness and the perpetual reiteration of a transcendent good. This is by no means a necessarily happier culture, but is a less pervasively anxious one. It is a culture in which unhappiness will not be experienced in terms of ontological insecurity. It is a culture without style, because it is a culture where the individual does not have to form symbols to express and contain anxiety. A good place to put anxiety is already established. Symbol formation is a far less costly process. The subject's sense of identity is enhanced by the extant social processes of containment of anxious feelings.

In a culture of disrupted social trajectories marked by an ambivalent (and at one extreme 'refusing') relation to inheritance, there is a disturbed relation to the external correlates of internal objects. There is a disruption of feelings of gratitude and a corresponding intensification of anxiety. This in turn disrupts the relation to the means of communication, as separation from and mourning of the internal good containing object is, at some level, relatively incomplete, leaving the subject unable to distinguish between internal and external worlds in a consistent way. This leads to a shift along the continuum of symbol formation away from 'symbols' and towards 'symbolic equations'. Anxiety is re-routed into new forms of expression whose modalities incorporate new styles of referentiality and whose hallmark is an intensity of feeling and experience, on the one hand, and lack of correspondence to approved models of reality on the other. Judged by the standards of former culture these new forms of representation are found to be indirect, illogical and unbounded. The boundaries between reality and symbols, whose job was to represent reality, are 'imploded'. Culture is informal and deformed.

Since an aspect of the refusal of inheritance is a refusal either to be serious or take seriously the established cultural rituals and their attendant symbolism—the orthodox narratives of life—the subject is likely to improvise a place to put the anxiety which is constitutive of his or her selfhood and seek out or make use of symbols of his or her own. Adolescence, the period in which the primary transitions of separation are replayed, will become a more intense and potentially unmanageable experience, claiming and extending its own versions of the psycho-social moratorium or provoking society to control it. The cultural logic of such a society will be the multiplication of difference and the pursuit of immanent, experiential goods. This is a culture of stylisation. Stylisation becomes a feature because members of such a society will work to make symbolic forms to help manage anxiety which will be unlike extant ones.

> Style...The private portion of the ritual. (Barthes, 1977)

> Style is the deference...which action pays to uncertainty. (Oppenheimer cited Fish, 1994)

> ...there are only styles, thanks to which man turns his back on society and confronts the world as objects without going through any of the forms of history or of social life. (Barthes, 1977)

What is style? This is an important question because one of the defining features of discussions of postmodern consumer culture is the emergence of 'lifestyle' as an analytic category largely superceding 'class'. It is worth exploring as the term 'lifestyle' is often used unreflectively, as it is in the technical discourses of marketing (Giddens, 1992).

It is interesting that 'lifestyle' is a condensation of two words which have been prominent in cultural analyses in the past fifty years. 'Style' has been the watchword of many defenders of popular culture, seeing 'style' as a mode of resistance to dominant ideological dictats. 'Life' was one of the names of the mysterious good at the heart of the literature nominated by F. R. Leavis as an antidote to cultural dissolution. Perhaps 'lifestyle' is a useful term because, like other condensations, it indirectly allows the access of censored thoughts into the explicit discourse.

Barthes describes 'style' in a number of ways relevant to the distinctions between a culture of inheritance and a culture of its refusal, and between a culture of gratitude and a culture of anxiety. For Barthes 'style' is the individual aspect of expression where language provides the shared familiar social aspect for communication. Style is performative, bodily and personal while language is abstract, social and 'given'.

In a culture where relatively unproblematic inheritance is the predominant mode of relationship between the generations, the distance between language and style is minimal. Another way of putting this is to say that when someone is not attempting to defy the 'gravity of the social field' (Bourdieu), the 'coition of words and things' performed by that person, through the form of expression, in thought and speech, or through material objects, is dictated by common social rituals of meaning and not in 'the private portion of the ritual', i.e. not in 'style'.

While Bourdieu and Barthes, in their respective discussions of Flaubert, both locate the work of style in one form of communication—writing—the argument can be applied to any social field or any cultural practice. The move from style as writing to style in general is already implicit in the etymology and subsequent usage of the word. Neither Barthes nor Bourdieu preclude the idea that literary production is a paradigmatic case for other kinds of cultural practice.

Style is, at least potentially, the expression of postmodern gratitude. Reflective identity work is the labour of postmodern debt. Meaningful action and power are not, of necessity, incompatible with a world of consumer lifestyles.

IDENTITY WORK

To define the mode of symbolic action which we see as distinctive to consumer culture we describe an emergent form of cultural 'work'. This is work whose object is the consolidation and opening out of the self in the face of a culture seen to offer, at various times, both a plenitude and a lack of satisfactory opportunities for identification. The 'object' of identity work is 'the self'. This selfhood needs work in direct proportion to the degree to which the trajectory implicit in inheritance is disrupted. Unlike other forms of work, which are directed towards transformation of the external environment in some way, identity work is directed, through, but not upon, external 'objects', towards transformation and expression of the self's relation to the external environment. The 'object' of identity work is the manufacture of forms of containment for aspects of the self left unmourned and volatile. It is the battle to maintain and apply ego strength, not by rigid defensiveness but in reflective confrontation with anxiety.

Identity work, unlike other kinds of work, is characterised by its intransitivity. It has as much to do with 'being' as it has to do with 'doing'. It is better seen as performative action as opposed to purposive action. As such a mode of action identity work is allied with the aesthetic and playful activity which is commonly seen as characteristic of postmodern cultural living. Yet it is useful to call it 'work' in recognition of a novel kind of seriousness and of its social value which lies in the fact that it is, in a certain sense, productive and even necessary. It is also worthy of the title work to distinguish it from the kind of 'lazy' mode of 'defensive', 'escapist' fantasy (see Chapter 6).

The identification of this intransitive orientation is at the heart of much recent theory which sees an increasing concern with the self as one of the distinctive features of contemporary culture. In addition to those authors we have already referred to, Sennett (1986) describes narcissism as the new Protestant ethic and describes the new subjectivities of 'artists without an art'. Campbell (1987) identifies the evolution of a consumer culture based on the Protestant asceticism of vocation into 'autonomous self-illusory hedonism' which brings about a culture of de-traditionalised modes of pleasure. Falk (1994) sees in the pursuit of external material goods an attempt to confirm an internal good object which is psychic in nature. Thompson (1995) talks about the self as a 'symbolic project' and Fornas (1995) uses the term 'identity work' in a way similar to our conception. These versions of the intransitivity of large proportions of contemporary social and cultural life are summed up sociologically in Beck's description of a

> ...new mode of societalisation, a kind of 'metamorphosis' or 'categorical shift' in the relation between individual and society, [whereby the] [...] individual himself or herself becomes the reproduction unit of the social in the lifeworld. (Beck, 1992)

The psychological correlate of this summary can be found in Elliott's discussion of multiple modes of 'postmodern containment' which together comprise a

> postmodern institutional system which structures and secures the containment and regulation of intersubjective affective states, rather than representing some of its ideological incarnations in which fantasy and desire simply play themselves out. (Elliott and Frosh, 1995)

We contend that advertising makes a contribution to this institutional system. While we are to some extent at odds here with the dominant tradition of the academic study of advertising, as we described it in Chapter 4, we can claim some affinity with one important source of that tradition. We noted in the previous chapter what we might call Barthes' 'other essay' on advertising (in contrast to his work on advertisements most discussed, 'The rhetoric of the image', which is more plainly structuralist in tone), where he wrote:

> By its double message, the connoted language of advertising reintroduces the dream into the humanity of the purchasers and [...] thereby transforms its [the object's] simple use into an experience of the mind. (Barthes, 1988)

If therefore we can describe and even measure the identity work offered to (or perhaps required of) the readers of advertisements, over a period of time, we have the possibility of exploring two issues. One is the question of whether the process of de-traditionalisation and increasing reflexivity has in fact been occurring as sociological observation and cultural theory suggest, and if so whether there have been moments of particularly rapid or profound change, or periods of relative stability and even retrenchment. The other is about the nature of this process, about the extent to and ways in which the individual is offered cultural materials to fashion an identity, at the same time as experiencing the de-legitimation of traditional identities. Without such materials sufficiently available in popular culture, we are pitched into identity deficit; we have an identity need, but cannot do the work to meet that need, as that work requires cultural as well as psychic raw materials. A study of advertisements, as popular-cultural material, may yield some insight into the extent and nature of the materials available.

Figure 6.1 Anxiety addressed directly and indirectly

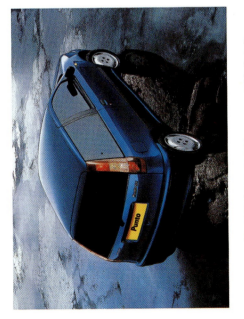

Figure 6.2 Anxiety: a direct appeal

Figure 6.3   Aggression and guilt

THE CAVALIER LS WITH ALLOY WHEELS. AND ABS, SO OTHER ROAD USERS HAVE A CHANCE TO ADMIRE THEM.

The alloy wheels which now come as standard on even the LS version of the Cavalier are no more things of beauty.

True, we crash test them for strength. Keep them in a hot, humid chamber to ensure against corrosion. Drive them for the equivalent of ten long years. And all to make sure they keep their looks.

But we also X-ray them for cracks and bubbles. Check to make certain enough air arrives at the brakes to keep them cool.

It's things like these which are at the hub of our thinking. With a Vauxhall, safety is paramount even on items that appear purely cosmetic.

In fact, just behind your shiny alloy wheels you'll find something called ABS, the anti-lock braking system that stops the wheels locking in a heavy braking manoeuvre.

We fit ABS as standard on all Cavaliers, from the top of the range to the bottom. So hairpin bends, dark country lanes and wet roads needn't hold any fears for drivers or their passengers. And the local wildlife can go safely about its business.

As part of our policy of safety throughout the range, the Cavalier, in fact, is equipped not only with ABS as standard but also with a full-size driver's airbag. And twin side impact bars. And bodylock front seatbelts.

After all, no matter how much we care about your Cavalier keeping its good looks, nothing compares with helping you keep yours.

THE CAVALIER FROM VAUXHALL

Figure 6.4 Separation anxiety

THE PEUGEOT 106.
LEAVE IT ALL BEHIND.

Blow the sheets, darn the socks, hang the washing. Why not take the dazzling Peugeot 106XT for a spin instead?

Having escaped from the daily grind, just sit back and relax while the 106 irons out the road. **THE PEUGEOT 106. LEAVE IT ALL BEHiND.**

With every 106XT we include a large measure of comfort.

Standard features include remote - control central locking, tinted glass, velour seat trim and integrated digital radio cassette.

The 3 and 5 door range of petrol and diesel models offers a wide variety of colours, all guaran- teed to run nicely.

So why bother with grubby socks when you can get clean away in a 106?

Call 0500 500 106 for further details, or visit your Peugeot dealer. **PEUGEOT**

Figure 6.5   Injustice and guilt

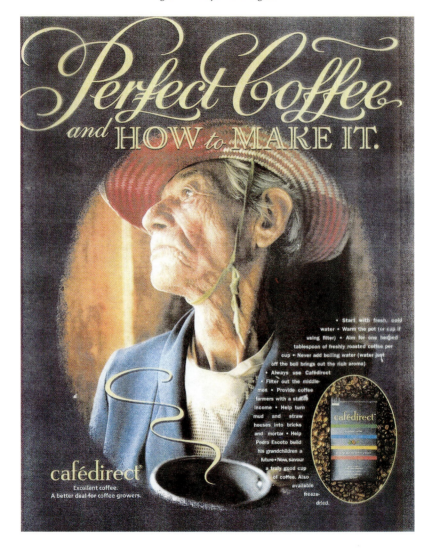

Figure 6.6   The victim survives

Figure 7.2 'Container' predominates

Figure 7.3 'Contained' predominates

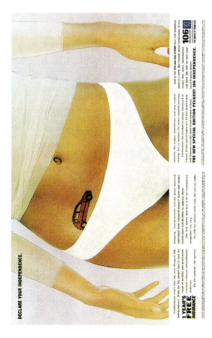

Figure 8.1 A simple practical message

Figure 8.2   A complex practical message

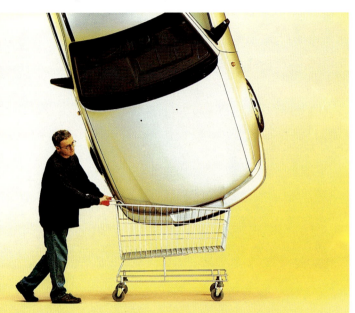

THE DAEWOO
30th ANNIVERSARY ·SALE
IS NOW ON.

1997 marks Daewoo's 30th anniversary of being in business. To celebrate, we're having a sale. As you'd expect, every new Daewoo still comes with the following comprehensive package:

1. WE DEAL DIRECT: More for your money as standard, including Electronic ABS, Driver's airbag, Power steering.

2. HASSLE FREE BUYING: Fixed prices, including delivery and 12 months road tax.

3. COMPLETE PEACE OF MIND: 3 year/60,000 mile free servicing including parts and labour.

3 years free comprehensive insurance, subject to status.

3 year/60,000 mile comprehensive warranty.

3 year Daewoo Total AA Cover.

6 year anti-corrosion warranty.

4. COURTESY SERVICING: Free courtesy car whenever yours is in for a service.

And as part of our 30th anniversary celebrations, every private customer purchasing a new Daewoo can choose one from any of the offers listed below. Written details for all offers available on request. Daewoo prices range from just £9,445 to £13,735 for the 3, 4 and 5 door Nexia and Espero saloon. To find out where your nearest store is, call us on 0800 666 222.

 1.) £500 worth of fuel vouchers.

2.) £500 cashback.

 3.) Choice of up to £750 worth of Daewoo electronic products.

 4.) £500 towards your deposit with Daewoo Direct Finance. Typical APR 11.2%.

SALE OFFERS AND 3 YEARS PEACE OF MIND? THAT'LL BE THE 🌼 DAEWOO.

Figure 8.7   A coping anxiety message

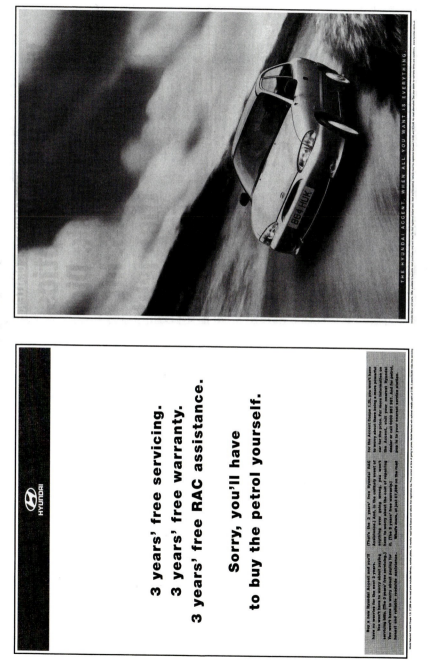

Figure 8.13   Not only practical

Figure 8.8   A status anxiety message

WHERE WALL STREET AND FIFTH AVENUE MEET.

Chrysler Fifth Avenue gives a higher return on your investment than any Cadillac sedan.

The distinguished Chrysler Fifth Avenue is a unique luxury car. With 49 standard features and a valuable 5 year/50,000 mile Protection Plan, it just may be the best luxury car value in America. In fact, re-sale reports show that the 1982 and 1983 Fifth Avenue retain more of their original selling prices than any similarly equipped Cadillac sedans.*

Luxuries abound: Standard 8-Cylinder Engine • Plush Pillow Seats with Passenger Recliner • Power Steering • Power Windows • Automatic Transmission • Air Conditioning • Power Front Disc Brakes • W/SW Steel Belted Radials • Premium Wheel Covers • Electronic Digital Clock • Special Sound Insulation • Rear Window Defroster • Halogen Headlamps • Dual Remote Mirrors • Premium Plush Pile

Carpeting • Trunk Dress-Up • Trip Odometer • Warning/Interior Light Packages • Padded Landau Vinyl Roof • And 30 additional features.

5 Year/50,000 mile Protection Plan

Your engine, transmission and drivetrain are protected for 5 years/ 50,000 miles, and the car's entire outer body is protected against rust-through for the same period.** Clearly, Fifth Avenue is an investment in luxury and quality. See your dealer for details. Buckle up for safety.

The best built, best backed American cars.

*Recent NADA Used Car Guides. **5 years or 50,000 miles, whichever comes first. Limited warranty. Deductible applies. Excludes leases. †Based on lowest percentage of National Highway Traffic Safety Administration safety recalls for '82 and '83 cars designed and built in North America, and a comparison of manufacturers' warranties for 1984 American models.

Figure 8.14   Exotic but practical

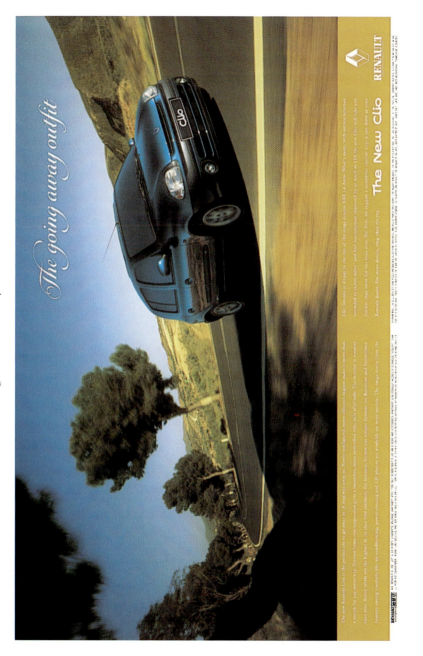

Figure 9.9   The distinctive consumer

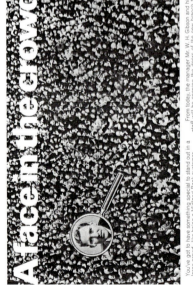

Figure 9.10   Diverse consumers

Figure 9.12   The consumer's whim

Figure 9.11   The cash machine as breast

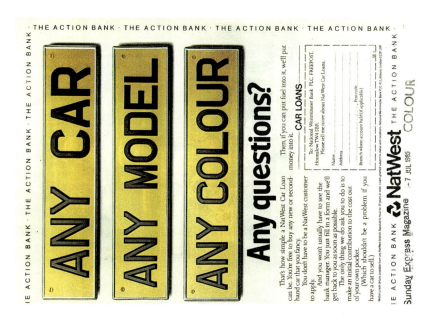

Figure 9.13 The consumer unbound

Head for the shops.

It could be clothes. A holiday perhaps. Or something new around the house.

You see them. You like them. You buy them.

Trouble is, doing everything in one go can sometimes leave your bank balance a trifle depleted.

That's why we hit upon a helpful idea called the Cashflow Account.

All you do is undertake to pay a certain sum each month. Anything from £20 upwards.

If the money should mount up, we pay you good interest on it.

But at the same time, it also guarantees you an instant overdraft.

It works this way. At any time, you can borrow as much as 30 times your monthly payment – up to £5,000.

Once the limit is agreed, you simply use your special Cashflow cheque book which is covered by your cheque guarantee card.

Or you can just take the money through a Cashpoint card.

Either way the money's always there, just waiting to meet your needs.

To find out more, clip and mail the coupon. In no time at all we could be picking up the bills while you pick up the packages. Or the interest, whichever takes your fancy.

We'll foot the bills.

A THOROUGHBRED AMONGST BANKS

Lloyds Bank

COLOUR Cosmopolitan

Figure 9.14 The consumer restrained

Figure 10.5   Coping with the unpleasant

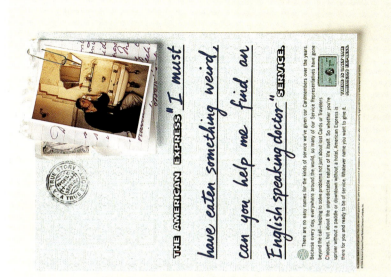

Figure 9.15   Animal tests = Social values

Figure 10.7   A balanced message for the universal citizen

Chapter 6

THE PSYCHODYNAMICS OF ADVERTISING[1]

The most distinctive feature of the approach we take to advertising and to the wider study of culture is its grounding in British traditions of psychoanalytic theory, the 'object relations' and Kleinian schools. We will not offer here a general outline of these rich traditions; good introductions to them can be found in Frosh (1991), Kohon (1986), Symington (1986), Rayner (1991), Rustin (1991), Elliott and Frosh (1995), and Greenberg and Mitchell (1983). Instead we will try to show through the example of their application to the study of advertising how we think they can contribute to understanding contemporary culture and its future.

Psychoanalytic influences in cultural theory are now quite commonplace, especially those derived from some French schools of psychoanalytic thought. Much of the potential of the British schools to enrich social and cultural analysis remains to be realised, although important work has already been done by Hoggett (1990), Minsky (1998), Rustin (1991), Young (1994) and other writers associated with the journal *Free Associations*. The work of cultural geographer Kevin Robins (1996) is of especial relevance here as he has drawn upon British psychoanalysis in discussing visual culture. The emphasis placed by the psychoanalyst Wilfred Bion on the unconscious sense of catastrophe, and the central importance in mental life of anxieties about the unthinkable, is used by Robins to suggest that in a richly photographic and televisual culture the consumption of images may be used in various ways to defend against these anxieties, e.g. by anaesthetically distancing oneself from television images of suffering, or by a flight into virtual reality. Following Morley (1995) Robins, like ourselves, seeks to steer a path between conceptions of the consumer as manipulated by a world of false images, and freely negotiating an identity from a genuine diversity of imagery. However, while drawing on an extensive body of theoretical and literary work, Robins does not link his interesting ideas to a systematic appraisal of a body of evidence about consumers' experiences or image content. As we have noted, this is a deficit typical of work in this area and is one which our study was intended to redress (though the testing of Robins' specific hypotheses about the importance of catastrophic anxiety in the everyday consumption of images would be particularly hard to design, given the intensive clinical exploration usually required to identify very primitive anxiety states).

One of us has previously suggested (Richards, 1994) that the psychic and emotional dimensions of popular culture can be helpfully understood using a present-day 'object-relational' formulation of Freud's concept of the reality principle. What we look for, and sometimes find, in our consumption of popular culture is a combination of both pleasure and restraint, that is of the pleasure and reality principles. We need both sensual enjoyment, and confirmation of our social being, of our ultimate subjection to a shared code. In this sense sport is a paradigmatic institution of popular culture, providing as it does intense experiences of both bodily pleasure and of rule-based social authority.

If advertising is able in at least some of its forms to offer a blend of 'pleasure' and 'reality', this would account in part for the way in which it has inserted itself so tenaciously into everyday experience. If advertising messages include something of both the 'Reality Principle' of modernity and the 'Pleasure Principle' of permissive and remissive postmodernity then—whatever their commercial purposes and effectiveness—the consumption of their images can be a form of cultural participation which confirms social membership while providing moments of delight.

ADVERTISING AND MENTAL ASSOCIATION

We will start with some basic axioms. One of the most fundamental ideas in psychoanalysis is that mental life is governed by the principle of association. Some other psychological theories have a similar starting point (including the otherwise very different theory of behavioural psychology), but a *specific* understanding of association is at the basis of psychoanalysis as a distinctive theory of mental life. According to psychoanalysis, all elements of experience have the potential to trigger off within the individual an associative process, in which one image or word or fragment of experience is connected in the individual's mind with something else outside of the given experience, which may lead onto something else, and so on. These connections may be highly idiosyncratic; they are the creative productions of the individual mind, and so will be guided if not fully determined by the store of contingent links which have arisen from that person's individual experience.

For example, if you have, say, been involved in or heard about an accident in which a Fiat was badly driven, this may colour your associations to Figure 6.1 (page 123), as might any negative association you might have to a dark blue car—perhaps an unpleasant neighbour or difficult colleague drives one. Then the striking black rear screen, for example, or the whole mean backstreet pose of the car, may take on a sinister meaning. The car becomes what you need protection against. You may not actually be aware of this configuration of meaning at work, but the effect—which might be vaguely noticed by you, or in more detail by a market researcher who questioned you—is that the advertisement fails to impress you positively, and may even leave you feeling that you don't much like the Punto, or Fiats in general.

So what may seem to another observer to be trivial or incidental details may to the reader of an advertisement be of great importance in shaping the overall emotional response to it. One of the problems that advertisers have is that there is no way of legislating for which details of an advertisement may register most in the minds of the public (hence the development of advertising as an extremely intensive crafting of the image, leaving as little as possible to chance or to 'mis'-appropriation or 'subversive' readings). Even then, other readings will certainly occur, as we have suggested for this Punto advertisement.

In clinical psychotherapeutic and psychoanalytic work, it is the idiosyncratic associations which are of most interest, because they say most about the specific inner world of the individual and so may help to understand why that person suffers in the particular way that he or she does. But in cultural analysis it is the regularities and patterns that we are more likely to be interested in, because they tell us about the ways in which and the extent to which our experience is shared, and is shaped by cultural dominants.

Because we do have common cultural experience, there will be such regularities and recurrent patterns, dominant associations which will be shared by many people within a given cultural context. Without any strong personal associations to the content of an advertisement, you will be likely to fall back on the store of publicly available associations to it and on received ways of sampling from these.

In this case, though the text is explicitly about car safety in accidents, the slogan (presumably addressed particularly to women buyers) obviously seeks to tap into the fear of violence; the Punto is your new 'bodyguard'. This is an area of conscious and, to some extent, realistic fear; there is no need for a subtle psychoanalytic exploration of meanings to tell us that many people, especially women, are fearful of violence in public places. However, the extent to which different individuals buy into the discourse of danger on the streets will vary. One person's greatest fear is another's occasional minor worry. Why do different people assess external dangers so differently? This happens because we bring different internal states of mind to our assessments of the external threat. As individuals we have different reserves of anxiety which may be mobilised by external threats.

ADVERTISING AND UNCONSCIOUS ANXIETY

Here we need to introduce a second basic axiom of our psychoanalytic approach: this is that the internal preoccupations of the individual, which will guide the process of association, are best thought of as *unconscious anxieties*. We are not talking here about the extent to which people should realistically fear violence on the streets; that is not the concern of psychoanalysis. We are talking instead about the kinds of unconscious anxiety which may cluster around the possibility of street violence. We all have reserves of paranoid anxiety; for all of us there is somewhere a darkness from which our killer may spring. We all have anxieties, however buried, about sexualised violence, about the possibility of sexual feeling becoming infused with murderous impulses; and we all have anxieties about being the subject of envious attacks by others who want what we have got. So we have a variety of unconscious anxieties which we can deploy in this connection; they will strongly influence our general fear of crime, and will help to shape our responses to an advertisement such as this.

Other advertisements which deal quite explicitly in anxiety, by referring directly to real dangers which people are consciously anxious about (such as the well-known Benetton advertisements), will have an effect determined both by the reader's knowledge of the threat to which they allude, and by the unconscious reserves of different sorts of anxieties which they may activate. The example in Figure 6.2 (page 123) is unusual in its direct reference to a psychic trauma, but our contention is that all advertisements, whatever their manifest content, will have their effect partly by provoking some anxiety. This is more often a function of the way our minds work, rather than—as in this case—being a deliberate strategy of the advertisement itself.

To some extent, then, our responses will be idiosyncratic, because they depend on particular experiences we may have had as individuals, and on the particular mix of unconscious anxieties pre-eminent in a person's mind at any one time. But since these anxieties are basically shared, common to us all, there will also at this level be regularities in the interpretation of advertisements. One of the tasks of psychoanalytic cultural research is the study of how unconscious anxieties may *consistently* shape our perceptions and actions, and what their *general* relationship is to our cultural forms and social processes.

Another difference between clinical work and cultural research is that in the former the associations which the patient or client has, whether they are to a dream or some event in the session, or are brought into the session from an experience outside, are likely to be brought into conscious awareness and made available there for reflection and assimilation. Indeed the making conscious of erstwhile unconscious associations is sometimes seen as the central principle of therapeutic work. One of the difficulties of applying psychoanalytic principles in cultural research is that the associations which people have to cultural artefacts, though we may assume them to be of great importance in determining their use and experience of these artefacts, may well remain largely unconscious.

However, despite these differences in how the associative processes of the mind may be investigated, the processes themselves are the same, whether produced on the analytic couch or while somebody walks past a poster advertisement, flicks through a magazine, or watches the commercial break on television. The core of these processes is the generation of links from the presented text or image to other words and images and to feelings. The associations which people will generate from presented images are not arbitrary productions. They will be guided strongly by the unconscious preoccupations of the individual— by, as we are putting it here, unconscious anxieties.

Some elaboration of the concept of unconscious anxiety is necessary here. Post-Freudian developments in psychoanalytic theory have greatly enriched and extended the descriptions of anxiety found in early classical theory, though Freud's fundamental insight that mental life is at one level a perpetual struggle with anxiety remains at the core of much psychoanalytic thinking. The first form of anxiety which Freud identified, castration anxiety, can now be included in a broader category of fears centring upon the idea that one is not entitled to, or not able to, become a sexually mature adult. To this category can now be added other categories of anxiety: anxieties about separation and loss; guilty fears about the consequences of our greed and destructiveness; anxieties about our capacities as individuals to be sane and not to be overwhelmed by experience; and anxieties that grandiose and omnipotent parts of ourselves may get out of control. These and other descriptions now constitute the expanded language which contemporary psychoanalysis has at its disposal for charting the forms and power of anxiety.

Unconscious anxieties lie, as it were, in waiting, ready to seize on elements of experience and use them as occasions for expression. In an important study of advertising, the only one prior to ours that made systematic and full-blooded use of a version of psychoanalytic theory, Haineault and Roy (two Canadian analysts writing in 1984) suggest that in the first mental response to an advertising image there will be an expression of an unconscious anxiety. 'Any representation', they say, 'is reducible to an intrapsychic conflict...all the following associations aim at reducing this tension...to the degree that they are capable of reducing the tension that the first association provokes'.

They argue this persuasively, at first in relation not to complex whole advertisements but to the much more condensed signs found in brand names. The name 'Lois', for example, a jeans brand, can set off two trains of association for French speakers. One is towards a wide domain of pleasure, via *loisir* (leisure). The other is notions of restraint, via *loi* (law), to which the nature of the product may help to add images of a particular kind of law—the harsh law of the cowboy Wild West. A strong tension can thus be created instantly, between thoughts of pleasure and libidinality, and thoughts of severe, possibly violent, restraint and punishment. This typical id *vs* punitive superego conflict may generate considerable anxiety, and the consumer will then presumably have a lot of psychic work to do in neutralising or resolving this conflict. Some advertisements (as in recent British campaigns for Marmite, Sun Alliance and the Abbey National) directly offer associations to the brand name, and may consist of little more than this. For Haineault and Roy, such advertisements would be attempting to pre-empt the possibility of a brand name becoming entwined with an intractable conflict or unmanageable anxiety.

Phonetic and other sensory characteristics of the advertisement call forth more associations than the semantic content of an advertisement, they say, because 'they speak to the primary movements, to the fundamental logics of the psychic apparatus'—the unconscious as a whole works by the principle of contingent association rather than by more meaningful links.

An advertisement will carry through its whole content this principle of setting up tensions, for which resolution is then sought through an associative chain, and the result can be very powerful. At this subliminal level of provoking associations, advertisements fit perfectly into the normal activity of the unconscious and so are guaranteed to elicit our involvement and consent. Advertisements with an abundance of images are, for Haineault and Roy, 'constructed like a phenomenon of the unconscious...What such an unfolding of images resembles most is phantasmic unfurling', as the mind elaborates whole sets of associative networks at once, a process they say is otherwise found only in dreams. Since they wrote, the proliferation throughout print and broadcast media of surreal and phantasmic content, especially in computer-generated imagery, has probably brought this dream-like quality to a lot more media content, but their analysis of what advertisements do can apply as much to the simplest poster, carrying just a name, as to the most extravagant TV creation.

They conducted a study of both 'static' (posters) and 'dynamic' (TV) advertisements. They report having examined thousands of posters from the 1950s on; they do not present systematic observations, though there are many interesting case studies in their rich but difficult book. We think there is much to be gained from the idea that a particular area of unconscious anxiety has been activated in associations to an image, and that other associations will be attempts to deal with that anxiety, by calling up other images which can somehow mitigate it.

One dimension of advertising in which this process may be especially intense is largely beyond the scope of our empirical study (though some account of it was taken in our advertisement coding procedures—see Chapter 7): the musical element of TV and radio advertisements. Music, of course, has tremendous power to evoke affects and associations of all kinds, and Haineault and Roy note that the soundtrack can play various roles in the total psychological configuration of an advertisement. The '...soundtrack can play a primordial role in the restitution of the necessary equilibrium between desire and inhibition at the heart of advertising' (1984). Despite the sensual qualities of music, this role is not necessarily on the side of desire; sometimes the soundtrack is a 'guardrail' against primitive associations to visual content.[2]

ADVERTISEMENTS, CONTAINMENT AND DEFENCE

Here we are introducing a third basic psychoanalytic precept: where there is anxiety, there will be an attempt to deal with it. Broadly speaking there are two kinds of responses to anxiety. It can be dealt with either by defence, whereby an anxiety is denied or displaced, or somehow warded off; or by containment, where it is acknowledged, confronted and managed constructively within the resources available to the individual, both inner, psychic resources, and external ones. The latter consist primarily of our relationships with others, in the reality of which we gain the support and strength to confront and contain our anxieties, and of the culture which we inhabit, which provides symbolic (and also material) expressions of the containment of anxieties.

To defend against anxiety is to deny, evade or suppress it. The old psychoanalytic concept of 'repression', as often understood, connotes a substantial part of the range of this broad concept, but by no means the whole of it. Psychoanalysis also recognises that defensive work can be carried out by states of mind which are on the surface anything but 'repressed' in the sense of inhibited and manifestly fearful. Of particular importance here is the concept of narcissism, with its implication that broad modes of relating to the world, in which the independence, agency and right to pleasure of the individual are emphatically asserted, are actually defences against profound fears of abandonment or rejection. Omnipotent states of mind, expressed in, for example, unrealistic confidence or a belief in the possibility of total control, are often a clear illustration of this kind of defensive organisation, but there is an infinite range of more subtle forms of flight away from terror or frustration into eroticism or illusion. Many of the critiques of advertising, as we noted in Chapter 4, have seen it as the social institution most responsible for the cultural credibility of these defensive flights.

In contrast to defensive responses are containing ones. The concept of containment is particularly associated with the 'post-Kleinian' work of Bion (1959/1997). We are using this notion very broadly here, and not engaging with some important levels of Bion's theory. The psycho-analytic concept of containment originated in clinical work with seriously disturbed individuals, though it was soon generalised to normal development. It referred originally to the process by which an anxiety was communicated from one person to another, and back again but in different form. The first person (patient or baby) felt the anxiety to be intolerable, and so projected it into another (analyst or mother). The second person is however able to understand (albeit perhaps not consciously) and tolerate the anxiety, and then returns to the first person a sense that the anxiety is tolerable. Through repeated experiences of this containment by another of the individual's feelings, through this to and fro of projections, most babies and some patients acquire their own capacity to process and tolerate powerful feelings.

In this form the process of containment obviously requires two minds in relationship with each other, which is not the case when an individual confronts a cultural process or product. However, some psychoanalysts extended the theory to include the ways in which social institutions, or even society as a whole, could be said to contain the individual, while Bion went on to apply the model of container/contained to processes within the individual, especially the development of the capacity to think. Richards (1994) has sought to understand the general meaning of much popular culture to the individual in terms of the containing function which the forms and institutions of popular culture, and the experiences they offer, can perform for their consumers or participants.

We think therefore that in the mental processes which an encounter with an advertisement may trigger, certain kinds of message content may serve a containing function, by reminding the individual of containing forces both within and without. This 're-minding' function is in effect a stimulation or confirmation of internal resources the person already possesses, or may be a demonstration of the presence in social or material reality of containing powers.

Bearing in mind the need to complement the concept of defence with that of containment, we therefore do not accept Haineault and Roy's *a priori* propositions that the *first* association will always define the main anxiety evoked by the advertisement, and that subsequent associations are usually about dealing defensively with the first anxiety-laden one. They propose that advertisements generally encourage us to use defences rather than to reflect on them or—in our terms—to react in a way more containing of the anxieties involved. They assert that the message structure of advertisements is modelled on defensive habits such as projection, displacement, denial and repression. Thus the classic Marlboro advertisements, for example, they see as displacing the fear of death, which should attach to the cigarette, on to the excitingly dangerous frontier territory in which the horseman sits. By invoking 'eternity', an advertisement for a watch denies time and mortality. A TV advertisement for Carlsberg lager has four simultaneous screens showing different types of people engaged in different activities, and they are saying 'we're different'. In the subsequent line, though, they say 'still we're alike: Carlsberg's my beer'. So the fact of difference is glimpsed, and the pains of separation and individuation are implied, but they are swiftly displaced by the reassurance that they can be avoided.

This defensive proclivity of advertisements is termed 'perversion' by Haineault and Roy, following a conventional use of this term in psychoanalysis. Perversion stems from the inability to accept the reality of one's own psychological separateness. Advertisements reinforce the perverse element in us all, they claim. In effect they are providing a sophisticated psychoanalytic complement to the cultural and moral critiques of advertising discussed in Chapter 4. Their affiliation with elite habits of criticism is shown in their discussion of the reasons for the perversion of advertising.

They do not explicitly blame 'mass culture', but instead implicate all of us: 'we are the authors of our own perversion', because we spontaneously search for defences against inner conflicts and fears. The unconscious is 'by nature lazy', and will 'lean in the direction of ease', which is away from the reality and sadness of separation. There is no class dimension to this analysis; the 'masses' are not being blamed by an elite. Rather the corrosive psychic impact of advertisements is attributed to the general human condition. However, there is a further step to their argument, which is to contrast advertisements with art, and in particular to contrast TV advertisements with great films. Both deal in what they call the great 'problematics' of humanity—individuation, power and sexuality (a recasting of the Freudian stages of psycho-sexual development). However, while art inhabits the problematic, allowing the audience to explore their anxieties about it, advertisements annihilate their subject: they set up problems *and* offer immediate solutions. So while art can be subversive of the evasions characteristic of everyday life, advertisements just concur with the evasions. An advertisement 'never modifies the content of an ideology or culture, but constantly consolidates it'. It offers 'a perversion to avoid a subversion'. So an implicitly elite position creeps into the Haineault and Roy analysis, as a moral gulf opens for them between 'art' and everyday life.

This approach rests on a simplistic dichotomy between everyday life (bad) and true art (good). Like much of the work previously discussed, it draws its credibility from an assumptive framework. Detached from those assumptions, it may be just as plausible to suggest that the Carlsberg advertisement contains anxieties about separation by pointing to the possibilities for human community (through a shared consumption practice), or that a watch advertisement which uses the word 'eternity' is alluding to ties of love with the capacity to mitigate the realities of death and separation.

Haineault and Roy's study is an important one, and the force of much of their analysis needs to be recognised; it undoubtedly provides a way of understanding the psychodynamics of many individual advertisements. Its shortcoming is in assuming that one mode of response is characteristic of all advertising, and in failing to consider the possibility that the call-and-response structure typical of many advertisements may be a vehicle for a measure of confrontation with anxiety and pain. We would agree with them that the need to deal with anxiety will loom large in some way in the reader's overall response to the advertisement, but we would want to point out the likelihood that associations to advertisements will contain a mixture of anxious, defensive and containing elements.

Their approach is also unbalanced at a metapsychological level. While the unconscious has to be understood as a field of associative activity, it must also be seen as the core of selfhood, as the medium in which the basic capacities to relate to others reside. In addition to the associative unconscious, there is the moral unconscious (Brown and Richards, 1998), the basic configuration of the individual's internal object-relations which will be fairly stable across time and from which the individual, unless very severely damaged, can draw experiences of goodness which are both projected out into the cultural world and reintrojected from cultural materials. We might say that Haineault and Roy over-emphasise process at the expense of structure, and so miss the morally creative or recuperative forces at work within the readers of advertisements.

Their approach can be contrasted with that of Falk (1994), who in his use of a Kleinian concept is closer to our own position, though his use of this concept is relatively limited. He suggests that advertising must invoke some notion of goodness in its presentation of commodities; in Kleinian terms, a 'good object', that is an internal representation of goodness, is being deployed. In a discussion of the history of patent medicine advertising, Falk notes that many products shifted from being constructed in advertisements as medicines to deal with ailments (i.e. to banish negatives), to being presented as pure positives, bringing greater vitality, energy, etc. to the well. The transformation of Coca Cola from a medicine to a 'soft drink' is a clear example of this development. While this is partly attributable to increasing restrictions on what could be claimed for the cure-alls, Falk contends that it also reflects a broader cultural shift. Advertising in general came to invoke a state of goodness, a domain of good experience, to which it then attached the commodity, rather than as previously laying the emphasis on the commodity to which it then attached some good value. As the consumer society developed, 'the experience of consumption and the consumption of experiences appear as mutual prerequisites for each other' (Falk, 1994), with the consumption of 'good' experience an increasingly central principle for living. While this does not distinguish genuine good objects, which are real sources of emotional sustenance and pleasure, from idealisations, which are defensive denials of bad elements, Falk's approach does help to lay the basis for one of the key propositions we develop in Chapter 7: that however indifferent they may be in their commercial purpose to their moral-psychological content, advertisements must make use of images of the 'good' which may play a positive role in the psychic work of association which is provoked in the minds of the audience.

To return to the Punto example in Figure 6.1 (page 123), we can now ask what kind of *response* to anxiety does it embody? We could say that in its suggestion that anxiety can be dealt with by rational measures to increase safety, this advertisement has a containing component, though in its promise of an individual 'bodyguard' and its suggestion that there is a complete 'answer', it is probably also giving succour to some defensive component, in the form of a phantasy that anxiety can be completely abolished.

In the example of Figure 6.3 (page 124) there is again, arguably, a containing resolution to the anxiety. Two anxieties are evoked, offering alternative positions to the reader, depending on which figure in the picture you identify with—rabbit or car. One is based on the fear of being helpless, transfixed like the rabbit, and the other is of being the powerful, aggressive force which destroys things in its path. The text then deals with the anxieties evoked by the picture, by stressing the braking capabilities of the car: we read that although there is danger, there is also provision against it, and against the misuse of power.

Incidentally, the intensive crafting of detail in advertisements extends, we believe, to the number plates of cars shown; our association to the one shown here was 'good luck'. While this may not match the advertiser's intention, it is necessary to explain somehow why other manufacturers' advertisements were using the same letters around the same time!

DEPTH PSYCHOGRAPHICS

In cultural research we are interested primarily in recurrent patterns of association, that is to say in figurations of anxiety and responses to it which can be traced across a whole culture, or which are at least characteristic of a specific social group within a culture. In the latter case what we are trying to do could be seen as bringing a depth-psychological dimension to the marketers' conception of 'market segmentation', or 'psychographics' as some of those approaches which use lifestyle and demographic information to map target markets are called.

This sees products as consumed by distinct groups of the population differentiated by demographic, social and cultural variables; we are trying to understand this in terms of differences in unconscious preoccupations, which will vary between different social groups. The major variables of age, gender and socio-economic status will set some quite firm parameters here, as will the nature of the particular product concerned and its location in everyday life: whether it is used in the context of domestic labour, family leisure, individual leisure, at the workplace or whatever. The price of a product will also affect which areas of emotional life it is likely to be relevant to; not surprisingly more expensive goods will on the whole command deeper emotional investments than cheap, repeat purchase ones, although this is not always the case. Some consumers may succeed in distancing their larger purchases from their more pressing emotional needs, which may instead find expression in more trivial or minor purchases—food, clothing, etc. (where of course the consequences of a 'neurotic' or impractical choice are less serious). It is doubtful though that any act of consumption can be cleanly separated from emotional life and carried out in a realm of purely calculative rationality. While advertising for housing, the largest purchase that most of us make, is relatively low key and factual, we can attribute this more to the predominance of the second-hand, one-to-one market in housing, and the weakness of brand identity (particular builders) in comparison to the importance of location, size and idiosyncratic features in influencing buyers of houses and flats.

As an example of the determining influence of segmentation factors on the emotional content of advertisements, we could take a number of television advertisements from a famous Bartle Bogle Hegarty campaign for Levi 501s. The predominant theme of most other advertisements in this long-running campaign is what we could describe as an Oedipal one, in that it hinges on a conflict between a young man and an older man in which possession of or the attentions of a woman are at stake. The advertisements (sometimes very explicitly, or we might say crudely) take the side of the younger man, and their narrative is the story of his triumph over the older one. This is not to say that the target market for 501s is just that of young men of the age of the hero (although males between 18 and 35 may indeed be the way that Levis define their core market for the 501). It is to say that when any male is buying jeans he is inhabiting a part of his mind, and a zone of everyday culture, in which the Oedipal struggle of youth is celebrated, in which the heroes are the individualist, sexual rebels of post-war American mythology. The advertisement expresses the adolescent phantasy of triumph over a jaded and discredited authority figure.

In these comments we are drawing upon no-one's associations but our own. Though we would be confident that these associations are not idiosyncratic, we are not satisfied with them as a means of securing our argument. If we want to do persuasive research into advertising, we have to accumulate data which is more than just the intuitive observations of we researchers. It has often been observed that the over-reliance on the writer's own responses to advertisements has dogged much of the theoretical writing about advertising of the last twenty years or more.

The most direct way of assembling evidence relevant to our enquiry would be to conduct large numbers of individual or group interviews in which we asked respondents to think and talk about their impressions of and feelings about a systematically-drawn sample of advertisements. A substantial chunk of the market research business is concerned with the pre- and post-testing of advertisements, i.e. with eliciting responses to them, and if the huge quantities of market research material could be archived and made accessible to academic researchers, it would be possible to build up a broad dataset on people's associative responses to advertisement content. However, as we describe in Chapter 7, we are taking another approach, which is to describe advertisement content in considerable detail, and to divide that content into categories which we can relate to certain areas of emotional life, to certain unconscious preoccupations and anxieties.

Let us sketch out some ways in which this might be done. If, for example, an advertisement shows a same-sex couple or group we can suggest that anxieties about homosexual impulses will be triggered in the minds of at least some readers; or, at another level, about the difficulties of forming good and lasting friendships with people of the same gender.

If an advertisement stresses freedom or independence (see Figure 6.4, page 125) then we might suggest that the type of anxiety which is active here is what some psychoanalysts and other psychologists call separation anxiety. Typically, advertisements dealing in this area are ambivalent, or adopt what we might call 'penny *and* bun' strategies. They hint at the possibility of both total freedom and complete security. It is not a great leap of the imagination to see the knotted sheets here as similar in appearance to an umbilical cord, and to note that the cord has not been cut—indeed, the car is pointing backwards to the (?maternal) washing machine. As such, the advertisement is more defensive than containing. It seems to suggest firstly that you *can* leave it all behind— forget all your responsibilities, and your debts to those on whom you once depended—while also, in the visual image, giving the reassuring signal that you can remain connected and belonging in the midst of your absolute freedom. It encourages a manic, omnipotent belief that one can have it all ways, without cost.

It will be evident that we are not just describing the textual content of advertisements; we are drawing on psychoanalytic theory to link this content to the psychic contexts in which it will be received and understood. It may be objected that the advertisement is just about the *positive* virtues of freedom and independence, and that it is just a Freudian obsession with the dark underside of things which leads us to suggest that it may also be about the *fear* of freedom. This objection, we suggest, overlooks the costs and pains of independence, and the struggles with fear which every individual has in the process of separating out from parents—of developing a sense of agency in childhood, and of self-assertion and breaking free in adolescence.

ADVERTISEMENTS AND THE MANAGEMENT OF GUILT[3]

We will extend our exposition of the psychodynamics of advertisements with a few case studies in a particular area of emotional life, namely guilt feelings. Amongst the different forms of public communication, advertising has a special relationship to guilt. It seems closer to it, more often linked with it, than many other kinds of mass media content, except for the massive output of drama concerning crime and policing where the content is explicitly about guilt. Advertisements are not usually *about* guilt, as such, but in contemplating them we are often put, or put ourselves, into states of mind in which an element of guilt can be discerned.

Sometimes this is the crux of the experience of reading an advertisement, and it is easy to see why, and to construct on the basis of it a loosely psychoanalytic explanation of the link between advertisements and guilt. This is the experience of seeing in an advertisement an overt attempt at seduction, at enticing the reader into an experience of pleasure or self-indulgence. Whether or not the reader or viewer consciously feels vulnerable to the particular seduction portrayed, various tableaux of desire and its consequences, and of the struggle between prohibition and licence, are installed in the mind of the reader, who can then inhabit any of the subjectivities potentially involved. There are those on one side who refuse, seeking to evade guilt (whether defined as resolute puritans or uptight prudes), and those on the other who give in and so have to contend with their guilt (who could be seen as the corrupt weaklings, the rational hedonists, or the ordinary mortals of weak flesh). There is also the seducer or seductress, who can be seen as trying to deal with their own guilt by drawing others into their sinful worlds.

On the basis of this kind of experience, we can then say that advertising is linked to guilt because of the remissive or provocative role it plays in relation to pleasure. The most effective guilt-inducing or guilt-relieving 'buttons' may be different for different people. For someone whose guilt is most easily focused on eating, it will be advertisements for luxury, sensual foods that will do the trick most often. For someone else with a guilty unease about their narcissism, it may be advertisements for cosmetics and clothing which evoke most guilt.

We can extend the argument more widely, and say that an advertisement does not actually have to adopt a seductive strategy to implicate its readers in a scenario of guilt. Nor does it have to be advertising a commodity that in itself can set up a struggle with guilt for the reader. It will do so anyway just by virtue of being an advertisement, because it is part of the common-sense of our culture that advertising is the voice of the consumer society, and that we are guilty about consumption in general. There are least two forms of this argument.

One is a more general version of the psychoanalytic approach; it suggests that all consumption is shadowed by guilt. Any time we take, consume or use something, we activate inside ourselves the fear that we are damaging, even destroying, the object we take, or its source. Obviously this is often literally true: the apple consumed is the apple destroyed. But for psychoanalysis, it is not the literal truth that counts, but the truth in unconscious phantasy. What or who does the apple stand for, that we are then devouring? Can we rely on the apple tree to produce any more apples, after we have taken its fruit?

The other is a sociological or cultural argument, involving an implicit or explicit critique of the consumer society. It suggests that we know of our *collective* guilt which derives from our membership of high-consumption societies—guilt about depletion of the earth's resources, or about the poverty and starvation endured by less fortunate peoples. All advertising, as an incitement to consume, represents this guilt, and may be taken as a cause of it, even as a major cause.

There are of course the long traditions of intellectual work in both Britain and the U.S., which we discussed in Chapter 4, that have posited advertising as '*the* iconographic signifier of multinational capitalism' (Nava *et al.*, 1997, italics original), i.e. as its symbol *par excellence*, and which have therefore assumed it to bear institutional or structural guilt, or guilt by association, for the excesses or intrinsic evils of that economic system. In this framework, the locus of guilt may shift from the consumer to the persons or institutions seen to benefit from that system—the capitalist class and its servants in the symbolic professions.

Nava herself offers an unusual hypothesis to help explain what she calls the 'incrimination' of advertising, its theoretical 'framing' as a social form 'beyond redemption'. She notes the interweaving of feelings about advertising with those about television (also frequently reviled as an attack upon 'culture'), and wonders if 'the construction of the ad as a very bad yet quite seductive object with extensive socio-psychological powers' is a displacement of a negativity felt more fundamentally towards television. Television is also associated with guilt—about the alleged passivity of the viewer, about consuming 'rubbish', about falling for its empty charms—and the overlap in feelings about the predominantly visual cultural form of advertising and the defining visual medium of our age is a significant one. The strongly visual nature of popular culture as a whole is brought into focus here, though we should not underestimate the auditory power of television, nor of the advertising soundtrack, especially when musical—what often used to be the specially written 'advertising jingle', but is now more typically the skilful use of already-known pieces of music, popular and classical, to anchor or to embellish brand values. Moreover the deep hostility towards advertising in intellectual culture long pre-dates the advent of television, and there is no obvious reason why a displacement of negative feeling from TV to advertising should take place. Nonetheless, at the interface of television and advertising there may be a site of especially strong potential for visually-mediated guilt.

We have therefore a number of ways in which advertisements and guilt are linked. They can be seen as the occasion for the consumer's guilt, whether about specific products or about consumption in general. And they are frequently themselves seen as 'guilty'. This incrimination of advertising has been conducted most elaborately via intellectual theorising but is also embedded in the more everyday, popular experience of advertising as a social institution.

There is however another relationship between advertisements and guilt, which will be explored in the next examples. This is one in which the advertisement acts as a cultural resource for the management of guilt. It does not gratuitously install guilt in the minds of people who perhaps might otherwise be innocent by turning them into greedy consumers. On the contrary it offers to those already beset with guilt (as an intrinsic property of the developed human mind) a momentary experience of managing that guilt, of dealing with it in a more or less effective way (see Richards (1994) and MacRury (1997) for earlier illustrations of this analysis).

Whether or not we give any credence to the incrimination of advertising, we can explore the psychoanalytic idea that the consumer is inevitably a guilty soul, with or without the impact of advertising. The guilt may be felt in relation to others or to the natural world. In the unconscious, to own or to consume can be to steal from a phantasied other, or to provoke the envy of others. It may be, as Marx declared, that in our relationship to goods we wipe from view the history of labour which is embodied in the commodity before us. It may also be, at another level, that this knowledge is inescapable, that we register unconsciously the effort which has gone into producing and delivering the commodity, or that we sense the relative privilege which our consumption represents. Of course, an increasing number of people are consciously aware of the human labour that creates the things we consume, as the emergence of the ethical consumer shows. It is not difficult to find a solid basis for this in the external world, given the level of exploitation that currently characterises much production globally and the massive inequalities built into the global market.

In view of this it is perhaps surprising that there are not more advertisements like the one for cafédirect (Figure 6.5, page 126) in which a *direct* appeal is made to the consumer's guilt about enjoying things at the expense of exploited people in other countries. Note that the advertisement cannot make too heavy or one-dimensional an appeal to compassion for others or to a sense of responsibility to unknown workers. That message is embedded in the text, and at the foot of the bottom left signature, rather than being in the headline slogan or in the rich visual design. The person pictured looks healthy and proud; the golds and browns and swirls are the stock elements of coffee advertising, and the advertisement's most prominent message concerns the sensual enjoyment of coffee. You are nearly half-way through the text before it becomes apparent that the instruction format is a humorous way of saying that to buy this coffee will enhance the well-being of coffee growers in an unspecified but presumably South American country. As well as his dignified image, the naming in the text of the man pictured helps present him to the reader as an equal, maximising the possibility of an empathic response while minimising the risk that the reader is overwhelmed with guilt about an impossibly bad situation, and feels helpless or unwilling to respond. (In this connection we might suggest that the television reporting of famine has been the most effective visual mobilisation of guilt in recent years, qualifying the claim that people do not respond if they are presented with unbearably guilt- or anxiety-inducing images.)

In the case of this advertisement, it might be cynically claimed that the pleasure of the British consumer must not be disturbed by the oppressive reality of life for many in South America. But it is a promotional not a polemical communication, and as such it is a well-balanced one.[4]

In this respect it differs from the advertisements most famously linked with the explicit arousal of guilt about world issues: the Benetton campaigns featuring posters with images of suffering—a dying AIDS victim, a dead Bosnian soldier's uniform, an oil-covered bird and so on (Falk, 1997). While these advertisements may well have extended the boundaries of commercial communication in a way that may prove of importance, their effectiveness as either commercial or political communications is in doubt. We would argue that this is because they provided no tension, and no possibility for containing the guilt and other distressing feelings they aroused.

The cafédirect advertisement is promising relief from guilt not by reading the advertisement, but by doing what it proposes, i.e. buying the commodity. This is relatively unusual, however; the more typical action of advertisements is to offer some guilt-management in the process of reading them. Take the example of the Gore-Tex advertisement (Figure 6.6, page 127). There is no real-world, historical or political guilt addressed by this message. Instead there is the feeling that in the ordinary roughness of life you are being routinely violent to something. One boot has keeled over under the pressure, or been carelessly tossed down, but the other stands up defiantly, and both, we are told, are still breathing. So you may risk damaging things, or perhaps people, as you crash about your business, heedless of the pain you may be inflicting. But—and this is the guilt-*management*—the objects of your violent indifference will survive, and will continue to provide you with vital support—their 'breathing' is not so much a sign of their survival but of their continuing to relate to you in a caring way.

The advertisement is for walking boots, and does not mention people. It is axiomatic for a psychoanalytic approach, however, that a relationship with an image of a person, or part of a person, always underlies the experience of relating to impersonal objects, since in the deepest levels of unconscious phantasy there are only interpersonal object-relationships. So the text of this advertisement will address the reserve of guilt which Kleinian psychoanalysis especially sees as universal and central to psychic functioning, the anxious guilt about whether our aggressive impulses have damaged others ('depressive' anxiety as it is called—see Chapter 7).

There are a number of other elements and complexities in the advertising message, as is often the case with the dense content of advertisements. The leading implication is that you the wearer have abused the boots, but the text talks about 'Mother Nature throwing' tough conditions at you, as if you, like the boots, are the victim. Normally it is Mother Nature we are worried about having damaged— depressive anxiety is crucial to environmental awareness—but an advertisement for walking boots is in a good position to invert that scenario because the product is associated with outdoor pursuits such as walking, which in turn are either associated with environmentally-responsible attitudes or are occasions for experiencing nature as something to be endured.

And the boots are above all *protective*. Rather like parents, they exist to be abused and relied upon for protection. The theme of protection, so common in countless advertisements for a huge range of different products, and which in Kleinian terms is a 'paranoid' anxiety, is interwoven here with the 'depressive' theme. And while some protection might involve a suffocatingly close relationship, and claustrophobic anxiety, this form of protection allows you to breathe. It provides you with intimate care yet spares you the shame of sharing or even experiencing your own smell, which is able to escape.

So there are aspects of the message here which are to do with insecurity and shame rather than guilt. But the signing-off statement takes us back to the theme of brutality and guilt. Get out and stay out, it says, invoking once again the reader's identification either with the bully or the uncaring one, saying those words, or with the victim hearing them—but we know it's a joke, a play on words, because in this context to get out and stay there is something pleasurable you want to be able to do, without your boots letting you down.

These nuances would be lost on most readers of the advertisement. Only keen walkers, people about to buy some boots, and people unnaturally interested in advertisements would be likely to read the full text and so be able to enter into the more complex multi-levelled elaboration of the message in their own thoughts and feelings. But what casual viewers of it are likely to be left with is the idea expressed in the slogan that important 'objects' can and do survive the treatment—the lack of care, the exploitation, the demands—which we mete out to them. It thus both evokes depressive anxiety and offers to contain it with this reassuring, humorous message.

The fact that advertisements are frequently humorous is not unconnected with their function of helping in the management of difficult feelings such as guilt. The most common form of advertising humour is the pun, which holds two meanings together and provokes or misleads the reader by proffering one reading (an undesirable or perhaps forbidden one) before coming down in favour of the other, desired or accepted meaning. The pun can contain both the anxiety and its resolution.

Many humorous advertisements are not puns in the literal sense of the word but involve the fusion of two contradictory or incongruent thoughts by visual imagery alone, or by a combination of word and image. In an interesting example, Volkswagen employed a guilt theme and use parodic humour to manage it. In this ad the car is shown as an object of scrutiny in a laboratory, with a number of scientists/ technicians inspecting it in different ways. The main text is the word 'Obsession' in large lettering. The ad is a full-blown example of 'intertextuality' *within* advertising, with the visual design, the lettering and above all the name itself being in imitation of Calvin Klein 'Obsession' cosmetic ads, and the further phrase '*laboratoires Volkswagen*' being a reference to another personal care brand ('*laboratoires Garnier*'). Unfortunately for this reason we are not able to reproduce this example in the book, as intertextuality can have litigious consequences—at the time of writing the image is the subject of a dispute between Volkswagen and Calvin Klein!

The humour here rests on the conjunction of two sets of incongruent elements: cars *vs* cosmetics, and objective, scientific/ technological assessment *vs* enraptured, awe-struck contemplation. There are four men at the back in scientific, scrutinising mode; a woman and man at the front, while also in white lab coats, are by contrast in rapture. The incongruence is between 'Germanic' technological excellence and a 'French' eroticism; the word 'obsession' can cover both. By placing the guilt-inducing idea of the erotic in a context of white-coated objectivity, it is transmuted into a more manageable and acceptable force. More specifically, the narcissistic preoccupation with appearance, and the sensual adoration of the car as beautiful object, are recognised and allowed some expression, and simultaneously put in their place. This place is at one level the neutralised, rationalised space of the technical inspection; at another level, it is the place of humour. In the advertisement as a joke, the narcissistic eroticism of the reader's enjoyment of the car is deflated by its presentation in laughable form.

It is perhaps like the obsessional symptom, which can never adequately match the desires it is an attempt to control or abolish.[5] In fact the symptom itself is a collusion with those desires: the obsession with cleanliness requires the person to be in continual and close relationship with dirt, by monitoring it; the obsession with safety requires the person to live in the constant presence of danger, anticipating the worst. Narcissism is not an obsession, in this technical sense of the obsessive-compulsive symptom, but a similar dynamic may apply; once the genie of narcissism is let out of the bottle, however self-mockingly, it may dictate the narrative. As with so much else in postmodern pastiche, the act of parody or mockery can be a way of *inhabiting* that which is parodied.

Notes

1. An earlier version of part of this paper was presented by BR and IM in September 1995 to 'Shouts from the Street', the First International Conference for Popular Culture at Manchester Metropolitan University.

2. Also see Frontori *et al.* (1989) for a rare published report of some consumer research using a psychoanalytic framework, in which the description by the Italian analyst Fornari of the 'primary ideas of life' (similar to Barthes' 'oneiric themes') was used to classify associations to advertising jingles and to select the optimum jingle for the intended market.

3. An earlier version of this section was presented by BR at a conference on 'Guilt and the Confessional in Visual Culture' at Middlesex University in September 1998.

4. In the terms of the values coding procedure we set out in Chapter 7, the 'balance' of this advertisement can be described as follows. There is a strong presence of both Social and Sensual values, fused together in the text and imagery so that the pleasure of the drink is interwoven with the reparation which, it is claimed, the consumer can make. There is also an element of the Practical, in the cheerful, brisk instructional style. We do not have a thoroughly tested version of our coding form for beverages, but it seems likely that this advertisement would have a high tension/identity work score, and be likely therefore to be quite effective.

5. This imbalance is reflected in our coding. This advertisement had one Practical value (durability, in the reference to the galvanised body), and one Container Social value (excellence: technical), giving a Container score of 2. It has three Contained Social values (excellence: finish, excellence: perfection, and appearance). The identity work score is –2. Arguably, then, on our coding analysis, it is not quite strong enough on containment; the potential flood of erotic and guilty associations to it may not be sufficiently matched by containing values.

Chapter 7

PSYCHO-SOCIAL CATEGORIES FOR THE STUDY OF EVERYDAY LIFE

This chapter describes the design of our own research. We have argued that much of the literature on advertising in social science and social criticism is based upon preconceptions about it, usually negative ones. Thinking has been dominated, and restricted, by the powerful intellectual traditions described in Chapter 4. Insufficient attention has been given to the actual content of advertisements, and so the creative development of theory that can come only from open-minded observation of the world has been hampered.

The work of Leiss *et al.* encouraged us to think that meticulous attention to the content of numerous advertisements might bring forth evidence of how culture was changing. No similar work had been conducted in the British context. The study conducted by Haineault and Roy had shown how psychoanalytic thinking could be used with a large sample of advertisements, but had not used systematic content analysis, and had been conducted in a Canadian context. We aimed to combine systematic quantitative content analysis of a large sample with a psychoanalytic approach to content *meanings*, and to do so within a framework for mapping cultural change.

We began with the following plan. The intention was that one of the product sectors chosen for study would concern a major item of consumer spending. Some preliminary research had been done on car advertising in the 1950s and 1960s, and that was seen as an appropriate line of enquiry to pursue, since the car is the first or second largest purchase for many British consumers and has long had a pre-eminent status in iconographies of the consumer society. The other product should probably, it was thought, be an item of more everyday repeat purchase mass consumption, since this would enable us to sample a different level of the social perceptions and identities which are the stuff of advertising copy. We chose milk as providing the sharpest contrast with the car. These two products could be contrasted to represent the broad cultural axes of technology/nature and male/female, as well as in the UK representing the contrast of intense, international branded competition in the case of the car with the quasi-state monopoly of milk retailing. However, it proved impossible to source sufficient numbers of milk advertisements to put together a sample of adequate size; it is likely that there simply were not enough different milk advertisements created. So, as described below, we diversified the study into the financial services sector.

Personal banking is now so widely distributed (88% of adults in the UK have a bank account—MAPS, 1997) that we can claim here to be studying messages aimed at a very broad spectrum of the British people. While car ownership is a mass phenomenon, the market for new cars (and therefore the key audience for car advertisements) is—though well over 1 million p.a.—not a majority one. However, the second-hand car market is influenced by new car advertising, and there is a substantial subculture of interest in cars, the gender bias of which is weakening. Overall then the communications we have studied can be said to be drawn from mainstream mass advertising, particularly since we have used the national press ('quality' and 'tabloid') as the main source of advertisements.

What follows is a description of how we developed methods for studying advertisements in each product sector. While this usually meant constructing a tool for the coding and analysis of the content of large numbers of advertisements, we also adopted at times a case-study approach, as a supplement to extensive coding. We begin with an account of our coding work.

CAR ADVERTISEMENTS STUDY

Description of coding form
This was the sector in which we began the study. The first task was to set our theoretical preconceptions to one side and to immerse ourselves in the content of advertisements, and to develop a method of coding that content which was

a) as uninfluenced as possible by our theoretical concerns, in that it did not privilege or marginalise certain kinds of content in an *a priori* way,

yet at the same time was

b) able to capture those elements and dimensions of message content which would be of interest within the framework of ideas about psychic meanings and cultural change which we were using.

This is an old and basic dilemma for researchers, and it is impossible to offer a general prescription for how it should be handled. The reader may wish to judge how well we have handled it in this case, by considering the coding form we developed which is given complete at Appendix 1. Our approach has been to code in as fine-grained and literal a way as possible, thus generating an abundance of data at the level of 'molecular' detail, which we are then able to process in a highly theorised way by numerous groupings of variables and by examining a number of 'molar' patterns.

The form begins with basic information about the source of the advertisement and the type of car being advertised. The main slogan is then recorded, and, if there is one, the signature—the phrase, usually found in the bottom right corner of a print advertisement, or in the final frame or voice-over of a TV advertisement, with which the advertisement signs itself off—often a corporate rather than product statement. If the advertisement includes a pun or other humorous element, this is then noted.

The next two pages of the form are the core of our attempt to describe the value content of the message: they list 48 values which provide a comprehensive categorisation of the values expressed or invoked in car advertising. The list was generated by scrutiny of a convenience sample of advertisements to hand, mainly from the 1990s and 1950s. The researchers drafted and revised lists until it was found that the categories established were comprehensive, in that no further advertisements contained elements that could not be coded, and mutually exclusive, so that for any possible value element there was only one correct coding. Detailed guidelines were prepared for coders on the use of categories.

Staying close to the empirical content of the advertisements, and seeking to order the categories in only a very basic, common-sense way, we arranged them into three groupings (see Appendix 1). The first grouping ('Rational') refers to practical considerations such as price, warranty, and all other kinds of product information, i.e. what material properties does the car have, or is claimed to have, which enhance its utility, or bring financial advantage to the owner? The second grouping ('Performance') refers to those features of the car (usually related to its speed or handling) which support pleasurable experience in the act of driving. These are mainly material/technical features, but this grouping shades into a more rhetorical domain, e.g. where it is simply asserted that the car is 'fast', without any reference to measured power or acceleration times, or where its 'responsive' feel is celebrated without any reference to the technicalities of suspension, chassis construction, etc. Where a rhetorical reference to speed is present alongside factual data on, say, engine design, both 'Rational' and 'Performance' values are recorded.

The third grouping is of 'Explicit values'. Even though we were moving here into a territory of less tangible features, coding of these values depended on the presence in the advertisement text of some explicit expression of the values concerned, i.e. we sought to keep inference and interpretation to an absolute minimum, though some element of judgement by the coders was inevitably involved in a small number of instances. This section consists of a wide-ranging set of social or cultural values. Car advertising deploys a rich language of diverse values, which was the reason for our initial interest in it; at times in preparing this list it seemed to us as if we were drawing up a comprehensive list of contemporary cultural values. While it does not include, for example, the range of what might be called political values (such as the principles of democracy, respect for law, beliefs about state intervention, etc.), and is limited in the vocabulary it gives for describing personal and familial relationships (there is nothing about respect for the other, and not much about loyalty or nurture, for example), it does encompass many of the values around which everyday social experience is organised, and in terms of which key tensions in life are often posed— for example between individuality and belonging, freedom and responsibility, control and release, and continuity and innovation.

A crucial distinction between this grouping and the first, 'Rational' set is that the values in this group are not tied to specific functional or material characteristics of the product; they are more abstract or rhetorical in quality. This distinction provided the basis for a number of coding choices. For example, if the theme of safety were used in an advertisement, for the 'Rational' variable of 'Safety' to be coded as present there had to be some reference to an actual feature of the car linked to improved safety (e.g. crumple zone, side impact bar, airbag), however slight or spurious the contribution to safety of that feature might be argued to be. If however the reference to safety were just to the *idea* or to the *feeling* of safety, then it would be coded as the 'Explicit value' of 'Protection'. The distinction we sought to sustain here could be expressed as that between the denotative and connotative, or between the material and the rhetorical.

As the study developed we came to think about the categories in a more theorised way, and accordingly to group them somewhat differently. We describe in this chapter how we applied two other groupings to the variables, one a tripartite scheme based on the Freudian categories of ego, id and superego, and the other a dichotomous scheme in which groupings of ego and some superego variables are merged to form one category, the 'container', which is then contrasted with the remaining superego and id variables understood as the 'contained'. The meanings of and rationale for these psycho-analytically-based groupings of the descriptive variables are also given below.

Next, we required the coder to make a judgement about which of all the variables listed under these three headings was dominant in the advertisement as a whole. This usually meant which one, if any, informed the slogan or was expressed in the main image, though at times a judgement of dominance was based on more subtle features of the advertisement's overall composition. Where a single entry could not be made because the dominant message concerned a tension between two forces, this was also recorded. (In fact there were relatively few entries here and this section does not feature in our results.)

The remainder of the coding protocol is taken up with recording further descriptive features, predominantly drawn from the visual content of the advertisement rather than the verbal text which (especially for print advertisements) is the main source of the values. We hypothesised that there might be psychological or cultural significance in how the car was portrayed (whether on display, or in use—and if the latter, in what sort of use), in what categories of people, if any, were shown, in the kind of location chosen, and in the kinds of activities pictured or implied by the setting.

Also we took note of some other features which our preconceptions led us to think might be of relevance. The first is the 'voice' with which the advertisement speaks, the kind of person or agency who is giving the voice-over or who the reader might take to be the source of the text. Understanding advertisements as a kind of public conversation, or alternatively as a source of authority, points to the importance of identifying the voices with which they are heard to speak.

Secondly we noted if the advertisement had a 'metonymic object', that is if there was something with which the product was equated. It would be of anthropological interest, we thought, simply to have a catalogue of those objects (animals, computers, people, etc.) with which cars were compared, and with which the reader was invited (at least implicitly) to identify the car.

Finally, we noted any registration numbers of cars shown. Combinations of numbers and letters create abundant possibilities for deliberate symbolisation, as well as for yielding meanings in unintended ways. Given also the large UK market in personalised number-plates, and also the possibility that advertising people may indulge in esoteric jokes, we thought that this simple piece of data collection may produce some entertaining and perhaps useful material.

After using this form on many hundreds of print advertisements (see below for sample details), we then turned our attention to television and cinema advertising. We found that the form was directly transferable to the task of coding the content of 'dynamic' advertisements, if we treated them as a series of single images. Each advertisement normally needs to be viewed four or five times so that the separate content of each scene or frame can be recorded. Consequently the number of variables recorded as present is often (though not necessarily) higher than for print advertisements. While there is some risk that the narrative unity and overall impact of a dynamic advertisement may be lost by this checklist approach, the same could be said of static, print advertisements.

Our response to this charge in relation to both types of advertisement would be twofold. Firstly, the meaning of all communications is to some extent carried by the detail of their content and execution. While the whole is greater than the sum of the parts, the greatness of the whole is derived from the particular choice of parts and their relation to each other, which by the simple aggregation or cross-tabulation of frequencies one is able to study. Secondly, a number of our variables refer to qualities which—though possibly located in just one element of the advertisement—may often be the theme around which the overall experience of the advertisement coheres. This would certainly be the finding of the focus group work we have done.

The coding form was designed to capture the full content of advertisements in an unselective way, with a minimum of conceptual elaboration. Having amassed a large quantity of such data, the task of interpreting it required us to think about the psychological and cultural meanings of the variables, and to devise ways of grouping them that would enable us to use the data to reflect on the issues which concerned us.

Values

Quite early on we became dissatisfied with the preliminary groupings of the main values on pages 3–4 of the form. We therefore sought to re-order them in a way that would be more consistent. Proceeding partly in a common-sense fashion, but beginning to make links with psycho-analytic theory, we divided the values into three different categories, which we termed Practical, Social and Sensual. Figure 7.1 below shows these categories.

PRACTICAL	SOCIAL	SENSUAL
	A:	
Price	Environment	*Quiet*
Finance	Family	*Comfort*
Warranty	Freedom (carefree)	*Solidity*
Insurance	Excellence (general)	*Speed/acceleration*
Inducements	Excellence (technical)	*Power*
Economy	Excellence (finish)	*Driving pleasure*
Safety	Tradition	*Excitement*
Security	Insulation/protection	*Appearance*
Space	Prudence	*Soothing*
Accessories	Belonging	*Self-indulgence*
Practicalities	Age	*Newness (pristine)*
Durability		
Manoeuvrability	**B:**	
Choice	*Freedom (liberty)*	
Reliability	*Transgression*	
Maintenance	*Newness (innovation)*	
Other technical	*Excellence (perfection)*	
	Individuality	
	Achievement/reward	
	Control	
	Distinction/exclusive	
	Youth	

Figure 7.1   Car advertisements: revised tripartite classification of variables and the container/contained distinction

The Practical category is made up of only those features which are of material or practical utility. The Sensual category comprises those features which provide or suggest a physical sensation or which promise a pure aesthetic experience. The Social is the largest grouping, including all those meaningful elements of advertisement content not included in the other two. Though we refer to all three categories as 'values', the Social category contains those elements which would normally be thought of as expressing social or cultural values, such as concern for the environment or a positive image of family life. Alongside these however are other elements which might not be seen as values but more as neutral or literal features, such as the claimed technical excellence of the car, or its possession of an innovative feature. We will argue that a psycho-cultural 'value' can be ascribed to these features.

There is a clear and intentional echo in these three categories of the classical Freudian schema of ego (Practical), id (Sensual) and superego (Social). Our Practical values, like the ego, are concerned with external reality, with instrumentality and pragmatic calculation. (They do not, however, include aspects of the individual's relations with other people, which is a key element of ego-functioning, especially in post-Freudian conceptualisations of the ego.) Our Sensual values include references which might be taken as expressions of the libidinal life of the individual when seen in classical Freudian terms, with the notable omission of sex as such. (This is rarely if ever mentioned explicitly in car advertising, so when alluded to is probably most frequently coded as 'excitement', with variables such as 'transgression', 'appearance', 'power' and 'youth' also available to register sexualised meanings.) The Sensual category also includes other features of advertisement texts or images which suggest either the gratification of regression into infantile dependence or experiences which, introducing psychoanalytic terminology, we would describe as narcissistic—psychically primitive (i.e. intense and developmentally early) experiences of the self as ideal.

Finally our Social values incorporate a range of elements which could be understood as aspects of the Freudian superego, while also including things which might be seen as beyond or contrary to the functions of that psychic apparatus as it has often been understood, namely the functions of restraint, prohibition and judgement. In fact, the superego in psychoanalytic theory is also concerned with loving guidance and protection, i.e. with images of positive authority, and insofar as these can be found in car advertising we include them here. But we also include here in the Social category a set of opposite values, e.g. those celebrating freedom and transgression, or those stressing the rewards due to, rather than the limitations on or responsibilities of, the individual.

In other words, any advertisement element that carries any kind of social value, in the sense of an explicit or implicit guide to conduct or to what ought to be valued in life, is included in this broad category. This led us to differentiate within this category between two types of value, in order to reintroduce a notion of the kind of psychic function which Freud so sharply captured in his concept of the superego. We do this, however, via another psychoanalytic concept, a very post-Freudian one—the concept of containment, as described in the previous chapter.

We noted that it is necessary to distinguish between two kinds of response to anxiety, defence and containment. Any message content which invokes the capacity to contain, or 're-minds' the reader of the power of external realities either to reward or constrain, is therefore included in our 'container' subgroup of Social values, those in ordinary type in the first rows of the middle column in Figure 7.1. As can be seen we have included here all features which refer to the existence of human collectivities and their achievements, not all of which explicitly carry meanings of authority or membership, on the grounds that the very existence of community and its infrastructure is, at least potentially, a containing force. Some of these variables, particularly 'family', may actually be seen in some contexts as a 'defensive' value, in the sense of socially or culturally conservative. We include it here as an instance (actually a very fundamental one) of social membership which though constraining is also potentially—if not always—profoundly supportive of individuals in their struggles to manage their anxieties.

It will be seen from the table that we group these Social values together with all the Practical ones in order to derive an overall 'Container' (CR) score. The Practical values are in a sense, at one level, psychically neutral, but within the broad definition of containment that we are using, an orientation to the material and practical features of the product is potentially containing.

Again, the critiques of advertising have often focused on the issue of the relationship of the advertisement to the material product. The crime of advertisements, it has been said, has been to deal in images and not in the actualities of the product. While we reject this stance on the grounds that it overlooked the intrinsically symbolic nature of all our dealings with goods, we do nonetheless see the presence of product information in an advertisement (whether or not there is also powerful symbolic content) as a sign that the advertisement is offering some invitation to engage with reality. Reality is the most powerful of containers; while denying us all sorts of libidinal satisfactions, it also limits the extent to which our most powerful and primitive anxieties can hold sway in the mind, since these anxieties stem from unconscious phantasies (e.g. that one has been rejected, or attacked, or has rejected or attacked someone else) which are based on scenarios usually far worse than the reality.

It may be objected that an intense attention to the mere practicalities of an object may be a defence against its dangerous symbolic meanings, and we would have to allow that this could indeed be so in the cases of some individual readers of an advertisement. Our aim, though, is to develop an overall way of conceptualising the psychic significance of advertisement content, and we propose that within the dynamics of the message and its reception as a whole, the presence of a Practical value adds to the potential for containment in the psychic work which the reader is likely to be engaged in.

Through similar reasoning, we combine the 'defensive' sub-group of Social values, which embody omnipotent or other narcissistic elements, with the full set of Sensual values to derive an overall 'Contained' score. All those features of an advertisement which reflect libidinal, regressive or idealising tendencies are here, whether in primary, 'id' mode (Sensual values) or in the service of defence (Social values).

We must admit that this last distinction, though embedded in our coding scheme, is one which perhaps can be reliably made only in detailed assessments of individual readers' responses to advertisements. For some variables the Social *vs* Sensual distinction is a moot point. It is a matter of nuance that, for example, the narcissistic value of 'Appearance' is coded as Sensual, while the narcissistic value of 'Excellence (perfection)' is coded as Social. However we think there are grounds for retaining the overall distinction, rooted in the idea that the Sensual category is about direct experience, analogous to the material/practical criterion for Practical values, while the Social category consists of symbolic, rhetorical features.

Figure 7.1 illustrates how individual variables were reclassified. Features in standard typeface contribute to CONTAINER score (CR); those in italics comprise the CONTAINED (CD).

Within the SOCIAL category, list A is of containing (CR) features, which express elements of limiting relatedness (in nurture, sustenance, support, protection, care, or experience), while list B is of contained (CD) features, which express elements of individualised gratification (in lack of restraint, in superiority, power, or beauty).

Figures 7.2 and 7.3 (pages 128 and 129) are examples of advertisements strongly coloured by Social A and Social B values respectively. In the Volkswagen advertisement (strong Social values), although there is a clear sexual element, protection is the dominant theme, and the possibility of a sexual relationship is mentioned with circumspection. In the Peugeot advertisement, however, the aggressively sexual gun-slinging stance of the part-object female is matched by a strongly transgressive text and by the 'freedom (liberty)' element present in the slogan.

Manifest anxieties

Alongside the grouping of variables into the three major value categories, there is a second major grouping we have developed. This brings in the important piece of psychoanalytic theory described in Chapter 6, the concept of unconscious anxiety. As an intermediate step, however, we found it fruitful to apply to car advertisements the more common-sense identification of 'Coping' and 'Status' anxieties that had been developed in the design of the credit card research (see below). These refer to a more conscious experience and a more everyday understanding of anxiety.

'Status' anxieties are those relating to social status and, more broadly, social identity; typically, they are focused on the question of whether one belongs or qualifies to belong to an elite or privileged group of some sort. 'Coping' anxieties relate to the possibility that life will be disrupted in some way, that there will be a problem that one does not know how to deal with or does not have the means to solve.

The majority of all the value variables could be assigned, *a priori*, to these two broad anxiety categories, according to the kind of anxiety which we judge that a variable is related to. Indeed it was possible to go further in this than we had done in the credit card study. There, owing to the limited sensual possibilities of the object itself (Chapter 10), it was not possible to determine whether a Sensual value was deployed in relation to a 'Coping' or 'Status' anxiety. With cars, however, the commodity offers a rich range of very specific libidinal and aesthetic experiences, a highly differentiated vocabulary of sensuality which can be mapped on to a typology of anxiety.

The allocation of variables to 'Coping' and 'Status' is shown in Figure 7.4. Two Sensual values were too general or mobile to be tied down, and are therefore regarded (like all Sensual values in the credit card study) as anxiety-Variable. A few Practical and Social values were placed in the anxiety-Neutral category, as they could be seen to relate to 'conflict-free' objectives on the consumer's part (e.g. to save money), though this is a debatable category and it may be preferable to classify all these non-anxiety-specific items as anxiety-Variable, like 'excitement' and 'self-indulgence'.

However, this is to work at a relatively superficial level, dealing in a fairly common-sense description of recognisable worries which are (at least potentially) present in conscious experience, and can therefore be described as 'manifest'. We sought to relate our data to a deeper level of psychic functioning, to hidden or 'latent' anxieties as theorised by psychoanalysis and as we discussed in Chapter 6. It can be seen in the first column of Figure 7.4 how we worked back from the manifest anxieties to identify a more complex categorisation of latent anxieties.

In doing so we have constructed categories in a somewhat eclectic way that would not find favour with those committed to the rigorous application of particular paradigms within psychoanalysis. Our aim was not to develop a logically watertight set of compartments but to create a register of qualities. Although we have quantitatively summed and compared the putative presence of these anxieties, we do not offer the results as a positivistic claim that these anxieties, as discrete and essential phenomena, have this measurable existence. Rather, we use the numbers (as indeed we also do for the manifest anxieties and the tripartite value system) to help us generate a detailed picture of the qualities of emotional and social experience which are at play, and of the patterns of interaction between, and change in the strengths of, these qualities.

Quantification conducted in this spirit enables us to use words like 'increasing', 'decreasing', 'strong', 'weak', and so on, with more precision and consistency than might otherwise be the case. It does not transport us to another level of observation or insight, radically different from or superior to that derived from purely qualitative data. Crucially, though—and this is our main reason for a quantitative approach throughout this research—it does enable us to work with observations of many hundreds of advertisements in a highly succinct and manageable way. The use of a simple checklist/frequency count of the kind we have adopted, though it obviously loses a great deal of information concerning the specific narrative and emotional impact of an individual advertisement, does produce quantitative data which permits the summary treatment of many hundreds of advertisements, covering visual as well as verbal content.

In moving from simple frequency counts to composite variables, we are seeking to restore some wholeness to the data, to reassemble the parts albeit in different configurations from those in which they appear in individual advertisements. Through our aggregated frequencies we hope to show how, over time and across the reading population, individual advertisements contribute to the building up of a complex public discourse which is basically about values and the management of anxieties.

Latent anxieties

To introduce briefly the categories of latent anxiety listed below, we will continue here from the remarks made in Chapter 6. Our scheme is based loosely on the Kleinian model of development. We will describe those elements of this model that are directly relevant to us, and not explain the full psychodynamics and the developmental processes involved. A number of sources can be consulted for fuller accounts (e.g. Symington, 1986; Segal, 1991; Hinshelwood, 1991).

According to basic Kleinian theory, there are two fundamental psychic 'positions', the 'paranoid/schizoid' and the 'depressive'. In the former, the subject has projected destructive feeling into the external world, and now fears retaliatory attack from a world felt to be full of dangerous forces. Values which promise protection from problems or from attack by sensory intrusions are responses to such paranoid anxieties.

Depressive anxiety stems from a more mature, integrated psychic state, in which destructiveness is owned by the individual who then fears the damage s/he may have caused to others, or to the external world generally. Values which can help to contain or defend against this anxiety would be those which convey the individual's commitment to taking care of others, broadly speaking, or which attest to the robustness and survival of the external world.

In Kleinian theory, the classical Oedipal stage of the Freudian developmental scheme is to some extent subsumed within the theory of the depressive position. The achievement of the depressive position in early emotional development involves acquiring the capacity to tolerate depressive anxiety, and to exist without the continual splitting off and projection of bad feelings. This achievement is then the basis for the child's acknowledgement and toleration of its exclusion from the parental couple, that is for the resolution of the Oedipus complex. However the concept of the Oedipus complex has rich and specific connotations of rivalry with parental figures, of the inevitable conflict of the generations, of the deep anxieties attendant upon these rivalries and conflicts, and of the psychic work of reconciliation underlying the handing-on of tradition. It thus offers a distinctive spectrum of feeling which is closely linked to our sociological analysis of the 'postmodern' (see Chapter 5). It is therefore valuable to retain as a separate category, one which affords a coherent grouping of (mainly Social) values.

Our typology of unconscious anxieties is given a stronger hybridity, however, by our inclusion of two other categories which overlap heavily with the paranoid group, in that they refer to anxieties of the earliest and most primitive sorts. The concept of separation anxiety is drawn from the body of work known as attachment theory, a blend of object-relations theory with developmental psychology and ethological theory. It refers, as one might expect, to the anxieties felt when the person or object on whom the subject depends has gone away, or is felt to be missing, or lost. Though this anxiety is more easily recognisable outside of psychoanalysis than the others, some detailed rationale for the values linked with it may be necessary.

The two Practical values ('Space' and 'Manoeuvrability') which we have, somewhat cautiously, placed in this category are there because the possession of space and of the ability to turn oneself around adroitly can both be seen as positive, containing ways of dealing with separation anxiety. They flag the subject's ability, in the context of the geography of the social world and the infant's mobility in it with which attachment theory is particularly concerned, to be independent, to be able to venture away from base and to claim its own space (see Richards, 1994, for a discussion of the significance of the car in relation to the infant's development of mobility). Lack of space, which spacious cars promise relief from, also evokes a claustrophobic anxiety, a fear that the needed object to which one is attached, and from which it is hard to separate, will be a smothering, controlling force.

The two Social values lodged here represent opposite sides of the emotional coin of attachment—the positive value of belonging, of having a secure base, and the positive value of being free of attachments and ties. We interpret the latter—our variable 'Freedom (liberty)'—as a defence against the fear of losing the secure base. Our rationale for this is in the *timbre* of absoluteness given to assertions of independence in advertisements, which almost always have an omnipotent, narcissistic quality: they promise illusory freedom from all ties, a transcendent liberty (in contrast to our other 'Freedom' variable, which we have grouped under 'depressive' anxiety, and which offers relief, usually temporary or conditional, from everyday chores and burdens, and so in Kleinian depressive mode acknowledges the limitations of reality).

This points to the final categories of anxiety, which are both 'narcissistic'. In Kleinian theory narcissistic states of mind are seen as an aspect, indeed a central one, of the paranoid position (in which the subject cannot really experience the other as a separate, whole object). Again, as with Oedipal anxieties, we deploy narcissism as a distinct category because of the distinctive qualities of mind which it connotes: the belief in the possibility of perfection, the idealisation, the omnipotence attributed to the self or to some force experienced as an extension of the self. The basic anxiety, which the narcissistic state of mind defends against, is about the individual's vulnerability and dependence on others. In imagining omnipotence or self-sufficiency, the narcissist seeks to avoid the reality of human interdependency, and the risks which that implies for everyone.

Also, as we discussed in Chapter 5, the concept of narcissism has figured importantly in debates about cultural change and the nature of the postmodern. However, we found that this descriptively powerful term cut across our distinction at the level of manifest anxiety between coping and status anxieties, and so we have two groups of values linked to narcissistic anxiety. In the first group, the narcissism is mediated through coping anxiety, and so the defensive responses are about retaining control and remaining untarnished. We also surmise that more adaptive, containing responses may be found in, e.g. the assertion of technical excellence, where the narcissistic impulse is lodged in the reality of human achievement. In the second group, the mediation is via status anxiety, and the defensive responses are about setting the individual apart from others.

The advertising of all consumer goods makes intensive use of values which can be seen to respond to these anxieties, whether by containment or defence. What we tabulate below is an attempt to specify, in one symbolically rich field of advertising, just how the language of advertisements can make links between product characteristics and

LATENT ANXIETY	MANIFEST ANXIETY	PRACTICAL	SOCIAL	SENSUAL
Paranoid	Coping	Warranty	Insulation/ protection	Quiet
		Safety		Comfort
		Security		Soothing
		Reliability		
Separation		Space	Belonging	
		Manoeuvrability	Freedom (liberty)	
Narcissistic		Maintenance	Excellence (technical)	Newness (pristine)
			Excellence (finish)	
			Control	
Depressive		Economy	Environment	Solidity
		Durability	Family	Driving pleasure
			Freedom (carefree)	
			Prudence	
Narcissistic	Status	Accessories	Excellence (perfection)	Power
		Choice	Individuality	Appearance
			Distinction/ exclusive	
Oedipal			Tradition	Speed
			Age	
			Transgression	
			Newness (innovation)	
			Achievement/ reward	
			Youth	
	Variable	Price	Excellence (general)	Excitement
		Finance		Self-indulgence
		Insurance		
		Inducements		
		Practicalities		
		Other techical		

Figure 7.4   Car advertisements: classification of variables into latent and manifest anxiety

unconscious anxieties, and so develop what marketers know as 'brand values', i.e. those sets of values characteristically used by individual brands to deploy against anxiety and so to make these links.

Whether or not our method of coding can establish that there are quantitative patterns in advertisement content which can be defined or even explained with reference to these categories of 'latent anxiety', it is a necessary part of a psychoanalytically-informed enquiry into culture to consider the possible connections between everyday life and basic unconscious phantasies, as psychoanalysts have described them. We will therefore return at various points to the anxieties listed here.

Sampling car advertisements
Firstly, we aimed to analyse at least 100 advertisements from each of 10 sampling points, at 5 year intervals from 1950 to 1995. Secondly, we wanted to take advertisements from different print media which would have different readerships. The media also needed to have been published throughout the period. We selected the following publications:

Daily Mirror
Daily Express
The Observer
The Times
Autocar Magazine
Motor Magazine

The British Newspaper Library was the main source of back issues of all publications, though some advertisements were obtained from the archives of the History of Advertising Trust and the Advertising Archive. At some sampling points it was not possible to collect 100 advertisements, so examples were sought from adjacent years.

The UK print sample is distributed across the time period as follows:

DECADE	RAW NUMBER OF PRINT ADS	PERCENTAGE
1950	223	18
1960	242	19
1970	287	23
1980	245	20
1990	252	20
Total	1249	100

Figure 7.5   Car advertisements: sample size by decade

We also coded a smaller number (57) of television advertisements, some archival but the majority from teaching materials of 1990s advertisements.

The U.S. sample of 329 advertisements was collected at the John W. Hartman Center Archives Special Collections, at Duke University in North Carolina.

STUDY OF ADVERTISEMENTS FOR BANKING SERVICES

The arrival of an additional researcher (JB) meant that we were able to extend the study into a quite different product sector from the two originally intended, namely personal banking services. This more than compensated for the lack of a large coded sample of milk advertisements. As a consumer choice involving frequent small and usually routine exchanges (writing cheques, going to a branch to draw or deposit), yet in relation to a vital 'substance' (money), the use of a bank has some parallels with the consumption of milk. Obviously there are differences: banking is a branded service, one consisting of a high degree of human interaction. It spans the lifeworld of the consumer from low-involvement transactions such as paying grocery bills to issues of major emotional importance, such as who can be trusted to look after one's life savings. It is traditionally a world of men and bureaucracy, not of women and nature. However it gave us an opportunity to assess whether the kinds of changes we observed in the field of cars were replicated in this traditionally very different area of consumer culture.

The protocol used to translate the advertisements into a systematic data set followed the path set by the car study, recording the same broad features, such as sampling details, slogans, signatures, the number and types of characters, what they were doing, and the setting they were in. Like the car study, an exhaustive list of the values and rhetorical strategies particular to banking promotion were developed from scrutinising a convenience sample of 100 bank advertisements drawn across the period from 1950 to 1990. It can be seen that there is a considerable degree of overlap (perhaps surprisingly so) with the categories used for car advertisements, though some important categories (such as advice, access and trust) are unique to the banking discourse. A copy of the coding form used in the study is at Appendix 2.

We attempted to move between a top down and bottom up approach to interpreting the advertisements. We introduced some broad conceptualisations to our interpretation of the advertisements, but we also allowed these conceptualisations to be reworked based upon what the advertisements revealed. It should be noted that on the coding form many of the values are provided with two columns, one labelled Practical, the other Social. This split echoed the distinction we had made in the car advertisements study between the denotative and connotative, or between the material and the rhetorical.

The separation between the three kinds of values was thus less clear than in the car advertisements study, requiring a close consideration of how what was superficially the same element could carry a Practical or a Social value. For example, 'Expansion', typically associated with renovation of either bank or home, was presented in two different ways. One 'Expansion' valued space, efficiency, comfort, and mobility for consumers. We saw this 'Expansion' as primarily practically based, appealing to the utility of space (though the amount of space required by individuals is always a historical socio-cultural construction). The other type of 'Expansion' valued the opulence and splendour of 'expansions', which we felt aligned more with a Social (and status-related) value. Similarly, the administration of finances was valued in two different ways. There were appeals which strongly connected budgeting to an obligation to others, and saw it as a mark of social character. In other appeals, financial management was presented as simply an instrumental concern of the individual. While these subtle distinctions are fairly easily made in advertisements which explicitly dramatise them, in other instances it was difficult to decipher these conceptual splits. If there was a sense that both values were being invoked, both were coded.

Other subtle conceptual splits were involved in the coding of Sensual values. Here we asked whether the value was attached to a specific and tangible banking feature, or whether the value was free-floating and could be connected to any number of broader psycho-social qualities. For example 'Time' was presented in some advertisements as a Practical value which reminded readers of the importance of saving and co-ordinating time in their banking practices. In others, the representation of 'Time' was more to do with the annihilation of time as a constraint. This was typical in advertisements which promoted cash machines, for example, for the instantaneous access to money which they offered. The presentation of 'Time' here refuses to acknowledge linear temporality and seeks to fuse action and its fulfilment. Similarly readers were sometimes offered 'Freedom' from some everyday, specific banking constraints, in a world of less complex banking practices. At other times, 'Freedom' was not attached to any specific feature, but rather implied a general sense of freedom from all worry. Likewise 'Safety' was presented both as a practical concern, for example in the prevention of theft, and as a rhetorical sense of overall protection from all risks.

Once the full range of elements identified in advertisements had been securely defined, and the differentiations described above had been clarified, it was then possible to take the full set of values and to group them, across the Practical, Social and Sensual categories, into the psychologically-grounded composite variables that we have described above in the car advertisements study. Figure 7.6 below shows how the distinction between 'Container' and 'Contained' was mapped onto the variables in bank advertisements, while in Figure 7.7 anxieties at the two levels of 'Manifest' and 'Latent' are plotted against variable sub-groupings.

Sampling advertisements: banking services

A total of 801 post-war British advertisements gathered across the decades 1950 to 1990 inform the banking case study. As the historical value of advertisements is just beginning to be recognised, archiving of advertisements is improving. However, documentary records are very

PRACTICAL	SOCIAL	SENSUAL
	A:	
Services	Advice	*Freedom (carefree)*
Access	Tradition	*Customised*
Time (rational)	Trust	*Pleasure*
Choice	Family	*Excitement*
Calculation	Community	*Power*
Inducements	Belonging	*Ease*
Growth (interest, accumulation)	Ethical	*Instantaneous (time)*
Expansion (space)	Protection	*Gratification in consumption*
Mobility	Prudence	*Security*
Guarantee	**B:**	
Full service	*Freedom (liberty)*	
	Innovation	
	Competition	
	Breaking tradition	
	Up to date	
	Self-reward	
	Achievement	
	Ambition	
	Expansion (luxury)	
	Distinction	
	Luxury	

Figure 7.6   Bank advertisements: classification of variables into container/contained

LATENT ANXIETY	MANIFEST ANXIETY	PRACTICAL	SOCIAL	SENSUAL
Paranoid	**Coping**		Protection	*Security*
Separation		Expansion (space)	Trust	
		Access	Belonging	
		Time (rational)	*Freedom (liberty)*	
		Mobility		
Narcissistic				*Instantaneous*
				Customised
				Ease
Depressive		Calculation	Community	
			Ethical	
			Family	
			Freedom (carefree)	
			Prudence	
			Advice	
Narcissistic	**Status**	Full service		*Power*
		Choice	*Luxury*	
			Distinction	
			Expansion (luxury)	
			Up-to-date	
Oedipal			Tradition	
			Break tradition	
			Innovation	
			Ambition	
			Achievement	
			Competition	
	Variable	Growth		*Excitement*
		Inducements		*Pleasure*
		Services		*Gratification in Consumption*

Figure 7.7   Bank advertisements: classification of variables into latent and manifest anxiety

fragmentary and systematic sampling remains difficult. We did our best to ensure a robust sample which reflected the widest variety of appeals, by sampling across the individual years, and having no fewer than 100 advertisements per decade.

The History of Advertising Trust (HAT) proved an invaluable source and the majority of print and all of the television banking advertisements were gathered at this archive. To supplement the HAT samples and top up decades with low numbers, additional print advertisements were drawn from a systematic selection of newspapers found at the British Newspaper Library. The television advertisements were coded from Telex and Television Register, two advertising industry affiliates which catalogue the promotional messages which appear on British television. While archives are excellent for finding historical documents,

DECADE	PRINT	TELEVISION	TOTAL	PERCENTAGE
1950	100	0	100	12.5
1960	137	0	137	17.1
1970	125	0	125	15.6
1980	189	56	245	30.6
1990	165	29	194	24.2
Total	716	85	801	100
Percentage	89.4	10.6	100	

Figure 7.8   Bank advertisements: sample size by decade and media type

contemporary examples were derived from other methods. Many of the late 1990 advertisements were clipped from the newspapers or coded from posters around the city. The breakdown of the number of advertisements per decade is provided in Figure 7.8.

CREDIT CARDS ADVERTISEMENTS STUDY

Towards the end of our study of car advertising, an opportunity arose to apply our general approach to a very different sector, namely credit cards.[1] One would not normally think of advertisements for credit cards as being very exciting or symbolically rich, although a well-known image was produced in the 'flexible friend' of early Access advertising. However, we gladly took this opportunity for two reasons.

One was that if we could find our overall conceptual approach validated in this very different, and probably psycho-culturally less rich, field of advertising, it would be evidence that the approach was of wide relevance across the field of advertising, and perhaps beyond. The other was that it provided an opportunity for us to test our approach in a commercial as distinct from an academic setting, to observe how our concepts might be understood and taken up outside of academia, and to assess how the understanding of what advertising is, and what it does, is influenced by the setting.

By this time we had come to think of the 'values' categories described in the previous section on coding car advertisements in the more theorised way referred to there, and so we structured the form from the start in terms of Practical, Social and Sensual values (see Appendix 3). As in the other product sectors, the form was drawn up after scrutiny of a convenience sample (in this case numbering around 50) of advertisements from the 1970s to the present. The Practical grouping is very similar to that in the 'Rational' set of categories on the car coding form, referring to actual product features. The variables equivalent to those we had in the 'Performance' grouping for car advertisements (some material, some rhetorical) are here incorporated into the Sensual grouping. The major change, as in our subsequent re-grouping of the car variables, is that the large 'Cultural' grouping has been redistributed, so that some of the values are regarded as Sensual and some (the greater number) as Social. To put this in Freudian terms, we had refined the 'Cultural' conglomeration to separate those which could be theorised as 'Superego' values from those with 'Id' affinities. Thus we made more obvious in the structure of the form a distinction which we did not use until the analysis stage in the car advertisements coding.

A further development which we introduced in this study was to introduce an orthogonal method of grouping the variables, i.e. another set of distinctions which could be used to group the variables and so produce a two-dimensional matrix. This grouping depended on what anxiety a variable seemed to be addressing. Thus each single descriptive variable could be grouped according to whether it was Practical, Sensual or Social, and according to what kind of anxiety, if any, it was judged to be linked to. A preliminary survey of advertisements in this field suggested to us that at a common-sense level, two major kinds of anxieties were commonly evoked or addressed. One we called 'Status' anxieties, the other 'Coping' anxieties.

As described above, 'Status' anxieties are those relating to social identity, and are often focused on the question of whether one belongs or qualifies to belong to a particular reference group. 'Coping' anxieties relate to the possibility that there will be a problem that one does not know how to deal with or does not have the means to solve, that life will be disrupted and one's individual inadequacy revealed.

It might seem at first sight as if these categories replicate those of Social and Practical values respectively. However we observed that any kind of value could be deployed in relation to either kind of anxiety; the 'anxieties' refer to spontaneous, pre-existing states of mind in the reader of the advertisement, while the 'values' are features of the product or its use. An advertisement having evoked a certain kind of anxiety, it may then also offer certain values which can be used to deal with the anxiety. Thus 'Status' anxiety may be managed with reference to a Practical value, i.e. an actual feature of the product (e.g. this credit card gives access to exclusive airport lounges), or with reference to a Social value, i.e. a connoted meaning of the product (e.g. this credit card is for ambitious people).

Unlike the coding systems we developed for cars and banks, there was an insufficient number of variables here to support their intricate

PRACTICAL	SOCIAL	SENSUAL
	A:	
Interest rate	Non-elite testimonial	*Pleasure*
Inducement	Universality	*Excitement*
Competitor comparison	Protection	*Power*
Wideness of use	Elite testimonial	*Ease*
Insurances		*Instantaneous*
Controlling expenditure	**B:**	*Freedom*
Other problem solving	*Convenience*	*Security*
Simplicity	*Exclusivity*	*Gratification in consumption*
Comprehensiveness of function	*Ambition*	
No spend limit	*Achievement*	
Exclusive benefits		
Guarantees, welcome, respect		

Figure 7.9   Credit card advertisements: classification of variables into container/contained

grouping into 'Latent' anxieties. The smaller sample size would also have meant that such subdivisions were of questionable value. In Figure 7.9 we show how the container/contained distinction is mapped onto the elementary variables.

Sampling advertisements: credit cards
This form was used on a sample of approximately 250 advertisements from the 1970s on. These were all print advertisements, and were not time-sampled in the systematic way that the car advertisements were collected, and precise dating and location of the media source were not available for a number of the examples used.[2] However, we were able to divide the sample into pre-1990 and post-1990 sub-groups, and to conduct time-split analyses which enabled us to make some observations on trends and to compare the development over time of different brands. The pre-1990 sub-group was smaller (approximately 37% of the whole sample).

The advertisements were basically a convenience sample, taken mainly from national newspapers and magazines. We sampled from national dailies such as the *Daily Mail* and *Daily Express* and one regional paper, the *London Evening Standard*, from the Sunday supplements, in particular *The Observer* and *The Times*, and from magazines including *The Economist*, some women's magazines and, in more recent sections of the sample, some of the 'style' magazines aimed at young men. A significant section of our sample (about 25%) was given to us by the client who sponsored this part of the research, and we do not have information about exactly where these advertisements were

DECADE	PRINT	TELEVISION	RADIO	DIRECT MAIL	TOTAL	PERCENTAGE
Pre-1990	94	0	0	1	85	39
Post-1990	108	34	8	1	151	61
Total	202	34	8	2	236	100

Figure 7.10   Credit card advertisements: sample size pre- and post-1990 and by media type

published. We classified a few of the print advertisements as direct mail as they took the increasingly common form of free standing inserts in the Sunday supplements. We also analysed a small number of TV and radio advertisements.

FOCUS GROUPS AND INDIVIDUAL INTERVIEWS

A small number of these were carried out in relation to the car (12 interviews, with print and TV advertisements) and credit card (4 focus groups, with print and poster advertisements) analyses, to check the validity of our coding categories, or their applicability to the responses of ordinary readers of the advertisements. Material from the groups and interviews is described in Chapters 8 and 10. Our basic procedure was to treat the respondents' statements as we had treated the advertisement texts, and to code them for the presence of any of the value categories and anxiety themes we had identified. We were thus able to test, in a very limited way, for two things:

i)   whether our category sets showed a reasonable fit with respondents' comments, or whether there were values and anxieties which were not encompassed by our forms, or which straddled or cut across two or more of our categories; and

ii)   whether our coding of particular advertisements could then predict the content and range of spontaneous responses which would be made to those advertisements.

ADVERTISEMENT CASE STUDIES

We also offer, in Chapters 9 and 10, some case studies of individual advertisements, to add to those presented in Chapter 6. We hope to show that our approach can contribute in a new way to the interpretive work undertaken by some of the influential academic critics of advertising. Indeed, despite our criticisms of the shortcomings of that work, we believe it to be essential to the overall task of understanding advertising. It is also the part of the scholarly endeavour which is most likely to attract the attention of a wider audience because of its closeness to the fullness and complexity of our individual experiences of advertising messages. In particular we think that the psychoanalytic dimension of our analyses brings a new sophistication and rigour to the long-standing tradition of using depth-psychological ideas to interpret advertisements.

RESEARCH QUESTIONS

The various composite variables which we created provide material which can be used to explore and elaborate, and in some cases to test, a number of theoretical formulations about the nature of contemporary cultural change. Drawing on the conceptual frameworks indicated in Chapters 5 and 6, and linking them with the empirical categories described in this chapter, we can identify a number of questions where we may be able to contribute to the answers, and some issues on which our data could be expected to throw some light. We have interpreted the work of a number of sociological theorists such as Bauman, Beck, Bourdieu and Giddens to mean that 'identity work' is increasing, and we can suggest that a number of measures of this work can be derived from our data. We would expect to see an increase in the 'identity work' offered to or demanded from readers of advertisements. If identity work is becoming more common and important in the culture as a whole, then advertisements overall should become more intensively concerned with it. They should reflect the kinds of identity-developing or -maintaining strategies and projects in which people are increasingly involved.

Our conception of 'identity work' also draws upon the psycho-analytic thinking described in the previous chapter, and its formulations about anxiety, containment and defence. We see this as complementary to more cultural or sociological definitions of identity; identity is based on both inner and outer resources, and the most powerful forms of identity are developed when the richest cultural resources are deployed in response to the deepest of inner anxieties.

Overall then we can consider identity work as taking place when there are changes in the strength or organisation of either values or anxieties, or when there are shifts in the dynamic tensions between opposing psychic forces.

Firstly it would be significant if there were changes over time in the relative prominence of the three major cultural value categories. While all three, like the Freudian categories of ego, superego and id to which they relate, are necessarily present in cultural life, their distribution and inter-relationships may vary and produce cultural processes of different quality, in the way that changes in the structural dynamics of the mind produce psychic processes of different quality.

The 'risk society' thesis can be read as predicting an increase in preoccupation with Practical values, and in this context therefore is possibly at odds with other versions of the 'reflexivity' thesis. The latter might be read in either of two ways. In one it predicts an absolute increase in the expressive values found in the Social and especially Sensual categories, on the grounds that these will be featuring more in public discourse as that becomes more concerned with monitoring meanings, and in particular is more attuned to subjective meanings. In the other it predicts a more even balance between the three value types, and also between 'Contained' and 'Container', in that reflective and creative psychic change could be seen as most likely to occur when this internal tension is at its height and the pressures and possibilities for new internal settlements are greatest.

Secondly we can consider the range of anxieties with which advertisements typically deal. How wide is the range of anxieties addressed by advertising, and is the range or focus changing? Following the broad notion that we have entered a 'postmodern', or therapeutic, more subjectively-oriented and expressive culture, we would expect that a fairly complete engagement of popular-cultural forms with the inner life of the individual is now taking place (though of course it may also have been the case previously, in early modern times, that all kinds of anxiety were routinely registered in popular culture). While this may be the overall picture, however, the strong pressure in marketing towards 'segmenting' the market, so as to target products and their advertising to the demographic groups most likely to be interested in them, may have led to a differential distribution of anxieties amongst advertisements for different products. This would follow if demographic variables such as age and gender were determinants of the kinds of anxiety which will predominate, which is a plausible assumption as we suggest in Chapter 6. However, as we point out there, while an advertisement may target a particular group it is in the public domain and available to be read by many people from other groups. It is possible then that the ways in which anxiety is 'aired' in the culture as a whole are skewed by the concentration of advertising upon certain demographic groups.

At a more general level, the pressure across the whole culture towards increased identity work could simultaneously result in a general convergence of advertising strategies towards advertisements with greater psychological intensity and potential for identity work. Also, while demography may still pattern the distribution of anxiety, we could predict some overall shifts away from certain themes, and towards others. Specifically, we would expect that in a more fluid, inclusive and less deferential society, anxieties about social status are in decline, while coping anxieties, e.g. about safety and reliability, are increasing, as the idea of present society as 'risk' society would lead us to expect.

Our hypotheses about the role of advertising in identity work and emotional management can be linked with the thesis developed by Leiss *et al.* and others, that advertising is in some important respects a modern or late modern equivalent to or substitute for religion, as a source of images of the transcendent and its place in everyday life. This idea is not easily tested against the usual range of observations that can be made about advertising as a social institution: its commercial role, its importance in the development of the mass media, and so on. Advertising does indeed play a key economic role with profound cultural consequences, but arguably so also do the stock market and the insurance industry, without this leading to theories that these institutions occupy a sort of theological space in our social world.

Many cultural critiques of advertising would assign to it a moral role which on the face of it is the antithesis of the traditional functions of religion. While religion is restraining, binding and moralising, advertising may appear to be a disinhibiting, atomising and a- or im-moral discourse. If however it now plays a role in identity-formation and maintenance, then there arises the possibility of it playing a more socially cohesive role, instead of acting as this assumed disintegrative force (and perhaps alongside a corrosive role in relation to outgoing forms of social connection). We must therefore consider the nature of the 'identity work' we claim advertising contributes to, in the various ways in which we have conceptualised it, as related to value profiles, to anxieties and their management, and to risk and reflexivity.

Notes

1. We are very grateful to Michael Brewer of Abram Hawkes plc for the opportunity to conduct this study. Our thanks are due to him and Amanda Fajak of Abram Hawkes for their contribution to the interpretation of our data, and also to Link Research for their support for the focus group study.
2. The Advertising Archive in London has a well-stocked collection of print advertisements for many products in a well-maintained archive, to which its owners, Larry and Suzanne Viner, have generously given us access. Many advertisements there though are dated only by year or decade and without details of where they appeared.

Chapter 8

DRIVEN BY PASSION? CAR ADVERTISEMENT CONTENT
1950–1998

This chapter begins by providing, as historical background, a brief summary of key developments in the British car industry during this period (which also flags up some major dimensions of the economic context for the studies reported in Chapters 9 and 10). It then goes on to examine our main findings about changes over time, describing and discussing frequency counts for individual and composite variables on the coding form, where these show any pattern which is of interest. Finally we refer to our interview data, which we see as a check on our coding.

RATIONALISATION AND INTERNATIONALISATION

The large number of mergers and acquisition which took place on a national level in the 1960s has been repeated in the 1990s at a global level. The car industry in the 1990s is continuing to pursue the strategies of globalisation and rationalisation begun in the 1980s. Most recently BMW's take-over of Rover (though now unravelling) and Ford's take-over of Volvo have brought the number of major volume European manufacturers down to five, apart from the European operations of Ford, GM and the Japanese companies. This globalisation has meant that increasingly companies are manufacturing not for continental and national markets but for world markets.

Tolliday and Zeitlin described the industry in the 1980s as being in the midst of a significant transition 'Between Fordism and flexibility' with globalisation and Japanese innovation in manufacturing processes leading the way in the developments away from the procedures of mass production (Tolliday and Zeitlin, 1992). One interesting aspect of this complex set of changes is identified by Maxton and Wormald in their analysis of the global car market (Maxton and Wormald, 1995). They chart an important re-configuration of the relationship between car manufacturers and component suppliers. Component makers now play a greater role in the manufacture of the finished car and have greater influence in the design and production process. This approach, pioneered in Japan, has seen ancillary component manufacturers change their status from 'slaves' of the big car makers to 'partners' (Maxton and Wormald, 1995). In this new relationship of delegated component design and installation, manufacturers and suppliers act as 'co-makers' (Maxton and Wormald, 1995).

There has been an increased interest in safety, and car design has been improved by some technical developments, such as airbags, which are becoming standard on most cars. The preoccupation with safety, which began in the 1960s following the work of Ralph Nader in the U.S., has steadily increased since then. This has been a theme of particular importance to advertisers in UK advertising at least. Interestingly however, a content analysis of German car advertising has found less evidence of any increasing use of safety themes in car advertising (Wachtel *et al.*, 1995)[1].

Although the 1990s has been a decade in which environmental issues have been more prominent in the minds of newly 'green' consumers, environmental considerations have not played such a forceful role in the purchase decisions or marketing strategies in the car field as we might have expected. While some legislation has restricted dangerous emissions and lead free petrol has become the normal choice of fuel, the industry has found it hard to address green issues head on in above-the-line advertising. Wachtel *et al.*'s study of German press advertising replicates our own findings with regard to the prominence of environmental claims (Wachtel *et al.*, 1995). These remain low on the agenda of advertisers even while 'green consumption' remains prominent in the minds, if not the practices, of consumers and legislators.

Perhaps this increase in anxiety, which is, however, not matched in any apparent decrease in car usage, is reflected in the amount of money now spent on advertising, which has increased considerably since the 1980s. In 1980 only £53.80 was spent on advertising for each unit sold, compared to £230 in 1994 (MEAL/Mintel, 1994). Such growth can, though, be explained by the decrease in perceived functional differentiation between products. Competitive advantage in the market today seems to depend on symbolic differentiation and the availability of extra features (especially those to do with safety). Though fuel economy remains an important consideration (Mintel, 1994), there is a move towards the financialisation of the car, as illustrated by the launch of the GM credit card. This developed the trend, which includes credit and leasing agreements, whereby car marketing offers a package and a relationship to the customer rather than a one-off purchase arrangement. A different indication of this broad trend can be found in the case of Daewoo whose successful entry into the UK market has had as much to do with innovative marketing and substantial after-sales packages as it has with basic product competitiveness.

CHANGES OVER TIME

Firstly we split the sample into two, such that sampling points up to and including 1970 were compared with those from 1975 on. This division maps on to Harvey's (1989) proposition that the transition to the postmodern condition can be located in the early 1970s.

There are some shifts in the incidence of variables from one period to another (both individual and composite variables) which constitute the core of our findings. In the following discussion and tables, we are considering relative frequencies, to control for differences in sample size and for variations in the number of messages contained in advertisements. This latter variation may be of some significance in itself, indicating differences in communicative strategy between more and less 'dense' advertisements. It is however irrelevant to our aim of tracking the relations of dominance and interaction between different kinds of values.

In the case of single variables, the relative frequencies are given by the occurrence of a variable as a percentage of the total number of occurrences of all value variables in the sub-sample. For the composite variables, they are derived as follows. In the case of individual advertisements, it is assumed that each advertisement will have a 'Value' content of 10, and each composite variable is then assigned a values score proportionate to the actual occurrence of its constituent single variables such that the proportionate scores of all the composite variables will add up to 10. In the case of the time-based sub-samples we derive an average raw incidence score for each composite variable (the sum of the total incidence of the constituent variables of each composite, divided by the number of advertisements). Within each sub-sample, these raw averages are then converted into proportionate scores such that they add up to 10. (Throughout the ensuing discussion, whenever we refer to a 'standardised' score we mean one which is calculated as a proportion of 10 by a method based on the above principle.)

The rise of the 'Practical'

Figures 8.1 and 8.2 exemplify two kinds of Practical advertisement Figure 8.1 (page 129) is a simple example of a univocally Practical advertisement, based on the variable of fuel economy. In the case of Figure 8.2 (page 130), a complex Practical advertisement, the Practical messages still lead, but are modulated a little by the gendered social image and by the bizarre presentation of the car as a physical object.

A fundamental finding from the complete UK sample is the increase in the relative frequency of 'Practical' values from the first to the second

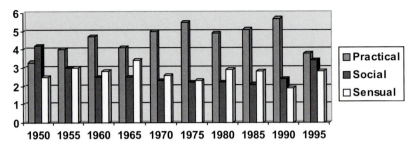

Changes in Practical, Social and Sensual Values over Time

Figure 8.3   Standardised incidence scores for different types of value

half of the period studied, from an average standardised score of 4.2 before 1973 to 5.1 after 1973. This gain is drawn equally from the Social and Sensual categories. Looking at the standardised scores at each sampling point (Figure 8.1), we can see there is an uneven but discernible rise across the whole period, with the exception of the sharp drop at the final point. We discuss later the possible reasons for the anomalous scores found on a number of variables in this final sub-sample.

Apart from the final column, we can see the overall rise in Practical as matched by a fall in Social, with a less regular fall in Sensual. This finding directly contradicts one of our hypotheses (see Chapter 7), that advertising would show an increasingly dominant symbolic and sensual content. It is also at odds with the findings of Leiss *et al.*, according to which a major trend in advertisements across this century has been away from the product, or more precisely towards embedding the product in increasingly rich symbolic contexts. If our findings speak of a more pragmatic, de-contextualised orientation to commodities (especially since the particular commodity involved here is the symbolically-laden motor car), they are certainly not what most contemporary understandings of recent cultural change would predict. A postmodern or late modern culture is not usually characterised as one in which consumers take an increasing interest in the mundane practicalities of things. This finding therefore demands close scrutiny.

When this trend first emerged we considered that it might be an artefact of either or both of two conditions. One is the division of labour between the media. The emergence in the UK of commercial television early in the period under study, the more recent development of commercial radio, and the expanding repertoires available to television advertisers as computer-based video technologies have developed, may all have led to a division of labour between media whereby the richer symbolic dimensions of brand imagery and product definition have migrated to the 'dynamic' modes, leaving 'static' (print) advertising to do more of the product-information work, i.e. to run the 'boring' advertisements which tell the consumer something factual about the product, and so to complement the emotional stimulation of, especially, the television advertisements.

The frequencies for our sample of TV advertisements give some support to this view. The Practical score at 3.1 is lower for these advertisements than for the whole sample. This sample is admittedly relatively small, and cannot support a longitudinal analysis, but it may be that the trend to the Practical is weaker or absent in TV advertisements. However a pre-eminence of Practical messages in TV advertisements was found in the banking sector (see Chapter 9), so there is no clear overall division of labour between the media.

The second way in which this might be an 'artefact' of sorts is in the possibility that minor features of the advertisements, which may go unnoticed by many readers, are inflating the Practical score and obscuring the fact that the primary impact of the advertisement is in the emotional or symbolic nature of its central image or slogan. The lists of Practical features sometimes found in small type at the foot of an advertisement, for example, might yield a number of frequency checks for Practical variables, but contribute little to the main cultural presence of an advertisement since most readers turning the pages do not read them. However, there was a way for us to check this because our coding form included a judgement of which was the dominant message in an advertisement. As described in Chapter 7, this was not at the level of individual variables but at that of the composite groups we began with. As these were then revised to form the Practical, Social and Sensual groupings, we cannot specify the complete relationship between the frequencies and the dominance of these categories. However the Practical category is very similar to that which we originally described as 'Rational', and our data shows that the 'Rational' content has increased in dominance. By the end 'of the 1960s it had overtaken the other two groupings combined, and it retained this dominance subsequently, even strengthening it slightly in the context of less frequent Practical values in the 1990s.

So we are left with the conclusion that the rising dominance of 'Practical' values is not a consequence of the research having focused mainly on print advertisements, or of our counting trivial elements in the advertisement without regard to their impact. The dominance is in

	1950s	1960s	1970s	1980s	1990s
'Rational' dominant	43	52	68	52	53

Figure 8.4   'Dominant' messages as percentage of total

frequency and impact. It appears that the discourse of car advertising, in print at least, has become increasingly oriented to practicalities, in a way that will certainly shape consumer experience in this sector, and may be of wider cultural significance.

The next step in the analysis is to examine which specific Practical variables are primarily responsible for this pre-eminence. To do this we grouped the sampling points in pairs to give profiles across decades (and thereby a possibly more reliable picture than by five-year intervals, when chance fluctuations may dominate the data). Several individual variables show clear overall rises throughout the period under study: Finance, Warranty, Other inducements, Security and Accessories. Low insurance and Safety also seem to be generally on the increase, despite dips in the 1980s. Price has a more fluctuating picture, and Economy is in decline after a sharp increase in the 1970s (a rise which was in all probability a response to the oil crisis), so it is not a simple matter of the advertisements reflecting a growing concern with saving money (as in Figure 8.1). Rather they reflect an increasing concern with what might be called the 'package' and 'gizmo' aspects of the product (Figure 8.2), which we can see in the context of a particular kind of consuming subject addressed by the advertisements.

The advertisements relate to the putative desire of the consumer for a commodity which will embrace a range of needs, a desire in which the wish for a prudent or achievable financial and maintenance package is linked with an interest in various in-car (and non-driving related) facilities. In other words the commodity becomes a site for the negotiation of an integrated and rationalised set of features many of which are unrelated to the basic functioning and use of the object itself. Of course the interest in accessories may be linked to powerful aesthetic or pleasurable experiences (the sound of a CD system, for example), but these will be registered elsewhere in our coding if the advertisement referred to them (e.g. if it mentioned the 'fingertip control' of a sound system or the 'hassle-free' period when all servicing costs are paid). As Practical features they are simply enumerated, often for the purpose of highly calculable comparison with competitors. But, we must stress again, getting the cheapest deal in simple terms is not what the frequency of these variables implies. It is rather a broader management of the consumer's affairs and a broader administration to practical needs for convenience and various technological devices. The advertisements offer an overall 'package' which is strongly coloured with implicit prudence, both financial and in relation to physical safety, but which in its concentration on practicalities is compatible with a diversity of socio-moral profiles.

Further analysis of relative frequency changes within Practical variables can develop this point. Figure 8.5 represents the central and peripheral aspects of rational propositions in car advertising as we have coded them. The inner circle holds those elements which are central to the experience of the car as a functioning product. These qualities cannot be 'bolted on', and are not likely to be presented to the consumer in the form of 'optional extras'. They are intrinsic to the everyday experience of the car. The outer circle holds those elements which to a greater extent can be seen as extras. Most can be added or taken away, though some (safety and the environment) are more hidden or intangible aspects of the car itself. To some degree the two categories are permeable, but for heuristic purposes they are distinguishable.

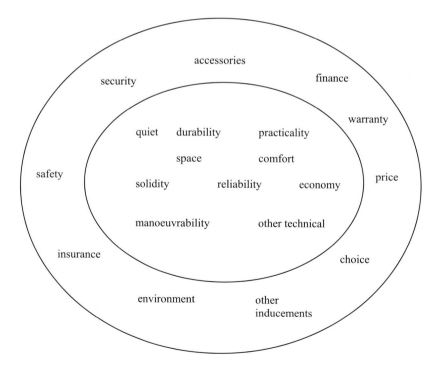

Figure 8.5 Core *vs* package

DECADE	1950s	1960s	1970s	1980s	1990s	WHOLE PERIOD
Core features	77	87	84	97	137	93
Peripheral features	133	123	126	113	73	117

Figure 8.6   Comparing frequencies of core and peripheral product features

Comparing the total frequency of claims across the whole sample for each group, we find that the inner circle is predominant. However we find there is a clear trend over time for more attention to be paid to the 'extras'. Figure 8.6 compares what might be called 'hierarchies of preoccupation' in each decade. We ascribe a number to each variable according to its rank in order of prevalence; the lower the overall score for a group of features, then the more frequent were the references made to those features relative to the other group.

In the 1950s the core features are strongly privileged. At this time the car was not fully established as a mass utility good; it was still in part a novelty, exciting in itself. Description of its basic functions held the reader's attention. However, this dominance begins to weaken in the 1960s. The 1970s again interrupt the trend; in the face of the oil crisis, 'economy' reasserted the primacy of core features. However accessories came to be more important in the 1980s, and by the 1990s the peripheral elements have come to have a major significance in the struggle to differentiate and promote the package. The accessorisation and financialisation of the car have proceeded to a point where 'peripheral' features now define the key parameters of the commodity.

It is possible that the very high ranking of these elements in the final 1990s sub-sample is connected with the way in which the 1990s reverse the frequency trend towards the Practical. Both may be linked to the relatively high frequency within this group of advertisements from the broadsheet press and from television. Rather like television, the 'quality' press has also tended towards advertisements with more Social and Sensual values than the average, and though there is no necessary connection messages in these media may also be more likely to prioritise features other than core utilities. So the swing to the periphery may be exaggerated in our data, but the overall trend is clear.

The changing nature of anxiety

A second major finding is in the shifts registered in the relative frequencies of different kinds of manifest anxiety. Status anxieties are seen to decrease, while Coping anxieties increase. The split-sample comparisons show a decrease in the total standardised Status anxiety score, from 4.1 to 3.2, and a rise in Coping from 4.0 to 4.4. In the second period there is also a rise in the proportion of variables which we judged to be anxiety-Neutral or -Variable, and here again we encounter the 'Practical' values of Finance, Low insurance and Other inducements which were important in explaining the rise of the Practical.

So at the level of what we are calling 'manifest anxieties', as well as at the level of values, we find a turn towards instrumental strategies and away from gestural ones. The world is presented increasingly as a place of danger and difficulty in which the satisfactory negotiation of everyday uncertainties and disruptions is the primary aim, rather than steering through the hazards of social comparison.

Figure 8.7 (page 131) is a high Coping advertisement. The owner of the Hyundai in this advertisement has to cope with buying his or her own petrol, but everything else seems to be taken care of. Little explanation is required to show how, in contrast, the American advertisement shown in Figure 8.8 (page 132) addresses Status claims and anxieties. While bearing numerous Practical and Sensual variables, the dominant message of this 1984 advertisement is 'swank'.

The finding that Status and Coping anxieties change places, with the latter becoming pre-eminent, can be elaborated in more detail if we also consider changes at the level of 'Latent' anxiety. Amongst Status anxieties, it is especially those related to narcissistic aspects of the person which are seen to decrease, while of the Coping anxieties all except those which are narcissism-related are on the increase. The overall decline in the frequency of those variables which we link to narcissism suggests that the move away from anxious concerns with status which is evident at the 'Manifest' level may have a deeper psychological underpinning. While this hardly disproves the 'culture of narcissism' thesis, it does suggest that the more grossly narcissistic tendencies in the late modern self do not find obvious confirmation in one place where such might have been expected, namely the texts of advertisements.

The other shifts to be observed in the overall standardised scores for the different kinds of latent anxiety are not large enough to be offered as clear evidence of trends. (Thus, although both Depressive and Paranoid categories show increases, while Separation and Oedipal anxieties decline, we will not claim that the Kleinian typology is becoming more relevant!) The movements within the Paranoid and Separation categories are too small to be interpreted. We will however note two features of the data. One is that a moderate 'de-oedipalisation' seems to have occurred from a peak in the 1950s. The other is that Depressive anxieties showed a smooth, gradual increase in relative frequency from 1950 through to 1985 (apart from a peak in 1975, again probably reflecting the oil crisis). Then, perhaps catching up with the more ruthless hedonism said to characterise the 1980s, they show a sharp drop in 1990, with some recovery in the most recent sample.

Overall, at the level of 'Latent' anxiety, the relatively small variances shown within each category indicate that there is a degree of stability in the patterns of anxiety evoked by advertisements in this sector. Psychoanalytically, this is what one would expect; the anxieties themselves are an unchanging phenomenon at the core of mental life. Moreover, a communicative form that is unrestrained as to its subject matter (apart from the need to make some reference somewhere to the commodity advertised), and that seeks to establish and retain the widest possible public interest in its messages, will be likely—in the range of messages produced within a given period—to tap into all the major basic unconscious dispositions.

Because of this, the identification of a more manifest level of organisation of anxiety may be important in bridging between analyses of cultural change and of psychodynamics, since at this level the relatively short-term impact of cultural changes may be more evident.

THE CHANGING MANAGEMENT OF ANXIETY

It may nonetheless be possible to indicate some deep shifts in the kind of unconscious subjectivity which the reader of advertisements is invited to inhabit. The rise in Practical values which we reported above is linked to another trend shown in the data, which is the increasing degree of containment, as defined earlier in Chapter 7. In the split-half comparison, the Container score rose from 5.4 before 1973 to 6.4 after, and the Contained score correspondingly moved from 4.6 down to 3.6. This was not due entirely to the rise in Practical and the fall in Sensual variables, however; over 50% of this movement is attributable to a relative shift within the category of Social variables, from the 'B' group to the 'A' group (see Figure 7.1). In the latter group there is a fairly steady decline throughout the period, apart from the sharp rise in the final period (see Figure 8.9 below).

The increasing containment applies to all types of latent anxiety. It also applies to both Coping and Status anxieties, though these have a very different baseline of containment. The latter show an excess of Contained over Container values throughout the whole period, so it

Social A and Social B as Proportion of Overall Container

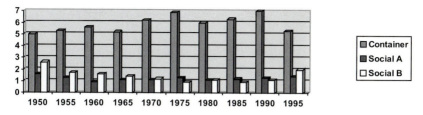

Figure 8.9   Standardised incidence scores for containment variables
N.B. influence of oil crisis, via Practical variables, in high Container score for 1975.

would be more accurate to say that Status anxieties become less uncontained over time. (Whether by their general nature, or by the ways in which we have operationalised them here, it may be that these anxieties are less amenable to containment, since there are very few psycho-social locations in which social comparison cannot engender doubt and insecurity. Effective competence, however, is achievable and is easily experienced as an intrinsic good and as a good-enough response to Coping anxieties.)

In addition to the turn to the Practical, therefore, we can identify a second broad shift in values, one within the Social category: a shift away from those stressing individualised gratification (B) and towards those expressive of the benefits of relatedness (A). For reasons described earlier, we have characterised this distinction as one between containing and defensive values, though we acknowledged the limitations of this postulated link between our variables and these major categories of mental life. One of these limitations was in the possibility that an individual reader could use a 'Social A' value defensively, e.g. the use of nuclear family imagery in advertisements is often taken to be in the service of psycho-cultural defences against the sexual and social anxieties accompanying social change.

However, the strengthening position of 'Social A' compared to 'Social B' does not rest on variables such as Family and Tradition, which show declines across the whole period, but on rises in Freedom (carefree), Excellence (technical) and Insulation/protection. So the containing power of the social is not tied to specific social arrangements, traditional or otherwise, but is instead inscribed into technology and its capacity, in its excellence, to lift burdens and to protect from dangerous and disagreeable experiences.

Some of the contribution to 'carefree-ness' may also come from financial packages. In all, what appears to emerge here is a construction of the subject as one who finds in the social a rationalised form of security. Whether through bureaucratic or technological means (financial services or engineering and design), an impersonal social matrix is established as the dominant meaning of the commodity, and within the protected space of which the individual consumer is able to negotiate his or her own customised relationship to the world.

To link these observations with some of the wider debates on contemporary culture, we can suggest that the consuming subject as addressed in these advertisements is more concerned with risk than with reflexivity. The effect of the rise in Practical and Social A variables is to reduce the tension, in the overall discourse of these advertisements, between Container and Contained, and thereby to reduce the scope for or the pressures towards expressive or reflective identity work, as we have called it. However, this is offset by the gain in the other form of identity work, that concerned with risk-reduction. The patterns observed in our data can be used to describe in a detailed way how the subject as consumer is implicated in risk society and what some of the preferred strategies for dealing with risk are.

We can extend this analysis through a consideration of differences between media, comparing a group of advertisements taken from the tabloid press (the *Daily Mirror* and *Daily Express*—365 advertisements), with others from the 'quality' press (*The Observer*, *The Times* and the *Sunday Times*—570 advertisements). Tabloid advertisements are recognisably different from those found in the 'quality' press. Across the whole time frame we have generally found a higher concern with practicalities in the messages. The mean score for aggregated Practical values in tabloid papers is 5.42 while in quality papers it is 4.38. This is reflected in the higher Container score for tabloid advertising which shows a mean of 6.47 against 5.65 for the quality papers. This difference is sustained despite the greater prevalence of 'Social A' values in the quality sample, showing that the constitution of tabloid advertising containment is relatively more to do with practicality than with Social values. In fact across the sample both sets of aggregated Social values ('Social A' and 'Social B') are higher for quality press advertisements, reflecting their greater tendency to place the car in a psycho-social setting as opposed to simply presenting the car against an anonymous background (47% as opposed to 25% in tabloids), to depict people, (48% as opposed to 38%) and to allude to a specific activity (53% as opposed to 43%).

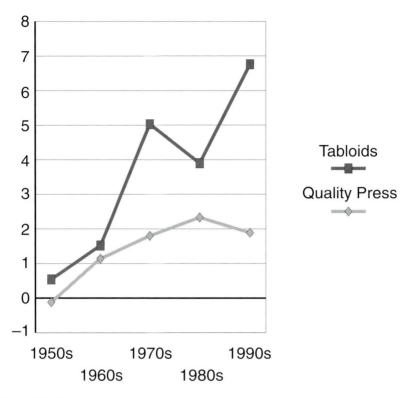

Figure 8.10   Containment scores: comparing media

The Sensual elements are also relatively less prominent in tabloid advertisements. As well as being richer in Social messages the quality press advertisements have the greater proportion of Sensual elements (2.52 as opposed to 1.91). We might have expected, given the relative neglect of social themes in the tabloid advertisements, that Status-based claims would be substantially lower in that sub-sample. This is not however the case. Tabloid and quality advertisements have almost identical scores for the Status variable (3.64/3.68 respectively) suggesting that when tabloid advertising has tuned into sociality, it has done so in the mode of Status-based claims. This suggestion is supported by the findings with regard to Coping. Considering the practical orientation of the rational elements of the propositions we might have expected Coping values to be higher than in the less pragmatic quality advertisements. This is not in fact the case. Overall Coping is higher in quality advertisements than in the tabloids (4.20 over 3.95).

The differences can be summed up as follows. Tabloid advertisements offer more containment than quality advertisements. This containment is constituted more pragmatically; there is less sensuality and less Contained material in the tabloid advertisements. When tabloid advertisements have addressed sociality it has been predominantly in the register of Status claims. Coping is lower than the average for tabloids.

According to one way of evaluating these different kinds of advertisements we can suggest that the quality press advertisements are more conducive to 'identity work' than the tabloid advertisements because there is more tension between the Containing elements of the message and those elements which are to be Contained. Tabloid advertisements, on the other hand, have tended to emphasise rational information and practical considerations over the symbolically richer aesthetic depictions afforded by quality press advertisements. While we might recognise the value of this pragmatism, which is strong evidence for the persistence of rational modes of decision-making in the age of all-consuming images, there is also a preponderance of status claims which suggest that aspiration plays a role in this sector of the marketplace alongside the strictures of calculation in the face of necessity and economy. We might therefore suggest, following Bourdieu, that the quality press is the location of the stylisation and aestheticisation which is characteristic of the new classes and their greater distance from necessity, while the tabloid press are attuned to more traditional readerships for whom status remains the dominant register of sociality but for whom pragmatism is the predominant mode with regard to consumption.

Following Bourdieu's terminology we might say that the quality press indicates the presence of readerships which enjoy a greater distance from necessity and that advertising reflects the different structures of perception which these playful and stylised dispositions bring to thoughts about consumption.

When the sub-samples are examined across the five decade groups, we see a significant divergence between them. This is most marked in relation to practicality. The aggregated Practical score has been higher for the tabloid advertisements across the board. But it is not until the 1970s that a significant gap developed. The quality advertisements maintain a fairly consistent practical score across the period while the tabloid advertisements have shown steep rises. The average difference between quality and tabloid advertisements on the Practical scores has leapt from an average 0.31 in 1950s–1960s up to 1.96 since 1970. At the same time the Contained score has gone down steadily in the tabloid sub-sample, from 3.18 in 1950 (when it was higher than the equivalent score in the 'quality' sub-sample of 2.98) to 1.51 in the 1990s sample. The consequence of this change is the strongly increasing difference between Container and Contained in the tabloids. In the same period tabloid 'Social A' scores have been largely consistent and always lower than the quality advertisement 'Social A' score.

This gives a historical dimension to the distinction outlined in the analysis of the sub-samples. The observations with regard to tabloid advertisements' hyper-practicality, the disproportionately rational constitution of their mode of containment, and the paucity of Sensual elements in the tabloid advertisements are increasingly found to be the case over time. This is no better indicated than by highlighting the containment scores for the two sub-samples in the 1990s. Tabloid advertisements show a score of 6.76, i.e. a very low tension. The quality advertisements show a score of 1.89, which shows a greater balance between Practical, Social and Sensual elements in the advertisements and hence a richer resource for the processes of the 'reflexive' kind of identity work to take place. The phenomenon which we identified as a large scale 'rise of the Practical' can be seen to be distributed unevenly across the sample. Pragmatism in car advertising has been on the increase since the 1970s but in particular it is on the increase much more rapidly in the tabloid advertisements.

This historical bifurcation suggests there is some intensification of a rich culture of symbolic consumption and of an aestheticised consumer ethic being consolidated among the readerships associated with the quality press. At the same time the readerships associated with the tabloid press are being fed a sparse diet of rational product information born out of an ethic of consumption rooted more in practical necessity and economy than in hedonistic self-styling. The introduction to the former readerships of colour supplements in 1962 will have contributed to this trend, given their suitability for aestheticised images. (It would be interesting to look now at the impact of the spread of these 'glossier' media to other readerships.)

TRIANGULATION WITH INTERVIEW DATA

It was possible for us to conduct a dozen interviews with car owners (or 'user choosers', who chose their own company car), in which we elicited their responses to a series of six advertisements. The interviews were conducted in the homes of market research recruiters, who had recruited the respondents in the usual way to a sample specification that produced a group mixed in age, gender and imminence of next car choice. We then compared their responses with our values coding profiles for those advertisements.[2]

Interviewees were initially asked simply to describe what they saw in the advertisements. The interviewer had a list of those elements of each advertisement which our coding procedures had identified, and prompted the interviewees for comments on or associations to any values not spontaneously mentioned, taking care not to suggest anything for which there was not a basis in the interviewee's own perception. The verbatim responses were then analysed by us as if they were advertisement texts, and were coded for the presence of the values listed in our coding form.

We thus produced for each advertisement a coding profile that averaged the respondents' reports of the presence/absence of each value variable, and could compare this both with our own coding profiles for the individual advertisements, and also with average profiles for that make (or 'marque') of car where our database had sufficient numbers of the marque in question. In each of the figures below (relating to two of the print advertisements used) the first profile is our own on the individual advertisement ('researcher's profile'), the second row is the marque average in our sample ('marque heritage profile'), and the third is the respondents' ('readers' profile'). In row 1 the figures are the raw incidence scores (except for '% difference', which like the standardised scores is a simple measure of the Container/Contained difference based on the relative strength of these two composite variables, and so is an inverse measure of tension). In rows 2 and 3 the figures are raw means, across either the marque sub-sample of advertisements (row 2) or across the interviewees' responses to the single advertisement (row 3). The

	PRAC	SOC	SENS	CR	CD	% DIFF	COPE	STAT	NEUT
1	1*	1	1	2*	1	+166	1	0	2*
2	3.1	1.5	1.8	4.1	2.2	+30	4.1	2.1	0.2
3	2	5	2	4	5	−11	3	4	1

Figure 8.11   Coding profiles for VW Golf advertisement. Asterisks show location of dominant value

	PRAC	SOC	SENS		CR	CD	% DIFF	COPE	STAT	NEUT
1	6	1	1*		7	1*	+75	6*	1	1
2	5.2	1.3	2.1		5.9	2.55	+29	4.9	2.3	1.2
3	5	2	1		6	2	+23	5	2	1

Figure 8.12   Coding profiles for Renault Clio advertisement. Asterisks show location of dominant value

advertisements themselves are seen in Figures 8.9 (Volkswagen Golf), and 8.14 (Renault Clio).

It can be seen that on the whole there is a reasonable fit between our coding profile and that derived from the interviewees. While this limited study can do little more than confirm that our coding procedures can meaningfully be checked against interview data with advertisement readers, it did give us confidence that those procedures do yield profiles that are consistent with common perceptions of the advertisement. The considerable scope that undoubtedly exists for individual readings of advertisements, including idiosyncratic or 'subversive' ones, is quite consistent with a high degree of commonality in registering the basic value content of the messages.

MAJOR TRENDS IN U.S. SAMPLE

We are undertaking further analyses of the data gathered in Section B of the coding form. We conclude here with a comparison of the major overall findings with the U.S. sample.

In some respects the trends there are similar, though less marked. In the U.S. time-split analysis, the gap between Container and Contained widens (from 0.6 to 1.0 in standardised scores). Coping anxieties rise while Status ones fall, but Coping was ahead of Status anyway in the first time period. However Coping-related narcissistic anxieties rise a little. The main difference between the UK and U.S., though, lies in the absence in the U.S. sample of a rise in Practical values (in fact, there is a very slight decline) and of a fall in Social ones. In fact there is a rise in Social values, matching the decline in Sensual, and this rise is equally in both A and B sub-groups. The wider margin of containment is therefore due very largely to the decline in Sensual values, though these are still at a higher level than in British advertisements.

The evidence therefore highlights the importance of national context in the production and interpretation of advertisements. Our data would confirm that in the fading importance of concerns with Status, British culture is becoming more like American, but in the increasing prominence of Practical values it is becoming less like it. The American consumer, even though, like the British counterpart, increasingly beset by Coping anxieties, may be turning—or is being led—more to social imagery than to a regime of practicality in order to find the containment which, we argue, consumers are likely to seek in advertising messages. A further study would be needed to confirm or elaborate this picture, in other product sectors as well.

Notes

1. With thanks to Marianne Markowski for assistance with research and for translation of this article.
2. We are very grateful to HPI Research of London, a leading market research agency in the field of car advertising, who resourced the interviews and discussed their results with us.

Chapter 9

GOING TO MARKET: BANKING AND THE ADVERTISING DYNAMIC

ADDRESSING THE CONSUMER: HISTORICAL OVERVIEW

In the post-war period, British banks changed from quasi-public to market-driven institutions (Burton, 1994). This transformation brought changing attitudes towards consumers which influenced both the quantity and quality of the banks' advertising. The banks arrived late to the promotional task in comparison to many other sectors, learning promotional tricks in the 1960s which retailing and foodstuff sectors had known since the 1930s; yet by the 1980s financial products were one of the best promoted goods on the British market. In their early years the banks had little incentive to market their goods the way other sectors had long been required to, for government regulation largely sheltered them from competition until the 1970s, and the banks derived most of their profits outside of the personal finance arena. They were secured from domestic industry, as the banks helped orchestrate the post-war development boom, and through international money management, particularly the handling of 'Euro dollars', the funds which America pumped into European economies to help their rebuilding efforts after the war. Profit also came from cycling OPEC oil funds into Third World economies.

Negative attitudes towards marketing also hampered the uptake of a consumer-orientated focus in the banking sector. The banks had played an important role for the state in the war effort, managing the economy. For their services, the banks were rewarded with state patronage that protected them from competition. This tight alliance might explain why some in the bank community conceived of the financial institutions as more of a public than market institution. (Money was also considered a privileged product, as some members of the banking elite were loathe to view the pound as a commodity. They found it difficult to accept that on the level of exchange and profit, bank loans or any of the other services provided were no different from a bar of soap, a box of chocolates, or a car.) Furthermore, 'selling' banking services carried an air of unrespectability.

However, by the late 1960s, the banks began to be drawn half-heartedly into a new structure of economics which encouraged, and was encouraged by, a new relational stance towards the consumer. Americanisation might be seen as one factor influencing the banks' softening stance towards promotion, as the co-ordination of post-war rebuilding funds from the U.S. brought British banks into intimacy with American financial marketing and business practices. Yet the experience of a different approach contributed to retrenchment as well as imitation. Mather, the president of Midland Bank, articulates the quintessential British attitude toward America—scepticism tinged with dispassionate interest—in his 1968 Cambridge address to the banking community:

> Our American friends seem well able to dress up and present mutton as lamb and I am quite sure we are learning the tricks...by a little clever twist here and there, conventional lending can very easily be made to look like an ingenious new scheme. Suitable advertising at frequent intervals, it all helps to burnish the image of banking inevitably tarnished from time to time in the eyes of the public.[1]

By the 1970s, the economic picture grew increasingly complicated for the banks. Traditional profit-making sources began to dry up as developing country debt reached insupportable levels and domestic industries started to shop for cheaper deals within the growing international money markets. These economic shifts weakened the ability of the state to regulate the financial markets in the traditional way. The 1980s saw the abandonment of the entire financial regulatory structure, as British banks were opened to domestic and international competition. Since 1963 the banks had competed in the credit market with American cards (see Chapter 10), but in the 1980s American banks were able to reach out for British customers in a variety of new ways. The traditional boundary between the bank and building society was effaced, as building societies became banks at the same time as the banks entered the mortgage market. A host of other sectors from supermarkets to car manufacturers packaged their capital base into financial services and offered them to people for sale. Not only did the banks need to find new profit-generating sites, but they also needed to fend off competitors. The personal financial market became the preferred target of the banks, but this shift in focus required the banks to rework their image, their services and their relationships to consumers. It was thus that over a short history of three decades, British banks increasingly moved from seeing themselves as a quasi-public institution to viewing their role as service providers selling commodities like the other shops on the High Street.

In this transition the banks increasingly opened up their traditionally closed organisational structure. Bank boards, once the privileged domain of those who had worked through the ranks and token aristocrats, increasingly welcomed staff from a diversity of other product sectors, who brought their expertise in selling other products. The banks also increasingly turned to the advertisers, and their 'specialised' knowledge of the consumer, to negotiate the transition they were experiencing.

In the beginning banks offered little money and were less than enthusiastic towards the marketing task, hence financial accounts tended to end up at the bottom of advertising agencies' list of priorities, the campaigns being of low status and sometimes used to train new staff. There was also a lack of marketing intelligence available to inform financial marketing efforts. Yet, as the banks began to take promotion more seriously, increased sums of money were devoted to marketing and advertising. A new financial marketing specialism emerged: financial service marketing textbooks were written, specialised training courses were given, and specialised consultancies arose. By the 1980s financial advertising spends were outstripping most other product sectors, and financial services accounts had moved to the top of advertising agency agendas.

CHANGES OVER TIME

As the banks become increasingly consumer-driven, promotional appeals became more individually directed, more pragmatic, and less morally instructive. We find the consumer addresses of our post-war sample falling into three phases.

Nostalgia and tradition largely influence the 1950s advertisements. They speak to an elite, conservative reader, in the discourse of class, public life, and heritage. Social status is celebrated and the banks are anchored within communal networks. Here we see the banks in their quasi-public role as the builders of community.

From the late 1950s through to the 1970s, the banks begin to make their turn towards a more consumer-orientated ethic. Advertisers use 'modernity' to reshape the banks' image. Tradition, the enemy of the 'modern', becomes the subject of ridicule—debased as the consummate symbol of backwardness, ineptitude, inequality and emotional distance. 'Modernity', on the other hand, signals a fresh structure of feeling, rooted in a sensibility of newness, efficiency, style, and friendliness. The neighbour-like 'manager' is introduced to personalise the institutional coldness of the bank. The advertisements take on a more vernacular, compassionate, and humorous voice, and public representations are increasingly supplemented by private images of family and peer life. Modernity not only emphasises a new personalised discourse; it brings a more democratic language to the advertisements. Copy is directed towards the 'universal', not the 'class bound' consumer. Social mobility is encouraged through the repetitive praising of ambition and achievement. The modern world is not just for the select few, but for all those willing to enter it. One of the glories and problems of modernity is the increased tempo it brings to social life. The social worlds depicted in the advertisements become increasingly fast-moving, and readers are instructed on the necessity of seeking convenient, time-saving measures. Timeliness and efficiency are aided by the 'wonders' of technologically advanced processes, which are unveiled with much fanfare. Fashionableness is also a hallmark of the modern, and we find the advertisements of the 1960s and 1970s admonishing those who continue to carry out pre-modern practices, while those who are able to adjust to the new 'tempo' and 'look' of the age find acclaim. Yet, the advertisements retain a patriarchal strain, administering fatherly advice on the need to budget for the sake of one's family. Prudence is held in high regard.

Towards the end of the 1970s some of the values of 'modernity' begin to be remade. The advertisements cease to use the word 'modern'. Emphasis turns away from the universal subject towards the uniqueness of the individual. In the mature marketplace of late modern Britain, consumers are addressed in the language of colleagues and business associates. Having achieved a considerable breakthrough into the market, the banks no longer need to articulate their soft and welcoming image so forcefully, and the spread of automatic tellers also alters the older notions of 'personal' service. In the face of an increasing array of complex financial services, friendliness becomes secondary to competence, as the avuncular manager is replaced by the more impersonal, but 'expert' advisor. Consumers are encouraged to view the banks as the medium through which to achieve their 'financial goals'. The banks are less likely to dictate what those 'goals' are, and instead lay out before consumers their optimal financial wares. The advertisements quickly get down to the basics of informing consumers of their options. The banks highlight their unique qualities, as competition over specialised service increases. Consumers are assured it is both easy and socially acceptable to change banks. The sphere of choice expands and consumers are encouraged to shop for the best deal. The normative values of fashion and status fade as readers are unleashed from the burden of having 'to keep up with the times' or the 'Joneses'. Consumers can now use banks on their own time schedules, as 24-hour banking increasingly becomes an industry standard. The moral discourse of saving for the family is replaced by the value of maximising one's returns and taking pleasure in individual consumption. Morality in the late modern period is more likely to be focused upon environmental and animal rights issues.

In the following section we present the findings of our content analysis on how values and anxieties have changed over the post-war period. We begin by looking at how Practical, Social and Sensual values altered, moving on to explore how manifest and latent anxieties were engaged, both over time, and in relation to specific brands. We then explore the levels of 'identity work' the advertisements might be seen as inspiring. The anxieties and container/contained measures enable us to gain a sense of how our 'inner worlds' have been variously engaged by promotion throughout the post-war period.

THE RISE OF THE PRACTICAL

As in the car study, we find that Practical values rise steadily over the post-war period (see Figure 9.1). Taken as a whole, Practical values register higher than Social and Sensual values, largely due to the increasing array of new services, the expansion of competition and the growing importance of technology throughout the post-war period. We followed the same procedure as Chapter 7 to test whether the high level of Practical values was a data artefact stemming from the large number of print advertisements contained in the study. Hypothesising that television commercials would be more sensuous and social, and print more pragmatic, we confirmed that Sensual values were higher in the television advertisements (1.2 print; 2.4 television), and Practical values

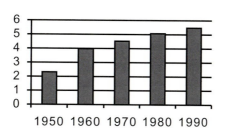

Figure 9.1   Practical values

were higher in print (4.6 print; 3.8 television). Only marginal differences were found in Social values (4.00 print; 3.84 television). These findings tend to confirm television's status as the more sensually orientated medium; however, the advertisements were not that much more Social, and still emanate higher levels of Practical values than Sensual.

Another factor encouraging high practicality might be the properties of the banking commodity itself. Because banking services have no concrete existence *per se*, it might be more difficult to package banking as a symbolic product, for it lacks the tangible and aesthetic qualities for the maximum generation of associations. This becomes more true as the banks de-materialise with automatic tellers. Yet we found examples of sensualised appeals that dispel the notion that banking services are only open to pragmatic packaging. However, these 'sex' appeals were rare, in the context of the overall 'business-like' focus of the majority of the banking advertisements. By and large the advertisements adopt instrumentalist orientations.

As Practical values rise, Social values fade. Social relatedness, images and references to togetherness and belonging steadily decline. References to individual gratification achieved through social relations climb in the 1960s, but return to lower than their 1950 level in the 1980s. Social addresses figure prominently in the 1950s, which were dominated by the characters of traditional class positions. This class structure is shaken in the 1960s and 1970s as the advertisements accentuate social mobility and the values of achievement, ambition, and distinction. Social values overall therefore remain relatively high. By the 1980s, direct reference to social position is de-emphasised, in favour of practical concerns.

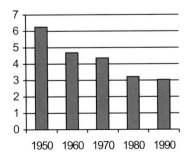

Figure 9.2   Social values

Sensual

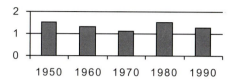

Figure 9.3   Sensual values

Sensuality scores are at their highest in 1950 and 1980, and their lowest in 1970. This pattern might be explained thus: 1950 advertisements emphasised creating a general impression for the first time consumer, constructing an ensemble of values in which pleasure, excitement, ease, and power were prominent. The high level of sensuality in the 1980s stems from a focus on 'gratification in consumption', as the advertisements link banking services to an expanded sphere of consumption. The drop in sensuality scores in the 1990s is perhaps a reaction against the unmoderated hedonistic ethos of the 1980s.

Overall, however, Sensual values are less subject to historical fluctuation, and are consistently less prominent than either the Practical or Social values (Figure 9.4). Our finding that the advertisements of the 1950s appear more highly stylised and sensualised than those of the 1990s perhaps confounds the view that the late modern period is

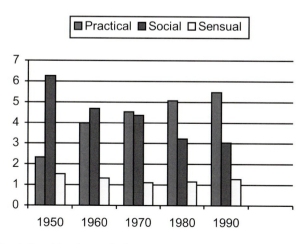

Figure 9.4   Practical, social and sensual values

captivated by a highly aestheticised communicational mode of hyper-real signs severed from their logical referents. The communicational mode of the banks becomes more, not less, logically orientated. Promotion of the late modern period is highly systematic, business-like, and orientated towards encouraging consumers to make decisions. These advertisements work hard to 're-mind' readers of their ego functions. Life is presented as a pragmatic project, requiring careful consideration and abundant information, and as extensively subject to choice.

THE CHANGING NATURE OF ANXIETY

The creative designers of financial advertisements encourage coping skills above all others. The discourse of banking advertisements requires engagement, action and the tackling of obstacles. Coping anxieties remain a dominant feature within the advertisements throughout the post-war period; however, unlike the car study, where coping anxieties were found to rise, here we find them in decline. Yet, like the car study, we also find a decline in interest in social rank. Status anxieties decline steadily over the post-war period from a high point in the 1950s, as banking promotion ceases to reinforce the salience of class placement. Appeals to status are replaced by values which are indifferent to anxiety or, more typically, not consistently related to either type of manifest anxiety.

Readers are increasingly confronted with a world of fluid opportunity and reward. The Sensual dimension is increasingly represented by the values of pleasure, excitement and gratification in consumption. These values are too mobile to be pegged to any specific anxiety. The growth in the anxiety-Variable category might also be seen as in keeping with characterisations of the late modern period as dominated by the joys of 'consumption' and the 'pleasure' ethic. In summary, over the course of the post-war period the advertisements increasingly paint a world within which social comparison ceases to be a primary concern, as attention is increasingly drawn towards the processing of information for the calculation of everyday choices, and the maximisation of benefit.

We find engagement with all latent anxieties in decline, except for a slight rise in some 'narcissistic' values. Unlike the car study, however, we find slightly less random historical variation. Paranoia follows the downward trend to the 1980s, but strongly reasserts itself in the 1990s, as the late modern advertisement finds the need to reassure readers that the world is not full of dangerous forces waiting to attack. The demise of separation anxiety through the post-war period might relate to both

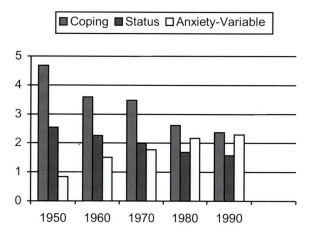

Figure 9.5   Manifest anxieties

the de-materialisation of the bank, and the increased levels of consumer sovereignty displayed in the advertisements. These assume a mobile and unattached individual, yet leave readers to their own devices in dealing with the psychic anxiety associated with dislocation and separation. The dwindling of social relations in the advertisements in general relates to the fading attention given to oedipal dynamics, which are at their height in the 1950s, but steadily decline over the post-war period. Banking promotion fed readers a desire for control, which we see as expressing a 'coping narcissism' anxiety, up to the 1990s when this anxiety ceased to be addressed in their advertising. In its place depressive anxieties strengthened, signalling a greater accent on caring for, instead of controlling the external world and others. We might see this turn towards depressive anxieties as linked to the ethical and charity marketing which has grown in popularity in the late modern period.

BRAND VALUES AND ANXIETIES

Having explored the sample as a whole, we turn towards an examination of individual banks. Our intention is to compare and contrast brand profiles, which are the overall impression individual banks make available to readers through their promotion. We seek to illuminate how brand profiles change over the course of the early and late post-war period, exploring how distinctive brands are, and isolating the banks which appear to be going against the trends found in the total sample. To undertake our branding analysis we selected seven banks: three major mainstream high street banks, Lloyds, Barclays, and

Midland (now HSBC), one upmarket bank, Coutts, which is distinguished by its elite clientele, including the Queen, the National Savings Bank which targets the opposite end of the market to Coutts, and two niche banks, the Co-operative, recently distinguished by an ethical banking identity, and First Direct, a relatively new player to the banking market specialising in telephone and computer banking services.

While our banks sample included a few corporate ads, we have not addressed corporate communications as such in this research. (The car and credit card samples contained even fewer advertisements not focusing on a specific product or product range.) However, given the very large spends on product advertising, we assume that both brand and corporate identities are built up substantially through the cumulative impact and aggregated messages of product advertisements.

We found that the strong emphasis placed on Practical values found in the total sample was particularly strong in the niche banks and National Savings, which consistently employed high levels of Practical values throughout the post-war period. It is somewhat surprising to find the three major high street banks registering slightly below average Practical scores. However, when we look at the time-split comparison, we find all of these banks recording much higher Practical scores in their post-1973 advertisements. Even Coutts, which registers the lowest Practical score of all the brands, placed more worth on pragmatics in the late modern period. There appears to be a growing convergence towards communication strategies rooted in practicality.

In terms of Social values, we find that Coutts breaks with the pack. Not only does this bank emanate consistently higher Social values than its rivals do, but it has done so consistently across the post-war period. All of the high street banks de-emphasise social appeals post-1973. The Co-operative and National Savings, on the other hand, display consistently below average social representations, with First Direct, our technology-driven bank, registering the lowest Social values of all the banks.

National Savings records the highest Sensual scores. In targeting individuals who are perhaps more reluctant, or unfamiliar with financial investment, National Savings plays down potential intimidation by de-emphasising social status, focusing instead on pleasure, excitement and ease. Barclays also records high Sensual scores, which might relate to their numerous youth campaigns. Like National Savings, Barclays emphasises pleasure, excitement and ease, though it also seeks to entice its readers with 'power' and 'security', values which are not found in

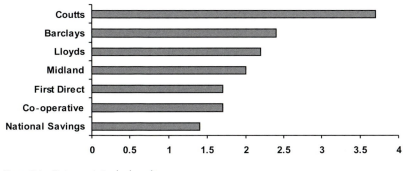

Figure 9.6   Status anxieties by brand

National Savings campaigns. Taken together these two banks have such abundant sensual scores they skew the mean, and the other brands are found presenting below average sensual scores.

Overall, Lloyds and the Co-operative have particularly strong Coping anxiety counts, but as in the sample as a whole this emphasis on coping anxieties is in decline. First Direct and National Savings placed the least emphasis on coping. Coutts projects status values far more than other banks, and even increases its representations of social standing in the post-1973 period, against the general trend towards down-playing social rank. The high street banks present the next highest levels of status—Midland the least of the three. The niche banks find little use for status in their appeals, and not surprisingly National Savings was the most likely to downplay awareness of social position.

We recognised in the total sample a growing emphasis on anxiety-Variable and anxiety-Neutral values. In our brand analysis we found the Co-operative and National Savings banks leading this trend.

In terms of latent anxieties, no gross differences emerge, but some brand-specific patterns are worthy of note. National Savings is relatively high on paranoid anxiety and low on depressive, possibly reflecting the financial insecurities and anxiety of its clientele. Coutts and First Direct were lowest on paranoia, with each having different reasons to see their customers as self-assured. Coutts was highest on narcissism. High numbers of youth-targeted advertisements might explain Barclays' significant attention to oedipal anxieties, whereas the Co-operative was least likely to engage with these maturational issues.

To summarise, our three high street banks are rather locked in step, presenting similar profiles, which rest in the middle of the road between Coutts' exaggerated status claims (which appear to have intensified in defiant response to changing values), and the more pragmatic profiles of the niche banks and National Savings. Next to Coutts, Lloyds presented the highest number of Social values; however, it was more likely to manifest them in images of togetherness, rather than appeals to ambition or achievement. Barclays' profile is very similar to Lloyds, with the exception of its increasing use of Sensual values. The promotion of the Midland has created the most distinctive profile, in being less timid about abandoning social and status appeals, by engaging its readers' pragmatic concerns, and emphasising depressive anxieties.

THE MANAGEMENT OF ANXIETY

We laid out in Chapter 7 our definitions of the 'container' and the 'contained'. One measure of the variable 'identity work' is the difference between container and contained scores. High 'identity work' can be seen as reflecting greater tension between psycho-social forces which, we have argued, engages readers in a process of active self-reflection. Low 'identity work' scores would indicate less space for this active work of selfhood, as messages would be dominated by either container or contained values. Dominant container values would indicate a discursive structure within which identity was more rigidly prescribed. Dominant contained values would point to the overriding of more materially and socially negotiated functions by libidinal needs.

We found that the tradition-bound advertising of the 1950s was the least likely to invite 'identity work'. These advertisements created less tension between psychic forces, for identities were securely inscribed through tradition. This discourse of tradition began to be broken down in the discourse of the 1960 advertisement. Here we find advertisers working towards freeing individuals from their older traditional practices. To achieve this change, the advertisements increase their emphasis on freedom, and pleasure, at the same time that container scores decline slightly. This realignment changes the ratio between the container and contained whereby identity work increases. The advertisements of the 1970s close down 'identity work', yet it is slightly reinstated in the 1980s. Here a growing emphasis on gratification in consumption and a valuing of individual satisfaction increases contained values again resulting in an increased ratio to the container and a more favourable environment for 'identity work'. In the 1990s 'identity work' scores decline again. The picture which emerges from the data is of a cyclical patterning with oscillations from decade to decade. These fluctuations cancel each other out in our time-split comparison

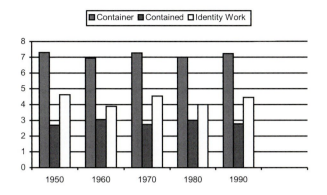

Figure 9.7   Levels of container, contained and identity work in banking advertisements by decade

and we find no difference between container/contained and 'identity work' scores in the pre- and post-1973 comparison.

This picture is different from the one of overall increase in containment that we found in car advertising. The evidence of small fluctuations here may suggest that 'identity work' is regulated by broader psycho-social forces, such that when the pressures towards 'identity work' increase, countervailing 'cooling' forces to begin to take effect. 'Identity work' might thus be seen as regulated by a cultural thermostat. However our data cannot support any firm observations; the overall fluctuations may be a chance effect of brand movements in different directions.

While we set out in this study to provide some answers about the nature of values in British society, as reflected in bank advertising, we appear to be left with more questions. We did not find conclusive evidence of a general shift towards a more post-traditional and therapeutic, reflexive society. We did find an overall decrease in Status anxiety related values, and a tendency to increased Practical values. However, we were unable to find evidence of an increased propensity towards sensuality, and observed an overall decline of Social values. Yet while it is true that the advertisements of the late modern period were much less likely to value togetherness and belonging, there was a positive side found to this orientation in the decreasing number of status claims. Also the increase in 'depressive anxiety' in the 1990s is indicative not of a turning away from morality, but a reinstatement of pro-social values after their eclipse in the 1980s. Narcissistic anxieties were found to be least important of all the anxieties addressed in the advertisements. While we could not confirm it concretely in our data, there is perhaps enough evidence cautiously to state that we are being unbound from some older social restraints, while in their place other containing forces appear to be instated. In the late modern period we are less likely to be held in order by superego guilt. The late modern bank 'holds' us by encouraging us to rationalise our needs and pointing us towards instrumental engagement with practicalities.

SUBJECT POSITIONS

To enlarge on the general findings described above, and to develop the concept of the 'subject positions' offered in advertisements, we will now move on to an account of how across the decades the kind of subjectivity typically assumed, addressed or cultivated in bank advertising has changed. Firstly, though, we can comment on the gendering of subject positions, and note that the banking sector continues to present itself as the domain of men. The only decade in which representations of women rose was the 1970s (arguably a period of strong, though contested, feminist sentiment, an awakening to many aspects of male domination). Representation of women actually declines in the 1990 advertisements as the financial experts who come to be frequently presented are usually men.

All advertisements invite us to take up a particular subject position—to acknowledge ourselves in particular ways. We link this here with the concept of re-minding, as used in Chapter 6, and we will attempt to put a 'face' on some of the subject positions of which bank advertising has re-minded us over the post-war period. Wernick argues that promotional discourse always assigns us to the subject position of consumer, but this leaves open a great variety of ways in which we can be addressed as consumers.

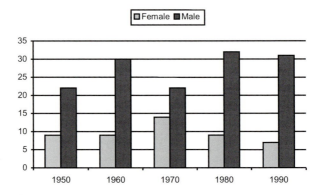

Figure 9.8   Percentages of advertisements with people

In looking at the subject positions offered by bank advertising we find a move away from identities rooted in community relationships and work, towards subjects who are increasingly individuated and possess greater and greater control over their desires and choices. This evolution to an increasingly more sovereign consumer did not unfold as an uncomplicated linear progression, but, rather, within the context of growing marketing intelligence, market expansion, and broader historical changes, each subject position revealed its limitations. As markets evolved, creatives learned the boundaries of the subjectivities they promoted, and altered them to meet new market realities. Sometimes advertisers created identities which made a distinctive break from past subjectivities. At other times older positions were simply supplemented by a new inflection. On the surface, the sovereign consumer model might be seen as the pre-eminent subjectivity for consumer culture, yet it, too, possesses its own contradictions and limits. As we shall see, in the 1990s there is evidence that some creatives are having success precisely by turning away from the sovereign consumer model towards a new community-orientated subjectivity.

The folk consumer: identity inscribed in traditional social networks and labour

A 1950 advertisement for Barclays, *Devon days—Devon ways,* is not reproduced here owing to poor image quality, but we will describe the vivid way it illustrates our first type. It presents an image of community bound through the act of roofbuilding. Identity here is inscribed within the guild-like tradition of shared labour. Subjectivity is positioned on the social map through regional identification. In other words, identity is invoked through the concreteness of place (Devon). The social convention of roofing, highlighted in both the image and copy of the advertisement, involves able bodied members of the community rallying together to repair or replace the roofs of each other's homes, or of community buildings such as churches or halls. The act of roofing bonds individuals together in the age old struggle of protecting themselves against the elements of nature. Roofing is not a form of abstract labour here, but a union between people, underpinning a community ethos. Some of the values here include sharing, belonging, tradition.

We are addressed as a social group in the advertisement. There is no sense of identity outside of the communal network or regional placement. The sponsoring bank aligns itself with the project of building community by showing its respect for the 'local tradition of country and townsfolk'. Traditional community practices are honoured, not disrupted. The copy notes that the sponsoring bank is interested in 'satisfying the traditional requirements of the community it serves'. The bank is marketed here as a total entity, not as a pragmatic service provider.

Broadly, the advertisement works to create a sense of stability, acting as a confirmation that what happened yesterday will happen again today. This stability of self and practice might be seen as placating the modern anxiety over continual change. In psychodynamic terms, oedipal anxieties are managed by creating a continuity between the old and the new in the handing down of tradition, and paranoid anxieties by firmly establishing the external world as benign. Identity is not in 'crisis' here, for it is plainly and harmoniously scripted within the community. We refer to this subject as the 'folk consumer'.

The classical superego is closely allied with the folk consumer. The self is tightly wrapped within the security of the community, and bound to the momentum of tradition. The foregrounding of the group leaves little room for individual freedom. A modern reading, which values mobility and agency, might view the community commitment portrayed here as a burden—an enslavement of the individual to the group. The advertisement does nothing to acknowledge or pacify the modern anxiety about the tyranny of the group, but rather assumes the reader will take the leap of faith necessary to read the words and image romantically, and thus nestle within the cosy communities symbolically constructed for the subject to inhabit.

The mass consumer: modernity, economies of scale, and mass consumption

This invitation to identification through personal group membership and practice fades in the 1960s as the modern individual begins to take flight from community shackles. Creatives lose their loyalty to the past and increasingly turn to the framing device of the present. More and more emphasis is placed upon the theme of modernity. Time is reworked, from the cyclical pattern of seasons to a linear succession approaching a continual betterment. This sense of time plays to the modern ethos of self-development, in which identity becomes more a process of self-construction. Life is no longer lived through the repetitive enactment of traditional practices, but is 'moving on'. To find a place in this new shifting sand will require a subject who is alert to 'keeping up with the times'. The advertisements make it plain that the desired identity is modern. To be a member of the modern tribe will require a new set of skills which displace roofbuilding. We are no longer praised for blindly following tradition, but for our choice of consumer goods and services. Ownership surpasses labour as the channel to identity. To be modern will necessitate knowledge of what is in and out of fashion, and the advertisements provide this important information, by dictating taste. Two 1960s advertisements provide some illustration of this.

In the first advertisement (for Lloyds), the television set is highlighted as a pre-eminent status symbol, and as the necessary *entrée* into modern identity. The introduction of new communication technologies throughout the centuries, from the printing press to computers, has been heralded as the sign of a new age, and the introduction of television to Britain in the 1950s was no exception. An antenna on one's roof signalled to the community that one had arrived. As a populist medium television was inclusive, uniting people through shared viewership rather than social background. Legitimate identity can now be gained from possessing modern consumer goods and engaging with services. However, one consumer good does not a modern make. While the television set is a good beginning, to be modern requires a constant array of consumer goods and services, including a cheque book. The banks begin to highlight specific services, over their general institutional character.

The advertisement plays upon anxiety about finding one's place in the modern condition: 'Have you ever reflected that you are too modern a person not to have a banking account?' We are praised for our television possession, at the same time as we are threatened by the reminder that modern identity is fragile and will require vigilant attention to ensure that one possesses the correct consumer accoutrements to be modern.

Another Lloyds advertisement continues the theme of educating people towards modern subjectivity. 'Old fashioned banking is out!', reads the caption below an image of a young couple holding a large piggy bank. The couple are positioned in front of a particularly clean-lined modern building. They look forward into the distance—the convention which gestures progressivism. The piggy bank is large, cumbersome, and looks awkward; it is a burden in the new, clean, modern setting. Past practices are denigrated, not applauded, as tradition no longer aids individuals in their quests for recognition.

Both of these 1960 advertisements script an aggressive appeal to change. The earlier respect for the sanctity of community practice and group identity is lost as the advertisements urge readers to update and transform. They appeal to rationality, providing us with 'reasons why'. To ease the transition to these new relations and identities, the advertisements (and a host of others from the 1960s) highlight friendliness. Instead of managing paranoid anxieties through the consistency of traditional practices, we are offered containment through reference to safety and privacy. Saving money is morally valued, and depicted as a difficult undertaking made easier by banking support. Appealing to the modern faith in technical excellence, we are provided with experts to guide us on our financial way. The universal subject is appealed to through the emphasis that there will be no social embarrassment around the amount of money presented to open a new account.

These advertisements illustrate a shift from a subject rooted in community to an appeal to a modern, universal individual, whom we refer to as the mass consumer. The subjectivity of the mass consumer is offered a new sense of liberty and freedom, which the folk consumer was denied. The mass consumers are encouraged to take hold of their own identity construction, yet they are also offered social containment, for the advertisements offer guidance in the projects of identity construction. Self-development is situated within uniform mass consumer goods. To be modern, in the context of the 1960s advertisements, was to be like everyone else, to possess what everyone else had, to undertake the practices of the mass. While large numbers of people still lacked the new goods and services of the growing British consumer society, the subject position of being modern provided a point of distinction. However, once large numbers of people had a television set and a bank account, the status appeal and perhaps also the identity value of uniform goods and services waned. And more profoundly, perhaps, the cultural valuation of membership of a bloc of consumers was changing, as a new drive for distinction and individuality began to emerge.

The distinctive consumer: the growing need to be recognised
The 1970 advertisement shown in Figure 9.9 (page 134) provides a summary of the central dilemma of the mass consumer, by underscoring the evacuation of identity which accompanies the sense of a growing mass. The people who surround the subject in the advertisement are not community members, but impersonal faces who swarm, overpower and eradicate the subject's identity. To contain anxiety about identity loss, the bank is presented as a distinctive site through which one can claim identity. The advertisement responds to the anxieties of non-recognition and impersonalisation through noting that the bank is able to recognise the subject as a unique and individuated person. The individual is elevated from the mass, through a rhetorical attention to distinction.

The second advertisement here, from 1975 (see Figure 9.10, page 134), continues the theme of social distinction, and creates a resolution which is successful enough to be taken up by a number of other advertisements of this decade. Group membership and emulation continue to be important, but the advertisement notably expands the range of subject positions (albeit in gender-stereotyped ways). Membership is reflected more through diversification. The image is a mosaic, a unity of separate entities. While a sense of community is still present, it comprises unique individuals bound together by their difference. The universal theme is continued, by the selection of characters who are neither extraordinary, nor elite, but everyday and typical. The pitch continues to be welcoming, for the subject is still positioned as timid. Typical of advertisements from the 1970s, a long list of options including insurance, cheque books, interest and safety, is offered to the reader. The advertisement remains reason-rich, continuing to appeal to a rational subject.

It also might be seen as more subtle rhetorically than its 1960s counterpart. The older style of address blatantly informed readers of what was in and what was out and expected them to conform. It assumed that modernity did not have to be justified. Here the reader is reasoned with through a 'critical mass' argument, which emphasises that more and more people are banking with the Royal Bank. It seeks to convince readers of the bank's positive qualities and trustworthiness through signalling that many people place faith in the bank. But the fear of conformity is addressed by presenting an image which registers diversity. The advertisement plays both to the desire for social belonging, and the need for individual distinctiveness.

The distinctive consumer and the problem of separation anxiety

As the distinctive consumer rises, so does separation anxiety. The 1970 NatWest advertisement (Figure 9.11, page 135) attempts to contain the fear of the absence or loss of the object. The foreboding of abandonment creates a preoccupation with closeness, time, and access. The advertisement refers to mother, the most psychically potent object of loss. Mother here is not recognised as an individuated being with her own needs and wants, but exists only to care for her child. She is an omnipresent giver who is available at any time, and does not require justification for the demands made of her. The advertisement 'reminds' us of the importance of the connection between mother and self for psychic survival. This desire for closeness to the giving capacities of mother is linked to the closeness and accessibility of money through banking technology. The advertisement centres on the notion of unlimited access, which is available 'anytime, day or night'. The image plays upon the theme of separation anxiety by using photographic techniques to fuse the consumer to the bank machine. The advertisement does not confront the inevitability of separation, but rather offers a regressive sense of unrealistic fail-proof support, an image of desperate unity created at a moment in history when subjectivities were becoming increasingly fragmented and competitive.

The sovereign consumer: freedom to consume

By the 1980s separation anxiety is eclipsed by a new emphasis on narcissistic anxiety, which emanates from yet another new consumer position. The subject of the 1980s advertisements ceases to be concerned with social distinction, instead being preoccupied with access to money and consumption. The bank ceases to market itself as a solid localised institution, and becomes increasingly transparent and virtual, an ever-present conduit through which money is accessed. (This shift to virtuality is on the basis of an increase in automatic and telephone banking services.) Subjective concerns shift from 'who' we are, to 'what' we want. Identity is offered through consumption, a theme encountered in previous advertisements, but the banks no longer dictate consumer choice. The advertisements promote access to money, but leave the individual relatively free to make their consumption choices. Luxury items are presented in the advertisements, but the items shown are not valorised over other choices as they were in the 1960s. The gold standard of mass goods which marked the modern identity in the 1960s is broken. There is no romantic community, no brazen modern position, and no 'uniqueness' for the subject to take refuge in, for the 1980s' subject has no need to be told who they are, they are simply reminded that they need money and they need to consume. The lack of social restraint and the deferral to this subject cause us to refer to the 1980 character as the 'sovereign consumer'.

A 1980 NatWest advertisement (Figure 9.12, page 135) constructs a home for the sovereign consumer. 'Any car. Any model. Any colour. Any questions?' illustrates the offer of a new freedom of taste. The copy notes, 'You're free to buy any new or second hand car that you fancy.' The individual is emancipated from the bureaucracy of taste, as now subjects are reminded to follow their own 'fancy', instead of being made anxious about whether their consumer choices measure up to modern standards. The advertisement projects a new attitude towards money by underscoring the simplicity of obtaining credit. The consumer is promised freedom from the stressful social ritual of being formally judged in person by the bank manager. These social conventions are rendered part of the horrors of the past. With these old social rituals out of the way, financial transactions can be undertaken with a new quickness. While the consumer is required to make an 'initial contribution' there is no reference to the amount, hence we can assume it is trivial. The Lloyds advertisement 'Head for the shops. We'll foot the bills' (Figure 9.13, page 136) also highlights the ease of access to cash and the freedom of consumption. The impulsiveness of the subject is acknowledged and celebrated: 'You see them. You like them. You buy them.' This emphasis on the caprice of consumption contrasts with the morally prudent saver of the 1970s.

We are no longer appealed to as timid consumers in need of reassuring, but as subjects capable of making our own decisions. A striking 1987 television advertisement illustrates the confidence of the new consumer. This sovereign consumer has no anxieties about meeting the manager, and actively seeks out and challenges authority. A young man in a suit enters the bank manager's office to find two bank representatives sitting behind a desk. He takes a seat and begins to state articulately that he will expect a sizeable overdraft with no penalties, preferred loan options, and no additional service charges. The managers listen to the man's demands in blinking awe. In a classic role reversal, it is the employees of the banks who are now presented as timid in the face of the sovereign consumer. They ask to be excused in order to check with their superiors, and upon their return, they inform the young man, to their own amazement, that all of his demands will be met. The consumer leaves with an air of confidence.

In portraying the instantaneous fulfilment of desires and a lacking of respect for established social relations, we take the 1980s advertisements to be symptomatic of the narcissistic position. Money becomes an extension of self which enables the effortless fulfilment of desires with minimum interference from others. As the banks become transparent, references to social relations and social bonds disappear. The relations surrounding money are now almost completely instrumentalised: money simply spills forth from machines, or is handed over when a form is filled out. We have discussed in Chapter 7 how narcissism might be seen as coping orientated or status orientated. The 1980s advertisements appeal to the 'coping' narcissist's desire to stand on their own unaided by social supports, and this position might be seen as the logical end point of the increased individuation of the consumer which began in the 1960s. Like all subject positions, however, this brazen narcissist comes with its own negativity: the alienation associated with an individuated life of consumption, and—shadowing the appeals to pleasure—a deep guilt (see Chapter 6).

The amalgamated consumer: old consumers made new
New subject positions offered in the 1990s react against the sovereign consumer. There is a reclaiming of older subject positions, which are refreshed for the times. For example, looking at a current (March 1999) campaign for NatWest one can see the reappearance of a 1970s appeal. The campaign follows the old theme of illustrating the lengths the bank will go to in order to provide access (returning to an engagement with separation anxieties). Bank employees are pictured on top of flying stunt planes or kicking it up in the chorus line to close the gap between the consumer and the bank. Also, the elite consumer is brought back, as many banks are promoting services to the high-end financial consumer. A central anxiety for these 1990s consumers is the fear that they are not taking full advantage of their money options. A recent advertisement showed consumers' pound notes slaving away, as if to provide evidence that the bank was making money for them. In the international money markets, money needs to work. It no longer has the luxury of sitting idly in a bank account, and readers are 'reminded' that they must keep their money in constant circulation. The consumer remains sovereign, but is now seen as in need of information upon which to base decisions. This renders the majority of the 1990s advertisements very high in Practical values, and low in Social, drawing on an eclectic mix of subject positions. However, a campaign unique to the 1990s appeared on the margin which is exceptional enough to warrant close attention, for it appeals to a new ethically concerned consumer, who might be considered the contradictory twin of the sovereign consumer.

The ethical consumer and the depressive position
Two advertisements from a 1990s Co-operative campaign (Figures 9.14 and 9.15, pages 136 and 137) speak to the ethical consumer. They offer strong appeal to the depressive position (see Chapter 6), by playing upon the psychic guilt associated with the belief that industrial-technological societies and consumer cultures are a threat to the sanctity and health of others and the natural world. The advertisements blur popular cultural forms to dramatic effect. Both of the images conform to the conventions of documentary news 'realism', and convey the sense of clandestine journalism and 'as it happens' truth. The advertisements also mimic the fund raising appeals of environmental

and animal rights groups. The bird image bears a marked resemblance to the infamous Benetton advertisements which similarly drew upon the theme of corporate pollution of the high seas.

The words which accompany the representations work hard to close out any rational justification for these acts against nature, by referring to 'needless' pollution and informing the readers that the rabbits are being exploited for the frivolous sphere of cosmetics—the shallow domain of women and surfaces. Although the reader is absolved from any direct connection to these senseless acts of destruction, because the blame is placed squarely on companies, the advertisements speak to a broad sense of social responsibility. They provide an antidote to late modern helplessness through an active way to combat destructiveness. This promise of the containment of badness is, though, relatively untaxing and calls upon minimum commitment.

The 'subject positions' offered by advertisements are therefore rarely stable. Contradictions with the wider culture soon arise, and subvert the commercial aim of communicating with target populations, and so push the creatives towards new modes of positioning the consumer. It will soon be possible to see how this process has worked out across the 1990s, and how significant an element the ethical position may be in the make-up of the 'amalgamated' consumer in the coming period.

Note
1.   1968 address to the Bankers Institute on the future of British banking.

Chapter 10

THE DEMOCRATISATION OF CREDIT

In this chapter we present the results of our study of credit card advertising, following the same broad format as in the previous two chapters. Firstly we sketch the history of the credit card, then we describe the main changes over time in advertisements for cards. We then consider differences between brands, and their relationship to overall trends. Finally we consider the evidence concerning audience responses gathered in a small number of focus groups; this small triangulation links coding procedures not with individual interview data, as in Chapter 8, but with transcripts of group discussions.

As described in Chapter 7, approximately 250 credit card advertisements from the 1970s on were coded. The sample included a number of advertisements for 'charge' cards rather than credit cards as more precisely defined; the difference is that with charge cards (of which American Express and Diners Club are the brand names) there is usually no limit to the amount of money which can be charged to the card, and the cardholder must repay the full amount charged at the end of each month, rather than using the card as a source of rolling credit.

HISTORICAL CONTEXT

We cannot here provide a contextual history going as far back (to 1950) as we have in other chapters, since these cards were not introduced to Britain until the late 1960s. Detailed accounts of historical and technical matters can be found in Stephenson (1993) and Goode (1974); Ritzer (1995) also has some useful background. The present-day credit card originated in the U.S. in the late 1940s, though earlier systems based on retailers' credit extend back at least to the beginning of the century. The modern credit card is issued by a financial institution. The present-day difference between credit cards narrowly defined and charge cards, though diminishing, stems back to their different origins. In 1950 in the U.S. the Diners Club organisation began to issue a card which was accepted by a network of hotels and restaurants (hence the term 'T&E' card—for travel and entertainment). The American Express 'T&E' card appeared in 1958. During the 1960s various American banks introduced and developed the bank credit card system, which soon consolidated into the two major rival networks now known as Visa and Mastercard.

The introduction in 1966 of the Barclaycard (licensed by what was to become the Visa service) marked the arrival of credit cards in the UK Barclays' British banking rivals joined forces to introduce the Access card in 1972, and quickly linked it to the American rival to Visa. Card ownership and use grew strongly into the 1980s, and an increasing number of people came to hold both of the two cards available. While Visa and Mastercard dominate the credit card market, a bewildering profusion of differently branded cards has developed, as more individual banks have launched their own cards linked to one of the two networks. A further level of branding occurs when organisations of various sorts link with banks to offer their 'own' cards to their members or employees. Many individuals have become multiple card-holders, such that the marketing task for the card issuers is as much concerned with achieving regular use as with recruiting card-holders.

At the same time the 'T&E' or 'charge' card has persisted, mainly in the business sector. Credit cards have raised their credit limits and so narrowed the gap between credit and charge cards, with the remaining distinctive features of the latter—fees, and a restricted number of outlets where the card can be used—being disadvantageous. Nonetheless the American Express card has continued to grow, and indeed during the 1980s entered the mass market.

The expansion of card use in Britain (where, compared to some other European countries, cards enjoyed a rapid growth rate—see Frazer, 1985) is clearly part of the general expansion of consumer credit which we have already discussed in Chapter 9. Hire-purchase had grown considerably in the post-war period (leading to its regulation in the Hire-Purchase Act of 1965), and bank loans were becoming more available (see Chapter 9), though store cards were slow to develop in Britain. However, the credit card brought an unprecedented scope and flexibility for the consumer seeking retail credit. Such was the rate of expansion of credit in the 1960s that a government report was commissioned (the Crowther Committee review of consumer credit was published in 1971), and the Consumer Credit Act of 1974 followed. This included a provision to give the Secretary of State powers to regulate what may appear in a credit advertisement. These regulations mainly govern what information and combinations of information must or must not be given in advertisements, but are not likely to influence the frequency of the variables we recorded (e.g. Sayer, 1988).

There was an initial pedagogic task of card advertising, in that a mass market had to be educated in the use of this new device and reassured as to its prudence and general moral character. In general though, despite

the fact that some of our focus group material suggests that some deep morally-grounded anxieties about card use persist (see below), advertising during most of the thirty or so years in question has been in a context of an expanding market where there are a few major competitors and very little difference between the products advertised. Given also the somewhat abstract nature of the commodity, one might expect that this is a sector in which advertisements have had to engage in especially intense symbolic work.

Given, further, the origins of charge cards in business use, we would expect that some of this symbolic work would be around questions of status, i.e. that the identity work involved would be linked to the competitive and aspirational modes of self-definition usually taken to be characteristic of much business culture. Like the mobile phone two decades later, however, the card rapidly passed from being a status business tool to a mass market item, a 'lifestyle' device adopted by many different kinds of people in their roles as active consumers. Card advertising should therefore add important new dimensions to the picture we have already derived from bank advertisements of how in this period more people have been drawn into more active, proactive and ambitious consumption through the expansion of credit and financial services. While that expansion has to be understood in terms of its economic and commercial drivers, it necessarily involves a substantial psycho-cultural change, which our research is intended to trace.

At the same time as it occupies an important place in the transition to a full-blown consumer society, and should therefore bear close examination for clues about the psycho-social nature of that transition, credit card advertising has not—with some exceptions—had a reputation for being very engaging. The functional and partly abstract nature of the commodity itself, as simply a means to acquire other more interesting commodities, both invites and yet also frustrates the copy-writer's talent for embedding the commodity in a rich symbolic matrix. Whether through the conservatism of the advertisers or the caution of the agencies, everyday impressions suggest that much credit card advertising has been dull.

CHANGES OVER TIME

Stable distribution of value types
As with the banking advertisements, and in line with everyday experience, the most common values across the whole sample were Practical ones. If we consider the raw (unstandardised) means, there is

an average of 3.4 Practical messages per advertisement, compared with 1.8 Social and 1.2 Sensual. There is also a preponderance of Coping over Status anxieties (the latter being less frequent than the Neutral/non-specific category as well), suggesting that despite the considerable historical loading of status on charge card brands, the card sector as a whole is one in which more anxiety is mobilised around the individual's performative competence than around his or her comparative social identity.

A time-split analysis was conducted, with 1990 as the split-line. This means the analysis is not directly comparable with those conducted in other sectors, but an earlier split was not possible given the time range of our sample. The analysis shows that this broad distribution between the three types of value has probably held since the inception of card advertising.

The shifts observed in this time-split analysis are not sufficiently large for us to interpret them as trends, and moreover lacking an interval series of sampling points we do not have an extended profile of changes in their distribution. We would not have expected to find here a replication of the trends in bank advertisements, with a dwindling of Social values, since the card as a product is by definition detached from the social matrix of the bank as an institution and so did not participate in the dispersal of authority from that institution. On the contrary, the card by definition is a *product* of that dispersal; it is positioned from its inception as part of the new, postmodern regime of consumption, in which the autonomous consumer putatively has instant access to goods, and has a choice of financial services.

In this context it is perhaps surprising that Social values have the presence that they do in our sample. Some of these reflect the need for any new product to be anchored in the terrain of the familiar, in some recognisable value context. In addition there was a need for the consumer to be educated in the use of this radically new product, especially in the early years when many consumers were not used to paying by any means other than cash. The educational task was carried partly by Practical messages, especially those of convenience and credit, tellingly captured in the famous slogans in Access advertisements about your 'flexible friend'—a morally as well as practically reassuring image. The presence and persistence of Social values suggests that the need to attach an aura of sociality to the commodity and its use is an irreducible task of the advertising communication, even when the commodity is as highly abstracted and individualised as the credit card.

Change in practical, social and sensual values over time

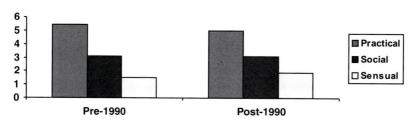

Figure 10.1 Standardised frequencies for different types of value

As we describe below, the small absolute gains in Social and Sensual frequencies (which as Figure 10.1 shows is also a relative gain for Sensual values) are the result of some brands making deliberate advertising choices that involved them in the use of more of these values in their advertisements. Later advertisements are therefore more likely to show a spread of values across the three categories, moderating the dominance of Practical ones.

Some individual variables show sharper changes. The Practical values 'Inducements', 'Interest rate' and 'Other anxiety-neutral' all show rises. The one Practical value to show the largest fall, 'Wideness of use', probably reflects the fact that as cards become more widely accepted and used, this is increasingly taken for granted. The largest rise amongst Social values is for Protection, with Exclusivity showing the largest drop.

There is no very strong overall effect here but the indications are that a risk-oriented concern with the integrated benefits of the commodity as manifold protection is once again a dominant theme in the discourse of advertisements in this particular sector. This observation is strengthened

Change in coping and status anxiety over time

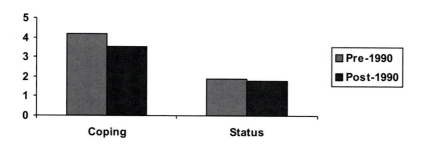

Figure 10.2 Standardised time-split frequencies for manifest anxiety

THE DEMOCRATISATION OF CREDIT

by a consideration of the 'manifest anxiety' scores, as presented in the next section.

Credit, cards and coping

Over time there is little shift in the pattern of relative anxiety frequencies when these are summed across the whole sample. What movement there is suggests a weakening of coping, but in relation to anxiety-neutral elements more than to Status.

However, this relative stability masks some quite marked changes within particular brands, which when examined suggest that there is in fact a strong cultural trend towards more coping and less Status anxiety, as we have found in other sectors.

The management of anxiety

The picture here is of a strongly containing message strategy dominating the sector both before and after 1990. The standardised container score for the whole sample is 8.5 before 1990, and 8.1 since. Across all brands (though see below) and in relation to all anxieties, a strongly structured frame of containment based on Practical values and on the 'Social A' value of Universality, is in evidence. The rise after 1990 of the further 'Social A' value of Protection adds to the strength of the risk-orientation, though its contribution to the overall container score is offset by rises in some contained variables, which we discuss below.

This convergence effect can also be seen in our measure of 'containment'. Overall this was very high, in relation to all kinds of anxiety. Across the whole sample there was a discernible though not very large decrease in the difference between 'container' and 'contained' scores, as seen in Figure 10.3 below (where the 'CR' score is a standardised one, so the corresponding 'CD' score will be 10—CR). The narrowing is greatest for the mass market credit card brands, which had

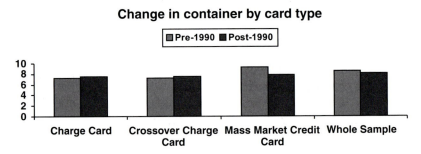

Change in container by card type

Pre-1990 Post-1990

Figure 10.3   Standardised container (CR) scores

very few contained elements in the first time-split sample. Indeed the two charge cards moved in the opposite direction, acquiring stronger containers and thus moving closer to the profile of the credit card.

Overall these data show credit and charge card advertising to be the most 'contained' of the three sectors we have studied, and as one might have predicted the least likely therefore to be the occasion for the kind of 'identity work' we defined in Chapter 7. However the movement towards more tension within the advertisements for the mass market brands suggests that advertising in this sector is moving towards a more balanced normative strategy, albeit one still more skewed than in the other sectors we have studied.

DIFFERENCES BETWEEN BRANDS

The commercial origin of this particular study meant that particularly intensive analysis was conducted of brand differences. This yielded some conclusions of considerable interest to our academic objectives, however. It was found that the advertisements for the mass market credit cards (within which we did not distinguish between ordinary and 'gold' varieties) and those for the charge card which had successfully 'crossed over' into a mass market showed very different anxiety profiles and trends from those for the other charge card, which had a declining market share. Essentially the credit card advertisements, which had always contained strong coping appeals, showed an increased predominance of these over Status-related elements. Those for the 'crossover' charge card showed an anxiety 'crossover', with coping replacing Status as the dominant appeal. Those for the other charge card, however, showed an inverse movement in which Status appeals moved to predominance from a previously more balanced position. It is not our concern here whether these trends in advertisement content are best seen as a cause or as an effect of their market share; the key point is that the dominant kind of identity work on offer through these advertisements is for a number of brands more about the management of coping rather than of Status anxieties.

It seemed therefore that our sampling procedure had led to a dominant trend being obscured in the overall sample. For brand comparison purposes we had ensured that there were substantial numbers of charge card advertisements, which had skewed the overall profile. When we disaggregated the sample it became evident that the brands with largest market share, which we knew also to have had by far the largest advertising spend, showed a clear shift from Status to Coping anxieties.

A related though more complex picture was present in relation to values profiles. In the overall sample, as we have noted, there was a convergence of standardised frequencies across the three values categories, indicating that messages were becoming more balanced combinations of elements of all three value types. This differs from our findings in the car and banking sectors. This intermixing trend would have been even more clear had it not been for the opposite trend shown in the advertisements of the declining brand. This showed a relative weakening of Social and Sensual content, when in the sector as a whole the 'maturing' of the market had provided a basis for a symbolic enrichment of this previously 'boring' commodity—at the same time as 'practicality' remained strongly dominant overall and continued to provide the main value basis for advertisement readers to engage with.

Brand comparisons with regard to container/contained scores also show an interesting contrast. As Figure 10.3 shows, a mass market credit card shows a shift which the two charge cards do not towards more 'contained' values, primarily. We understand this as another aspect of the same market convergence which has led to most cards becoming strongly Coping-oriented. In this case, we assume that the overwhelmingly container-based strategy of earlier years was proving unsustainable once cards had become commonplace and brand competition has intensified; there is perhaps a minimum of libidinal interest which advertisements must evoke once a market has 'matured' to the point where it is no longer satisfied just with information. We would expect the overall level of contained values in this sector to stabilise at this level, as the intensity of anxieties about risk in relation to financial matters is likely to restrict any further closing of the CR/CD gap to the levels seen in other sectors.

FOCUS GROUP DATA

Four focus groups were conducted, a basic aim of which (as with the individual interviews conducted about car advertisements) was to establish whether consumers' perceptions of advertisements were in the same terms as ours. If our conceptual approach is a valid one, it ought to be possible to confirm that the values/anxieties matrix is consistent with the spontaneous responses of target consumers. If in the course of even a small number of groups it was to be found that the matrix offered a framework for the consistent and comprehensive recording of respondents' descriptions of the advertisements and their associations to them, then this could be taken as such confirmation.

Four groups of around eight people each were recruited such that each group was made up of holders of the same card. One mass market card in fact had two groups differentiated by age, i.e. under and over 35 years. (It was felt that some homogeneity of experience and social status would be most likely to facilitate discussion.)

The groups began, before any advertisements were shown to them (indeed, before they knew much about what the groups were about or what product they related to), with an innovative use of projective stimuli. Three specially commissioned drawings were shown to the groups. They were of social situations in which the use of credit or charge cards is common: a department store, a restaurant and an airport. The drawings showed some social interactions in an ambiguous way. The basic principle of projective testing is that when shown an ambiguous or abstract stimulus and asked to imagine what narrative or figurative content it might have, the respondent will answer in terms guided by their unconscious phantasies, since the actual external material prescribes no particular answer. The main content of a response must therefore come from inside the respondent rather than from the stimulus. Projective techniques have a long history in market research as well as in clinical work; they have been used to explore consumers' feelings about goods and brands. Our purpose here was to use them to map out the values and anxieties likely to be mobilised in those situations where this particular kind of product, a credit or charge card, was likely to be used.

The respondents were asked to imagine what they thought might be going on in the scenes depicted, and to construct a short story around each scene. They wrote down their responses privately to each drawing in turn, then were asked to tell the group what they saw. Next, four print advertisements (selected to embody different values/anxieties profiles) were shown in turn, and respondents asked to write down their reactions to the two which had most impact on them (one positively, one negatively). Again, they were subsequently asked to read out what they had written, as the basis for a group discussion.

For both the projective stimuli and the advertisements, the material produced by individuals and in group discussions was plotted onto coding forms of the kind used in the advertisements coding study. The coding and plotting procedures are not strictly equivalent. While we have consistent ways of weighting the elements in an advertisement, the written and spoken responses of interviewees cannot be so easily weighted, especially in group data. Repetition by someone of a particular response might, for example, represent the importance or

	PRAC	SOC	SEN	CR	COPE	STAT
Readers	3.3	3.8	2.9	5.4	3.9	1.2

Figure 10.4   Standardised focus group responses to all stimulus materials

complexity of an element in the image or advertisement, or might reflect a repetitiousness. So we did not use this data in the same quantitative way as with the advertisement coding, to derive profiles for each message or stimulus, but instead we wanted to establish whether the content of respondents' comments and associations could be handled by our coding form. In the car advertisements interview study, we were able to produce 'reader' profiles for each advertisement, since for each individual interviewee it was possible make the binary yes/no decision for each variable. Here, a group could produce a number of 'yes' responses. Rather than comparing our own coding profiles for each individual advertisement with those derivable from the group data (as we compared 'researcher' with 'reader' profiles in the car study), we produced an aggregate profile from all responses in all groups, including to the projective stimuli (Figure 10.4).

While obviously unable to check readings of specific advertisements, this method arguably was a more exacting test of the overall adequacy of our coding framework to capture the full range of relevant responses, since it included associations not only to advertisements but to situations of product use.

The material elicited in response to the projective stimuli gave substantial confirmation of the appropriateness of the coding matrix. All values expressed could be meaningfully located in one of our three value categories. The relative distribution of values is different from that which our coding procedure found in our advertisement sample, with Social and Sensual values both being more frequently registered here. Both the projective stimuli and the actual advertisements shown released more values of these kinds in the associations of the groups than were recorded as features in coding. Most of this can be attributed to the reiterative quality of group discussion; further work would be necessary to establish whether these 'reader' frequency distributions are a good index of 'dominance', in the sense of showing which were the values with most impact (see Chapter 8; we did not score this variable in the credit card study), or whether people talked more about these kinds of values not because these were the most powerful elements of the advertisement but because they are more easily talked about, or generate more conversation, than the Practical.

Approximately 90% of the anxieties detected were of the coping or status types, with coping strongly dominant overall. The exceptions were those underlying more dramatic responses with story-lines involving, for example, crime and imprisonment, exile, lost children or potential violence. These anxieties (linked to feelings of guilt, insecurity or aggression) are of universal importance, but are not specifically related to the product-related dimensions of the scenes shown, i.e. to the use of cards.

In three of the groups the responses to the advertisements shown did however bring out a new specific (and negative) Practical value, related to coping anxiety, which we had not previously identified: the possibility of sinking into ever-greater debt. It may be that an attitude towards credit combining fear with disapproval may have more residual life than we had supposed.

One of the advertisements (for American Express: see Figure 10.5, page 137) also elicited another kind of negative response, one linked to an old fear amongst advertisers: the possibility that a negative element in the advertisement, even when proposed as the problem to which the product is the solution, may dominate the reader's experience of the advertisement and colour associations to the product. Though some respondents were impressed by the idea of strong practical support from a card company in such circumstances, others were alienated by a strongly negative Sensual value, carried in the presentation of debilitating illness in an apparently rough place.

	PRAC	SOC	SEN	CR	COPE	STAT
Researcher	2	5	2	7	5	1

Figure 10.6   Coding profile for 'sick' advertisement

The best-liked of the advertisements used was the 'O'Shea' one for Visa (Figure 10.7, page 138), chosen by us for use in this study as an outstanding example of universalistic, coping-oriented social values, linked to clear Practical and Sensual statements.

	PRAC	SOC	SEN	CR	COPE	STAT
Researcher	3	3	3	7	7	0

Figure 10.8   Coding profile for 'O'Shea' advertisement

The practical is in the promise of very wide and easy use, while the sensual elements are in the explicit reference to drink and the connotation of the pleasures of Irish rural life. This is also what the respondents saw in it, most often expressed as the fusion of the modern with the traditional, enabling the convenience of modern life to be taken into the most humble backwater, there to enjoy the simple folk pleasures.

We end this chapter with this advertisement because it also captures an important dimension of the whole expansion of credit, of which the Visa card is of course a major component. From being a cosmopolitan, sophisticated differentiator of a culturally specific identity, with connotations of 'business' and wealth, the card has come to be an all-purpose item for the 'everyperson'. It can sit comfortably in humble places or sophisticated ones, and it is a bridge joining a modern, abstract regime of convenience to an endless variety of culturally specific settings. Like the identity offered to the card-holder, the card is mobile without limits, culturally omnivorous, respectful, and oriented to the simple, basic things in life while having a wordly competence. Credit is the right of the universal citizen.

Chapter 11

Most advertisements are highly ephemeral, yet in their efforts to catch the eyes, ears and minds of the public they are finely attuned to the values of their time. Like other fleeting entertainments, such as those provided by reportage of the private lives of public figures, their light narratives will be stamped with the weight of the anxieties which bear upon many of their readers, and with the kinds of hope and reassurance that at any particular time we offer to ourselves. While it cannot be proved that they do this with accuracy, we argued in Chapter 2 that the position of the advertising industry in relation to its clients (for whom it must appear to know about consumers) and to the extensive labours of commercial research give good grounds for assuming that advertisements do embody a high degree of cultural sensitivity. We saw in Chapter 3 that while for some students of advertising this means that advertisement content follows repetitive cyclical patterns, in keeping with cultural cycles, for others the elements of repetition are subsumed within a process of change in which history does not repeat itself; instead new configurations of values and new communicative strategies are seen to emerge. Our own empirical data points in this latter direction. We have found some progressive shifts in value content, and some changes which we think cannot be ascribed to fluctuation.

Moreover, as publicly available cultural materials, advertisements can be used by readers as inputs to the everyday work of identity-development and identity-management. In Chapter 4 we extensively reviewed the dominant paradigms in the social and cultural theory of advertising, and found them to be negligent of this important dimension. We set out to understand the content of advertisements in a way that was oriented primarily towards the subjective, psychic context of their reception, or more precisely the psycho-social context. This requires taking a broad view, and seeing advertising as one of the social spaces within which low-key but complex dramatisations of contemporary predicaments can be found. 'Identity work', as we developed the idea in Chapter 5, is about exploring and trying to resolve these predicaments, and is centrally concerned with anxiety and its management. Anxiety is both social, as the cultural consequence of de-traditionalisation, and psychological, as an intrinsic property of the mind and a crucial factor in individual development. At the individual level the process of mental association is constantly generating anxiety and seeking ways of dealing with it, and in providing rich materials for associative work, advertisements will inevitably play a part in the everyday management of anxiety and therefore of identity work (see Chapter 6). While it might be objected that advertisements embody the particular anxieties (both cultural and personal) of the people who create them, we would incline to the view that advertising creatives—as cultural intermediaries—are adept at expressing wider concerns and aspirations. In this sense advertising *is* a mirror, as Fox and, in a different way, Marchand have suggested (see Chapter 3). Moreover the social presence of the advertisement creates a space, in front of the advertisement so to speak, in which the anxieties of readers are mobilised.

A psychoanalytic sociology can yield a complex set of categories for mapping cultural values and differentiating between modes of identity work, as we hope to have shown in Chapter 7, and these categories should be of relevance in many fields beyond advertising. When used as a framework for analysing advertisement content, they yield data from which we can draw one major conclusion. This is that in all three product sectors we have studied, Practical values are the strongest element of the advertising message. Moreover they are increasing in strength in the car and banking sectors. We therefore conclude that an orientation to the good or service as a practical entity is much stronger than many theoretical characterisations of late modernity might predict. While the trend towards deeper immersion in the practical may not be found in a study of television advertisements alone, the evidence we have is sufficient for us to suggest that in one dimension at least our relationship to goods is developing towards a kind of neo-materialism or neo-pragmatism. To some extent we might see this as encouragement for the current awakening of sociological interest in materiality and in the importance of objects, though since two of the sectors we studied were of non-material, financial services we could not comfortably discuss many of our findings in those terms. The 'materialism' of which our advertisements speak is a broad one, including a concern with interest rates and warranties as much as, if not more, than with the material object in itself. Moreover it is not a narrow utilitarianism; the aim of the advertisements seems to be to posit the product, or the financial institution, as providing a wide-ranging package of supports, guarantees, facilities, etc., such that the consumer feels held and protected against life's uncertainties and dangers. The commodity is

the medium through which the containing power of a wider social fabric is brought to the individual.

This trend is accompanied by one much more in tune with common-sense and theoretical prediction, which is the decline in status-related anxieties relative to those which we have termed 'coping'-related. This reinforces both the familiar sociological picture of de-traditionalisation and de-classification, and the less familiar idea that an important contemporary response to these processes is the adoption of a pragmatism which is broad in scope but also very attentive to the detail of the ways in which the commodity can help deal with life's problems.

The somewhat different position of credit and charge advertising in relation to these trends, with neither Practical nor Coping values showing absolute increases over time, can be understood with reference to the specific features of this sector. The very high practical content of the earlier advertisements had to give way a little when a richer symbolic discourse for this very abstract good developed, while our analysis by brand indicated that a reduction in status anxieties was in fact occurring in the sector as a whole.

Our prediction in Chapter 7 from the 'reflexivity' thesis that the tension between 'containing' and 'contained' elements of advertisements would increase, i.e. that the frequencies of variables in these two categories would converge, was not borne out. There was a slight movement towards greater equality of forces in the card advertisements, but from a base of very high containment. There are two possible ways of interpreting this finding. The first is that the kind of reflexivity which we sought to capture in the 'container/contained' score, involving the activation of a wide range of cultural and psychic elements and the possibility therein of new combinations of elements and of new 'settlements' between different kinds of values, is not occurring in the sphere of consumption, at least not in the sectors we have studied. The second possibility is that this idea may be of relevance in these sectors, but that we failed to operationalise it adequately, either because the concept of containment is not relevant to the notion of reflexivity, or because our attempt to map it onto our coding categories has not succeeded.

We think the latter version of the second possibility is the most likely, and hope in further work to clarify this issue. It does not, for example, seem very plausible to suggest that the dynamic between restraint and release has ceased to be of consequence in these fields of consumption. In the work of Elias (1994) such a dynamic is seen to be central to the process of modernisation, and consumption is a major field in which it is played out. Both the car and money are objects around which we might expect there to be continuing deep tensions between libidinality and social discipline. And in fact our 'container/contained' scores could be taken to indicate that such tensions are indeed present, to a considerable degree. The problem is that they appear to be waning, as the 'container' grows in relative strength. By the same token, the prediction that growing 'reflexivity' would mean an increase in Social and Sensual values was also not borne out.

For now, we can say with some confidence that while we have not produced evidence that advertisements directly address the more emotionally- or personally-inflected forms of reflexivity, we have shown that a reflexive orientation to risk is growing. Products are becoming increasingly presented as antidotes to excessive or unnecessary risk, and we may infer (assuming that advertising creatives do know something about their audiences) that choice between products—and perhaps more importantly the individual's ongoing relationship to the product once bought—is experienced as an opportunity to reflect upon risk and to plan for its management.

In our conceptual framework we could be said to have proposed two forms of 'identity work', though at first in the analysis of our coding data we gave that name to only one of them, not anticipating the strength and complexity of the other. Both assist in providing security in an uncertain world. One is a labour of stylisation; it is the blending of all kinds of values into a 'lifestyle' in Giddens' sense, the restitution of containment in the face of disrupted inheritance (see Chapter 5). This was what we attempted to measure in our 'container/contained' scores, and did not find to be increasing. The other is more a labour of calculation, the attempt to measure and manage inherent risks, and to predict and play off the costs and benefits of different choices. This we have found to be a strong and increasingly important component of the work which advertisements invite their readers to do.

Our finding of a pragmatic focus on the commodity and its features can be compared with the historical analysis of Leiss *et al.* Since our coding methods were different a direct comparison is not possible, but our data provide grounds for proposing that their four-phase account needs some elaboration. We may have entered a fifth phase of marketing characterised by a fifth cultural framing of our relationship to goods, one in which the 'product code' as Leiss *et al.* term it (see Chapter 3) has returned to prominence. All three 'codes' (product, person and setting) continue to be important but the product code now

has pre-eminence. Perhaps this is best conceived of as a development within their fourth phase of 'lifestyle' marketing and 'totemic' framing. Consumers remain thoroughly schooled in richly social ways of imagining and relating to goods and services (i.e. in the person and setting codes, which also account for a proportion of our sensual values category), and crucially marketing is still based on segmentation and the targeting of selected groups. However the rhetoric of individuality now has such a hold on the public imagination that an invitation to identification with the group is no longer the preferred way of addressing the reader of advertisements. The uniqueness of each individual consumer must instead be acknowledged and given pre-eminence. Since it is in the actual use of the product that people will be most aware of their unique configuration of need and desire, a return to the product and its features could be consistent with the intense individualisation of the late modern consumer.

We have argued that consumption as a sphere of action has taken on a greater role in the work of individual identity formation. This trend might be indicative of an encroaching privatism which is damaging to common culture and social cohesiveness. But it can also be viewed as symptomatic of a less ominous dynamic: one whereby individuals and groups are afforded a more plastic public sphere arranged not simply for self-indulgence and defensive escapism, but instead, for reflexive contemplation, consideration and judgement of action and identity, communal or otherwise. Advertising contributes to the ways in which the consumption of everyday objects can, in a very basic way, be thought-provoking as well as simply gratifying. We have proposed that advertising, conceived as a dynamic structure, can afford occasions for the elaboration of personal and collective experience around three axes: pragmatic, moral and sensual. To use the term of Leiss *et al.*, our three 'codes' of advertising (Practical, Social and Sensual) contribute to consumer society's provision of everyday ceremonials in which libidinal investments are modulated by the simultaneous assertion of containing experiences and structure. Alongside advertising's appeals to moral sense and to the senses, it has maintained and sometimes increased its provision of rational information about the materiality and pragmatism of the good. Our evidence is that advertising has more than maintained the function traditionally claimed for it by its defenders as an informative resource in the marketplace. Advertising continues to speak to the consumer's interest in calculation and comparison.

As we have conveyed above, an important finding has been that the composition of containment has changed. While containment has

CONCLUSIONS: THE RE-EMERGENCE OF THE RATIONAL CONSUMER

retained a flavour of morality, advertising has increasingly reasserted rational modes of product representation alongside the moral messages and sensual appeals. One explanation for this complex phenomenon lies in the re-emergence of a conception of the consumer as rational. This conception is very different to that implicit in economic theories of *homo economicus* or in Marxist accounts of rationality and use as an occluded 'nature'. The persistence of the rational conception of consumption has survived not solely as critique but also as practice. This is nowhere better illustrated than in the continued success in the UK of the consumer magazine *Which?* and its associated publications. Aldridge (1994), noting that *Which?* has a circulation of nearly a million, describes the magazines as producing a 'socially constructed' rational consumer and an implicit mode of consumer virtue which is spartan and pragmatic in relation to goods rather than, for instance, spiritual, or critical of consumption. *Which?* seeks to construct a readership which is rational, goal oriented, forward looking, disciplined, and ascetic. This character set is a far cry from the selfish, hedonistic 'playboy' culture which Bell (1979) diagnosed, and from the playful self-indulgence which postmodernism attributes to the modern consumer.

This of course is not the whole story. But it is relevant for us in that the 'character-set' Aldridge describes does not appear to be on the decline, at least not in the sectors where we have looked. We suggest that there are two ways of looking at the resurgence of rational claims in advertising. One is that the consumer movement, with *Which?* as a vanguard publication from 1957, has inflected the general format of consumer publicity. Rationality is one more seam of authentication which advertising has appropriated in much the same way as it has appropriated various sub-cultural spheres. Rationality, in the form of the 'sub-cultural' approach to consumption developed by the consumer movement in the 1960s, has been absorbed into the discourse of advertising, with beneficial effects for the quality of advertising discourse and its capacity to perform its containing functions.

We would in a way be agreeing here with those critics of advertising who see it as devouring all discourses and sign-systems, incorporating them into the meta-discourse of marketing. However our contention would also be that in so doing advertising modifies itself, and diversifies the experiences available to its readers. Some agendas and rhetoric of the consumer movement have thus been absorbed into advertising, significantly influencing their content, without of course neutralising that movement as a social force. This is part of the general trend during the

248   THE DYNAMICS OF ADVERTISING

period we have studied for business, at least at its marketing end, to be more responsive to ethical and political issues raised by social change.

Secondly we propose that the rational consumer is more resilient than most critiques of postmodern consumer society suppose. The presence of fact and pragmatism in the discourse of advertising is testament to the validity of a characterisation of the contemporary consumer who holds rational action amongst a repertoire of reflexive abilities as he or she negotiates the everyday. The idea of a repertoire must be stressed here; we do not propose that our findings or the theoretical ideas we have developed can be taken to supplant well-documented reports and established ideas about important cultural trends of this period. We would not doubt that there has for example been an 'expressive revolution' in the advanced consumer societies, and that this has occurred in a number of linked but distinct modes or dimensions—in connection with feminism, as part of the growth of 'therapeutic culture', in the form of 'New Age' sub-cultures, and in the mundane practices of consumption itself. The theoretical and empirical report we have been working up in this book serves rather to indicate the need for analyses of overall social change to recognise the new modes of rationality also embodied in the 'postmodern' consumer, and to register the complex variability with which these modes may contribute to narcissistic or integrative tendencies of the self.

These two explanations—in terms of a social movement, and in terms of psycho-cultural conditions—are by no means separate. The ability of individuals to function as 'rational consumers' both supports and is supported by the vitality of the consumer movement. The broad cultural trend represented by the many rationally-minded consumers is however a larger factor than the specific social movement represented by consumer publications and organisations.

That there can be a tension between consumer power and certain kinds of practical orientation can be shown through a consideration of the recent history of banking advertisements. Here the consumer movement has been pitted *against* a certain kind of practicality, the 'hard sell' approach to the marketing of credit which characterised some messages of the 1980s. In these, functional features such as the ease and speed of obtaining credit were dominant, and the criticism evoked led to a more circumspect approach with more prominent 'health warnings'. The implication is though that the role of campaigning consumerism, while not always extending the boundaries of the 'Practical' in advertisements, is at least influential in pressing the engagement with practicality into more detailed and risk-aware modes.

More generally, we surmise that the orientation of the advertising industry is pre-eminently towards the markets it has defined as its target, with the possibility of a pressure-group backlash at most a secondary consideration. On this view, which we argued for in Chapter 2, the trend to the practical is led primarily by research and by the intuitive guesses of advertisers, both of which must have produced support for the belief that people are favourably disposed towards information-rich advertisements which identify or even explain practical features of products. In the banking sector this preference would have been central to the whole process by which the banks 'went to market', since it provided the basis of the new strategy for advertising messages, one needed to replace the fading appeal of the bank as traditional authority. People increasingly wanted facts and figures, not the experience of a social inheritance which either they could not claim for their own, or they have refused.

We do not therefore take our data as evidence of a cyclical return to earlier 'hard sell' communicative strategies, but as an indication of a new development around the incorporation into current strategies of a risk-oriented mode of identity work. The participation of advertisements in this work is in itself neither a good nor a bad thing. It will not be essentially a contribution either to the degradation of the self, or to its enhancement. However our method of value analysis does suggest that the contemporary self is more stable and anchored than might on one set of views have been expected (see Chapter 5).

In general we might expect a discourse of practical reality to offer some containment of anxiety, but it will depend in any individual advertisement on the place of the Practical elements within the whole values profile. If we return to the Freudian root of our three value categories, we would say that ego functions are potential containers for the individual's anxieties, but that they need to be integrated with or at least able to co-exist with a range of superego features and id processes.

We should perhaps repeat that it is not our intention to adopt a tendentiously pro-advertising position in reaction to the critical dogmas we reviewed in Chapter 4. As Leiss *et al.* point out, the important debates to be had about advertising are not about whether one overall moral judgement or another can be applied to it, but about its actual content and effects in specific contexts. Foremost amongst these is the question of advertising and children; most of our discussion has assumed an adult reader, and our review of the literature has not included work on advertisements aimed at children. But for some critics of advertising it is its impact on children which is the most worrying

area. We would find much to agree with in that concern, though it must be noted that some of the ill-founded preconceptions which have underpinned the literature about advertising in general may be especially strong in debates about children, where a belief in the innocence of the reader can be especially strong (see, for example, the study by Roy Fox, 1996). There is no reason to assume that the basic psychodynamics of advertisements when read by children are any different from those which we have discussed in relation to the adult reader. Yet the longer-term impact of these dynamics may be different for young children, for whom the boundary between reality and illusion is not so firmly drawn, even for the increasing numbers with (unlike Fox's respondents) high degrees of media literacy and scepticism. We take from Campbell's rich thesis on the origins of consumer culture (Campbell, 1987) the idea that consumption is intrinsically, to some degree, based on illusion, on the hope for a better, more complete and satisfying experience from the next commodity. Campbell links the rise of the consumerist ethic to Romanticism and its precursors, and to the longing for an unknown fulfilment. The adult consumer is able, usually, to moderate this yearning (which psychoanalytically would be seen as ultimately a narcissistic one) by constantly returning to the world of actual possibilities (by subordinating the narcissistic ideal to the ego's reality orientation). The question then is not how to make our relationships to goods free of illusion, by purging them of unconscious longing, but how to tether that longing to some pegs in reality. Advertising, especially in the more varied forms of marketing discourse which have developed in recent years, has the potential to contribute to this, whatever the immediate concerns of those involved in producing it. It may contribute through a manifest emphasis on the pragmatic and on coping with life situations, and through its deployment of containing social values. If it is to do this effectively, though, it must also seduce us, not in the sense of conscripting us to its commercial aims but in the sense of fascinating us with its imagery and its words, of engaging us through its vivid representations of desire.

Of late advertisements have sought to seduce us partly through their use of self-parody. While this strategy—in everyday life as in advertisements, where it is increasingly common—may be sometimes no more than seduction or ingratiation, it may also at times be a sign of an emergent awareness of self and others, and of a stronger sense of social reality. It may also reflect a recognition amongst advertisers that in the earlier history of the modern advertising industry its professionals ascribed to their audiences a level of cultural dignity below their own.

However, though self-parody may be a sign that a 'learning' process of some sort is under way as advertising acquires more cultural maturity, it is very far from the consummation of such a process.

We do not suggest that advertising is moving towards a more coherently positive social role, and do not expect it to develop to any more coherent condition than it is currently in. As a product of or element in a set of dynamic processes at several levels, it has never been in a coherent condition, and the more that boundaries between promotional practices and other communicative activities become blurred or overrun, the more variegated advertising is likely to be. Perhaps the main point of our critiques of other work in this area, and of our own proposals for the theory of advertising, is that we should be very sceptical of any claim to have fixed the nature of its cultural influences. It is as open-ended, at least, as the process of adolescent development to which we have linked it.

The processes of association, which we have presented as the means by which advertisements exert their influence, are compatible with any kind of role for them as public or social communication. In our empirical work we have tried to specify how the content of advertisements might guide or constrain the associative work which readers do. We have found that a tripartite category system for the description of values, based on the Freudian model of mental agencies, has considerable power in enabling us to describe changes in advertisement content, at the level of a broad historical mapping of mass advertising. They also have some use in relation to sectoral analyses such as between brands and readerships, though more detailed studies would be required to extend such analyses beyond the few preliminary attempts we have reported here. We would like to suggest that these categories may also be of much wider use, in analysing other forms of communication and perhaps other phenomena such as goods themselves.

APPENDIX 1: CODING FORM USED FOR CAR STUDY

1.	Case:	Date:	Source:	Coder:

2.	**Identification**	
	a) Publication	
	b) Date	
	c) Page(s)	
	d) Product	
	e) Agency	

3.	**Product class e.g. Mini, super mini, medium, large, etc.**	
	a) A Mini size	
	b) B Small	
	c) B/C Lower medium [Escort]	
	d) C Upper medium [Cortina]	
	e) C/D Large [Carlton/Scorpio]	
	f) D [Super deluxe cars]	
	g) Sports Car	
	h) Range of models	

A: TEXT

4.	Identifying Slogan
	Signature:
	Pun / Humour / Wordplay (indicate)
	Other Notes:
	Logo ?:

7.	Explicit Values		
	a) Family		
	b) Freedom (liberty)		
	c) Freedom (carefree)		
	d) Excitement		
	e) Transgression		
	f) Newness		
	g) Excellence of car		
	g) (i) Ex Technical		
	g) (ii) Ex 'Finish'		
	g) (iii) Ex Perfection		
	h) Traditional		
	i) Appearance		
	j) Individuality		
	k) Achievement/reward		
	l) Soothing		
	m) Self-indulgence		
	n) Insulating/protective		
	o) Control		
	p) Distinction/exclusive		
	q) Prudence		
	r) Belonging		
	s) Youth		
	t) Age		
	u) Newness		
	v) Other		

5.	Rational		
	a) Price		
	b) Finance (HP)		
	c) Warranty		
	d) Low ins prem.		
	e) Other inducements		
	f) Economy (mpg)		
	g) Environment		
	h) Quiet		
	i) Safety		
	j) Security/lock/alarm		
	k) Space		
	l) Accessories		
	m) Comfort		
	n) Practicalities		
	o) Durability		
	p) Manoeuvrability		
	q) Choice		
	r) Solidity		
	s) Reliability		
	t) Maintenance		
	u) Other technical		

6.	Performance		
	a) Speed / accl		
	b) Power		
	c) Road holding / handling / driving pleasure		

11i	Image [Car in Use]		
	a) Single car		
	b) Multiple cars		
	b) (i) Multiple serial		
	b) (ii) Multiple typological		
	c) Part(s)		
	i) Cabin		
	ii) Boot		
	iii) Engine		
	iv) Skeleton		
	d) No image of car		

11ii	Image [Car Portrait]		
	a) Single car		
	b) Multiple cars		
	b) (i) Multiple serial		
	b) (ii) Multiple typological		
	c) Part(s)		
	i) Cabin		
	ii) Boot		
	iii) Engine		
	iv) Skeleton		
	d) Car absent		

8.	Dominant Themes		
	a) Rational		
	b) Performance		
	c) Values		

9.	Tensions/Conflicts		
	a) Head & heart		
	b) Appearance/reality		
	c) Divided self		
	d) Couple conflict		
	e) Intergenerational conflict		
	f) Power & responsibility		
	g) Power and control		
	h) Power and prestige		
	i) Other conflict		

B: ILLUSTRATION

10.	General		
	a) Colour		
	b) Black & white		
	c) Photograph		
	d) Illustration		

14. Location / (Backdrop)

a) Blank background	
b) Abstract design	
c) Surreal	
d) Naturalistic	
i) House & garden	
ii) (Air)ports/stations	
iii) Metropolitan	
iv) 'Small Town'	
v) Suburban	
vi) Rural	
vii) Exotic	
viii) Unlikely	
ix) Non specific	
x) Other nat	

15. National Location

a) Indeterminate	
b) English	
c) Scottish	
d) Mediterranean	
e) U.S.A	
f) French	
g) German	
h) Italian	
i) Scandinavian	
j) Japan	
k) Other	

13. People

a) 1 Male od	
b) 1 Male	
c) 1 Male with child(ren)	
d) 1 Female od	
e) 1 Female	
f) 1 Female with child(ren)	
g) m/f Ambiguous	
h) Nuclear family	
i) M/f couple [male owner /driver]	
j) F/m couple [female owner / driver]	
k) 2 Males (or more)	
l) Bystanders	
m) 2 Females (+)	
n) 2 Couples	
o) 3 or more other	
p) Male & female (not couple) [M/od]	
q) Female & male (not couple) [F/od]	
r) Body part (e.g. hand) [Male]	
s) Body part (e.g. hand) [Female]	
t) NONE	

17.	Connoted Area/Field/Style of Life (continued)	
	e) (ii) 'Country' sports	
	e) (iii) 'Popular' sport	
	e) (iv) Upper-class society	
	e) (v) Female environment	
	f) Art	
	g) Travel / transport	
	g) (i) Holiday	
	g) (ii) Travel (other)	
	h) Engineering / technophilia	

18.	Time Perspective	
	a) Futurity	
	b) Present	
	c) Nostalgia	

19.	Authority/Register/Citation	
	a) Disembodied corporate voice	
	b) Representative of company	
	c) Celebrity	
	d) 'Real' people testimony	
	e) Autocar / journalists	
	f) Child	

16.	Depicted Activities	
	a) Shopping practical	
	b) Domestic practical	
	c) Shopping leisure	
	d) Domestic leisure	
	e) To work	
	f) At work	
	g) Driving	
	h) Car care/admiring	
	i) Purchase (of car)	
	j) Non specific	
	k) Sport participation	
	l) Other	
	m) N/A	

17.	Connoted Area/Field/Style of Life	
	a) Business	
	a) (i) Commerce	
	a) (ii) Professions	
	a) (iii) Symbolic professions	
	b) Industry	
	c) Military	
	d) Craft	
	e) Lifestyle sport & leisure	
	e) (i) Outdoor pursuits	

g) Woman owner / driver	
h) Woman passenger	
i) Passer by	
j) Expert scientist	
i) Competitor	
k) Other	

20.	Metonymic Object

Number Plate	

Further notes / Observations

APPENDIX 2: CODING FORM USED FOR BANKING STUDY

ID:		Source		Publication		Publication (cont.)		Agency		Bank		New Services
Year:												
	1	HAT	1	Times	20	Sunday Telegraph	1	Meal	1	Lloyds	1	Saving account
	2	Library	2	Daily Mail	21	Financial Times	2	O&M	2	Barclays		
	3	Casual	3	Observer	22	Cosmopolitan	3	CB	3	NatWest	3	Mortgage
		Medium	4	Independent	23	Sunday People		**Invitation:**	4	Midland	4	Cheques/chequing acct.
	1	Newspaper	5	Daily Record	24	News of the World	1	Telephone	5	B of Scot	5	Travellers cheques
	2	Magazine	6	Guardian	25	You	2	Coupon	6	Yorkshire	6	Interest
	3	Television	7	Daily Telegraph	26	Weekend Guardian	3	Drop by	7	B of Glasgow	7	Safety deposit box
	4	Pamphlet	8	TV Times	27	Daily Record Glasgow	4	Literature	8	Clydesdale	8	Tax-relief
			9	Star	28	Yorks Eve Post	5	None	9	East Anglian	9	Automated telling
			10	Sun	29	S Wales Echo			10	Royal	10	Automatic bill paying
			11	Daily Express	30	Ideal Home			11	Co-operative	11	Various Access cards
			12	Evening Standard	31	Birmingham Eve Mail			12	Coutts	12	Branded services
			13	Sunday Times Mag	32	Newcastle Eve Chron			13	TBS	13	New forms of financing
			14	Radio Times	33	Good Housekeeping			14	First Direct	14	Club membership
			15	Mail on Sunday	34	Woman's Weekly			15	First National	15	Overdraft
			16	Sunday Correspondent	35	Mirror			16	Girobank	16	Financial planning
			17	Car					17	AIB	17	Insurance plan
			18	Today Weekly					18	Citibank	18	Telephone banking
			19	Sunday Mirror					19	Alliance	19	Computer banking
											20	Drive-thru
											21	Executor
											22	General

Advice:	Rat.	Rhet		
1			Expert	Knowledge, experienced, specialised/
2			Prescriptive	You should/you can't do without/a necessity/do it now
3			Personal	Friendly/helpful/caring/customised/spends time/listens/in person
4			Informal	Informative/reasonable/able to clarify/flexible
5			Non-elite test	

Tradition			Manager	
1	Founding father		Present	1
2	Longevity		Not needed	2
3	Anniversaries/bdays			
4	Consistent			
5	Other			

Modernity I:		Modernity II:	
1	Breaking tradition	1	Impersonal/standardised
2	Pro technology	2	Anti-tech
3	Busy, active lifestyle	3	Confusing/complex
4	Universality	4	Rootless/unstable
5	Other	5	Other

Accessible:		Time:		Other rational incentives
1	Convenient	1		No waiting competitor comparison
2	Simple	2		Need to be ahead inducements to subscribe
3	Coverage	3		Time means money controlling personal expenditure
4	To cash			24 hrs welcome respect
5	Limited			Extended hours

Choice		Freedom		Trust	
1	Consumer driven	1	Mobility	1	Honesty
2	Flexible	2	From worries	2	Other
3	At your own pace	3	Financial constraints		
4	Diversity	4	Bank as organiser		
5	Limited choice	5	See for yourself		
6	Customised				

Security		Prudence		Status			
1	Guaranty	1	Practical	1	Expansion	6	Sponsor
2	Safety protection	2	Common sense	2	Luxury	7	Giving
3	No risk	3	Worth	3	Exclusivity	8	Hard work
4	Privacy	4	Plan for future	4	Distinctive	9	Team work
5	Comfort	5	Budget	5	Ambition		
6	Stable	6	Efficient		Achievement		
		7	Accumulate		Novel		

Psycho Conflict		Social Appeal:		Family	
1	Integrated	1	Belonging reference to specific group or person	1	Maturity
2	Sides self-indulgence	2	Critical mass: reference to sheer number,	2	Nuclear
3	Sides self-restraint	3	Social shame/embarrassment	3	Generational (bank part of family tradition)
		4	Aspiration	4	Other

Tension/ Conflict						
Integrated	1	Modern	2	Tradition	3	Competition
Integrated	1	Technology	2	Service	3	Building societies
Integrated	1	Expertise	2	Customer knows best	3	Other banks
Integrated	1	Saving	2	Loan	3	General
Integrated	1	Family or tradition	2	Independence	3	

	Sensual
1	Pleasure
2	Excitement
3	Power
4	Ease of use
5	Speed/instantaneity
6	Freedom/independence
7	Security
8	Gratification in consumption
9	Fear
10	Frustration/anger

	Activities
1	Shopping leisure
2	Domestic leisure
3	Walking to bank
4	Working at bank
5	Counting money
6	Travel
7	Other

	Target:
1	Non gender explicit
2	Men
3	Women
4	Parents
5	Students
6	Young people
7	Retirees/seniors
8	Ethnic group
9	Other

	Location
1	Blank
2	Abstract
3	Surreal
4	Office
5	Street scene
6	Front of bank
7	Inside bank
8	Home
9	Yard
10	Rural
11	Exotic
12	Other

	Field Gifts:
1	Business
2	Commerce
3	Professions
4	Symbolic professions
5	Industry
6	Craft
7	Outdoor pursuits
8	Popular pursuits
9	Family life
10	Upper-class society
11	Middle-class
12	Lower-class
13	Art
14	Television
15	Holiday
16	Other

	Products:
1	Initial deposit
2	Calculator
3	Magazine
4	Dis magazine
5	Free booklet
6	Entry in draw
7	Other

1	Holiday
2	Cars
3	Fur coat
4	Hi fi
5	Renovations
6	Education
7	Other

Characters	
1	None
2	Female
3	2 Female
4	3 or more Female
5	Male
6	2 Male
7	3 or more Male
8	Male/Female
9	Nuclear family
10	Bystanders
11	Non Caucasian
12	Other

Role			
1	Mother	9	Ambiguous grouping
2	Father	10	Friends
3	Staff	11	Butler
4	Child	12	'Every day'
5	Young person	13	Father/son
6	Baby	14	Mother/daughter
7	Family	15	Mother/child
8	Couple	16	Mother/son
		17	Father/daughter
		18	Elderly lady
		19	Elderly man
		20	Animal
		21	Cartoon figure
		22	Partial body
		23	Hand

APPENDIX 3: CODING FORM FOR CREDIT AND CHARGE CARD ADVERTISEMENT ANALYSIS

1) GENERAL INFORMATION		SPSS ENTRY NUMBER					
	Case Number		Source		Date		Coder

2) ADVERTISEMENT IDENTIFICATION						
a) Medium	TV ☐	NEWS ☐	RAD ☐	DM ☐	POST ☐	a1) Specify Newspaper / Magazine
b) Date of advertisement						

3) PRODUCT SPECIFICATION		
Brand *(e.g. Natwest, Amex, Co-op)*	Service if applicable *(e.g. Visa, Switch, Delta, Mastercard)*	Goldcard Yes ☐ No ☐ Both advertised here ☐
Corporate service advertised	Yes ☐ No ☐	

4) TEXT: MAIN FEATURES	
a) Slogan	
b) Call to action	
c) Signature	

5) PRACTICAL / RATIONAL / 'EGO' CONSIDERATIONS	
a) Interest rate	
b) Inducement to subscribe	
c) Competitor comparison (if mathematical)	
d) Other 'anxiety' neutral features (specify)	
e) Wideness of use (expressed as matter of fact)	
f) Insurances	
g) Controlling personal expenditure	
h) Other problem solving (specify)	
i) Simplicity	
j) Comprehensiveness of function	
k) Other 'coping' feature (specify)	
l) No spend limit	
m) Exclusive benefits (specify)	
n) Guarantees welcome, respect	
o) Other 'status' features (specify)	
q) Other anxiety-related features (specify)	

Notes on coding this section

6) SOCIAL / TRADITIONAL / 'SUPEREGO' CONSIDERATIONS	
a) Non-elite testimonial (specify who)	
b) Other 'anxiety-neutral' value (specify)	
c) Convenience	
d) Universality	
e) Protection (card as shield / umbrella)	
f) Other 'coping' values	
g) Exclusivity	
h) Ambition	
i) Achievement	
j) Elite testimonial (specify who)	
k) Other 'status' values	
l) Other anxiety related values (specify)	

Notes on coding this section

7) SENSUAL / LIBIDINAL / 'ID' CONSIDERATIONS	
a) Pleasure	
b) Excitement	
c) Power	
d) Ease of use	
e) Speed / intantanaeity	
f) Freedom / independence	
g) Security (card as bed / duvet)	
h) Gratification in consumption	
i) Individuality (tailor made)	

Notes on coding this section

8) SETTING: SCENE / OBJECTS and OTHER CUES	
a) Business (specify if possible)	
b) Business travel / entertainment	
c) Leisure shopping	
d) Leisure sport	
e) Leisure cultural	
f) Other leisure	
g) Other setting (specify)	

9) PERSONS PRESENT OR REFERRED TO	
a) Peers	
b) Authority (e.g. boss)	
c) Subordinates / service personnel	
d) Family	
e) Partner	
f) National identity	
g) Other (specify)	

10) DESIGNATED SPHERE OF USE	
a) Business	
b) Personal consumption	
c) Personal finance management	

Bibliography

Abercrombie, N. and Longhurst, B., *Audiences* (Sage, 1998).

Adeney, M., *The Motor Makers: The Turbulent History of Britain's Car Industry* (Collins, 1988).

Adorno, T. W. and Horkheimer, M., *The Dialectic of Enlightenment* (Allen Lane, 1944/1973).

Aldridge, A., The construction of rational consumption in *Which?* Magazine: the more blobs the better?, in *Sociology* 28(4), 899–912 (1994).

Alford, C. F., *Melanie Klein and Critical Social Theory* (Yale, 1989).

Arnold, M., *Culture and Anarchy*, J. Dover Wilson, ed. (Cambridge University Press, 1988 edn).

Barker, N., *From A to B: Tales of Modern Motoring* (BBC, 1994).

Barthes, R., The rhetoric of the image (1964), in *Image, Music, Text* (Fontana, 1977).

Barthes R., The advertising message in *The Semiotic Challenge* (Basil Blackwell, 1988).

Baudrillard, J., *Simulations* (Semiotext(e), 1983).

Bauman, Z., *Intimations of Postmodernity* (Routledge, 1992).

Bauman, Z., *Postmodernity and its Discontents* (Polity Press, 1997).

Beck, U., *Risk Society: Towards a New Modernity* (Sage, 1992).

Beck, U., Giddens, A. and Lash, S., *Reflexive Modernisation: Politics, Tradition and Aesthetics in the Modern Social Order* (Polity, 1994).

Beck-Gernsheim, E., Life as a planning project, in Lash, S., Szerszynski, B. and Wynne, B., eds, *Risk Environment and Modernity: Towards a New Ecology* (Sage, 1996).

Bell, D., *The Cultural Contradictions of Capitalism* (Basic Books, 1976).

Berger, B. M., *An Essay on Culture: Symbolic Structure and Social Structure* (University of California Press, 1995).

Berger, J., *Ways of Seeing* (Penguin, 1973).

Bion, W. R., *Taming Wild Thoughts* (1959/Karnac, 1997).

Bion, W. R., *Attention and Interpretation* (Karnac, 1993).

Booker, C., *The Neophiliacs: A study of the Revolution in English Life in the Fifties and Sixties* (Collins, 1969).

Booker, C., *The Seventies* (Collins, 1980).

Bourdieu, P., *Distinction: A Social Critique of the Judgement of Taste* (Routledge, 1989).

Bourdieu, P., *An Invitation to Reflexive Sociology*, translated from the French by L. J. D. Wacquant (University of Chicago Press, 1992).

Bourdieu, P., *The Rules of Art* (Polity, 1996).

Bowlby, J., *Attachment and Loss*, Vol. 1: *Attachment* (Hogarth Press, 1969).

Bowlby, J., *Attachment and Loss*, Vol. 2: *Separation* (Hogarth Press, 1969).

Bowlby, J., *Attachment and Loss*, Vol. 3: *Loss, Sadness and Depression* (Hogarth Press, 1969).

Broadbent, S., Accountable Advertising, in Institute of Practitioners in Advertising, *Marketing Appraisals* (October 1997).

Brown, J. A. C., *Techniques of Persuasion* (Pelican, 1963).

Brown, J. and Richards, B., The humanist Freud, in Elliott, A., ed., *Freud 2000* (Polity, 1998).

Burton, D., *Financial Services and the Consumer* (Routledge, 1994).

Buttle, F., What do people do with advertising, in *International Journal of Advertising* 10(2), 95–110 (1991).

Campbell, C., Consumption as communication: a critique, in Nava *et al.*, eds, *Buy This Book: Studies in Advertising and Consumption* (Routledge, 1997).

Campbell, C., *The Romantic Ethic and the Spirit of Modern Consumerism* (Blackwell, 1987).

Churchill, R., Advertising and civilisation, in *Scrutiny* 12, 60 (1944–5).

Cook, G., *The Discourse of Advertising* (Routledge, 1992).

Cronk, J., *The Third Age of Marketing* (Admap, September 1995).

Davidson, M., *The Consumerist Manifesto* (Routledge, 1992).

Dichter, E., *The Strategy of Desire* (Boardman, 1960).

Dichter, E., *Handbook of Consumer Motivations* (McGraw-Hill, 1964).

Dornbusch, S. and Hickman, L., Other-directedness in consumer-goods advertising: a test of Riesman's historical theory, in *Social Forces* 38 (1), 99–102 (1959).

Douglas, M., *The World of Goods: Towards an Anthropology of Consumption* (Allen Lane, 1979).

Eagleton, T., *The Illusions of Postmodernism* (Blackwell, 1996).

Easterlin, J., Does economic growth improve the human lot?, in Reder, M. & David, P., eds, *Nations and Households in Economic Growth* (Academic Press, 1984).

Elias, N., *The Civilising Process* (Blackwell, 1994).

Elliott, A. and Frosh, S., eds, *Psychoanalysis in Contexts* (Routledge, 1995).

Empson, W., Marvell's 'Garden' in *Scrutiny* I, 236–40 (1932).

Falk, P., *The Consuming Body* (Sage, 1994).

Falk, P., The Benetton Toscani effect, in Nava *et al.*, eds, *Buy This Book* (Routledge, 1997).

Featherstone, M., *Undoing Culture: Globalisation, Postmodernism and Identity* (Sage, 1995).

Fish, S., *There's no Such Thing as Free Speech* (Oxford University Press, 1994).

Flaubert, G., *Sentimental Education* (Penguin, 1970).

Fornas, J., *Cultural Theory and Late Modernity* (Sage, 1995).

Fowles, J., *Mass Advertising as Social Forecast: A Method for Future Research* (Greenwood Press, 1976).

Fowles, J., *Advertising and Popular Culture* (Sage, 1996).

Fox, R. F., *Harvesting Minds: How TV Commercials Control Kids* (Praeger, 1996).

Fox, S., *The Mirror Makers. A History of American Advertising* (Heinemann, 1984).

Fraser, W. H., *The Coming of the Mass Market, 1850–1914* (Macmillian, 1981).

Frazer, P., *Plastic and Electronic Money: New Payment Systems and their Implications* (Woodhead Faulkner, 1985).

Friedan, B., *The Feminine Mystique* (Penguin, 1982).

Frontori, L., Paris, A. and Ventura, I., Association technique and jingle analysis, in *Proceedings of the ESOMAR Congress, 448–60* (ESOMAR, 1989).

Frosh, S., *Identity Crisis: Modernity, Psychoanalysis and the Self* (Macmillan Education, 1991).

Gane, M., ed., *Selected Interviews: Jean Baudrillard* (Routledge, 1993).

Giddens, A., *Modernity and Self-identity: Self and Society in the Late Modern Age* (Polity, 1991).

Giddens, A., *The Transformation of Intimacy: Sexuality, Love and Eroticism in Modern Society* (Polity, 1992).

Gifford, C. H. P., Advertising and economic waste, in *Scrutiny* 3, 168–74 (1934–5).

Goffman, E., *Gender Advertisements* (Macmillan, 1979).

Goldman, R., *Reading Advertisements Socially* (Routledge, 1992).

Goldman R. and Papson, S., *Sign Wars: The Cluttered Landscape of Advertising* (Guilford Press, 1996).

Goode, R., *Consumer Credit Act 1974* (Butterworth, 1974).

Greenberg, J. R. and Mitchell, A., *Object Relations in Psychoanalytic Theory* (Harvard University Press, 1983).

Haineault, D. and Roy, J., *Unconscious for Sale: Advertising, Psychoanalysis and the Public* (University of Minnesota Press, 1984).

Hall, S., *Culture, Media, Language: Working Papers in Cultural Studies*, 1972–79, in association with the Centre for Contemporary Cultural Studies (Hutchinson, 1980).

Hall, S. and Whannel, P., *The Popular Arts* (Hutchinson Educational, 1964).

Harvey, D., *The Condition of Postmodernity* (Blackwell, 1989).

Haug, W. F., *Critique of Commodity Aesthetics: Appearance, Sexuality and Advertising in Capitalist Society* (University of Minnesota Press, 1986).

Hedge, M., IPA takes critical look at advertising research, in Institute of Practitioners in Advertising, *Marketing Appraisals*, (April, 1998).

Hinshelwood, R., *A Dictionary of Kleinian Thought* (Free Association Books, 1991).

Hoggart, R., *The Uses of Literacy* (Pelican, 1957).

Hoggart, R., Where is it all leading us, in Wilson, A., *Advertising and the Community* (Manchester University Press, 1968).

Hoggett, P., *Partisans in an Uncertain World: The Psychoanalysis of Engagement*, (Free Association Books, 1990).

Holland, N., *The Dynamics of Literary Response* (Oxford University Press, 1968).

Horowitz, D., *Vance Packard and American Social Criticism* (U.N.C. Press, 1994).

Inglis, F., *Raymond Williams* (Routledge, 1995).

Jameson, F., *Postmodernism or the Cultural Logic of Late Capitalism* (Verso, 1991).

Jhally, S., *The Codes of Advertising: Fetishism and the Political Economy of Meaning in the Consumer Society* (Routledge, 1990).

Katz, E., Mass communication research and the study of culture, in *Studies in Public Communication* 2, 1–6 (1959).

Key, W. B., *Subliminal Seduction* (Signet, 1974).

Klein, M., *Envy and Gratitude and Other Works 1946–1963* (Virago, 1988).

Kohon, G., ed., *The British School of Psychoanalysis: The Independent Tradition* (Free Association Books, 1986).

Lacan, J., The mirror phase, in *New Left Review* 51 (1971).

Lasch, C., *The Culture of Narcissism: American Life in an Age of Diminishing Expectation* (Warner Books, 1978).

Lash, S., *Sociology of Postmodernism* (Routledge, 1990).

Lash, S., Szersynski, B. and Wynne, B., eds, *Risk Environment and Modernity. Towards a New Ecology* (Sage, 1996).

Lash, S. and Urry, J., *Economies of Signs and Space* (Sage, 1994).

Lears, J., *Fables of Abundance. A Cultural History of Advertising in America* (Basic Books, 1994).

Leavis, R. and Thompson, D., eds, *Culture and Environment: The Training of Critical Awareness* (Chatto & Windus, 1964).

Lee, M., *Consumer Culture Reborn: The Cultural Politics of Consumption* (Routledge, 1993).

Leech, G., *English in Advertising* (Longmans, 1966).

Leiss, W., Kline, S. and Jhally, S., *Social Communication in Advertising: Persons, Products and Images of Well Being* (Nelson Canada, 1990).

Leymore, V. L., *Hidden Myth: Structure and Symbol in Advertising* (Heinemann, 1975).

Lury, C., *Consumer Culture* (Polity, 1996).

Lury, C. and Warde, A., Investments in the imaginary consumer: conjectures regarding power, knowledge and advertising, in Nava *et al.*, eds, *Buy This Book* (Routledge, 1997).

MacRury, I., Advertising and the modulation of narcissism, in Nava *et al.*, eds, *Buy This Book* (Routledge, 1997).

MAPS, *Marketing Financial Services to C2DEs* (Market Assessment Publications, 1997).

Marchand, R., *Advertising and the American Dream. Making Way for Modernity 1920–1940* (University of California Press, 1985).

Marcuse, H., *Eros and Civilisation* (Abacus, 1969/1972).

Martineau, P., *Motivation in Advertising* (McGraw-Hill, 1957).

Mather, L. C., British banking: changes and challenges, in The Institute of Bankers, *The Future of British Banking* (Cambridge Seminar, 1968).

Mattelart, A., *Advertising International: The Privatisation of Public Space* (Routledge, 1991).

Maxton G. P. and Wormald, J., *Driving Over a Cliff: Business Lessons from the World's Car Industry* (EIU/Addison Wesley, 1995).

McClelland, D., *The Achievement Motive* (Wiley, 1976/1954).

Menzies Lyth, Isabel, *The Dynamics of the Social: Selected Essays*, volume II (Free Association Books, 1989).

Mick, D. G., Consumer research and semiotics: exploring the morphology of signs, symbols, and significance, in *Journal of Consumer Research* 13(2), 196–213 (1986).

Mick, D., Levels of subjective comprehension in advertising processing and their relations to advertisement perceptions, attitudes and memory, in *Journal of Consumer Research* 18, 411–24, (1992).

Mick, D. G. and Buhl, C., A meaning based model of advertising experiences in *Journal of Consumer Research* 19(3), 317–38, (1992).

Mick, D. G. and Politi, L., Consumers' interpretation of advertising imagery: a visit to the hell of connotation, in Hirschmann, E. C. ed., *Interpretive Consumer Research* (UT: Association for Consumer Research, 1989).

Miller, D., ed., *Acknowledging Consumption* (Routledge, 1995).

Miller, P. and Rose, N., Mobilising the consumer—assembling the subject of consumption, in *Theory, Culture & Society* 14(1), 1–36 (Sage, 1997).

Minsky, R., *Psychoanalysis and Culture: Contemporary States of Mind* (Polity Press, 1998).

Mintell Marketing Intelligence, *Report: Cars* (Mintel International Group, 1994).

Morley, D., *Television, Audiences and Cultural Studies* (Sage, 1995).

Mort, F., *Cultures of Consumption: Masculinities and Sosial Space in Late Twentieth Century London* (Routledge, 1996).

Mulhern, F., *The Moment of Scrutiny* (NLB, 1979).

Myers, G., *Words in Ads* (Edward Arnold, 1994).

Myers, G., *Advertisement Worlds. Brands, Media, Audiences* (Edward Arnold, 1999).

Myers, K., *Understains* (Comedia, 1986).

Nava, M., Consumerism reconsidered: buying and power, in *Cultural Studies* 5(2), 157–73 (1991).

Nava, M., *Changing Cultures: Feminism, Youth and Consumerism,* (Sage, 1992).

Nava, M., Blake, A., Macrury, I. and Richards, B., eds, *Buy This Book: Studies in Advertising and Consumption* (Routledge, 1997).

Nava, M. and Nava, O., Discriminating or duped?, in *Changing Cultures: Feminism, Youth and Consumerism* (Sage, 1992).

Nevett, T., *Advertising in Britain: A History* (History of Advertising Trust, 1982).

Nixon, S., Advertising executives as modern men: masculinity and UK advertising industry in the 1980s, in Nava *et al.*, eds, *Buy This Book* (Routledge, 1997).

O'Barr, W. M., *Culture and the Advertisement: Exploring otherness in the World of Advertising* (Westview Press, 1994).

O'Donohoe, S., Advertising uses and gratifications, in *European Journal of Marketing* 28 (8/9), 52–75 (1994).

O'Donohoe S., *Leaky boundaris* in Nava *et al.*, eds, *Buy This Book* (Routledge, 1997).

Orwell, G., *As I Please: The Collected Essays, Journalism and Letters of George Orwell*, Vol. III (Penguin, 1892).

Packard, V., *The Hidden Persuaders* (Pelican, 1957).

Packard, V., *The Status Seekers* (Pelican, 1959).

Packard, V., *The Waste Makers* (Pelican, 1960).

Pateman, T., *Language, Truth and Politics* (Jean Stroud, 1980).

Poster, M., ed., *Jean Baudrillard. Selected Writings* (Polity Press, 1988).

Quilligan, M., *The Language of Allegory: Defining the Genre* (Cornell University Press, 1979).

Rayner, E., *The Independent Mind in British Psychoanalysis* (Free Association Books, 1991).

Reeves, R., *Reality in Advertising* (MacGibbon & Kee, 1961).

Richards, B., *Disciplines of Delight* (Free Association Books, 1994).

Richards, B., Popular culture in Kennard, D. & Small, N., eds, *Living Together* (Quartet, 1997).

Richards, T., *Commodity Culture of Victoria England: Advertising and Spectacle, 1851–1914* (Verso, 1991).

Riesman, D., *The Lonely Crowd: A Study of the Changing American Character* (Yale University Press, 1961).

Ritzer, G., *Expressing America: A Critique of the Global Credit Card Society* (Pine Forge Press, 1995).

Robins, K., *Into the Image: Culture and Politics in the Field of Vision* (Routledge, 1996).

Rose, M., *The Post-modern and the Post-industrial. A Critical Analysis* (Cambridge University Press, 1991).

Rose, N., *Governing the Soul: The Shaping of the Private Self* (Routledge, 1991).

Ross, K., *Fast Cars, Clean Bodies* (MIT, 1995).

Rustin, M., *The Good Society and the Inner World: Psychoanalysis, Politics and Culture* (Verso, 1991).

Sayer, P., *Credit Cards and the Law* (Fourmat Publishing, 1988).

Schudson, M., *Advertising: The Uneasy Persuasion* (Basic Books, 1984).

Scott, W. D., *The Psychology of Advertising in Theory and Practice* (Small, Maynard, 1913).

Sennett, R., *The Fall of Public Man* (Faber, 1986).

Segal, H., Notes on symbol formation, in Segal, H., *Dream, Phantasy, and Art* (Routledge, 1991).

Sinclair, J., *Images Incorporated: Advertising as Industry and Ideology* (Routledge, 1989).

Slater, D., *Consumer Culture and Modernity* (Polity Press, 1997).

Stephenson, G., *Credit, Debit and Cheque Cards Law and Practice* (Central Law Publishing, 1993).

Stern, B., Literary criticism and consumer research: overview and illustrative analysis, in *Journal of Consumer Research* 16, 322–33, (1989).

Symington, N., *The Analytic Experience: Lectures from the Tavistock* (Free Association Books, 1986).

Tanaka, K., *Advertising Language: A Pragmatic Approach to Advertisements in Britain and Japan* (Routledge, 1994).

Thomas, D., Cinema advertising in Bullmore, J. J. D. and Waterson, M. J., eds, *The Advertising Association Handbook* (Holt, Rinehart & Winston, 1983).

Thompson, D., Advertising God, in *Scrutiny* I, 241–6 (1932a).

Thompson, D., A cure for amnesia, in *Scrutiny* II, 2–11 (1932b).

Thompson, J. B., *The Media and Modernity: A Social Theory of the Media* (Polity, 1995).

Thomson, A., Advertising control: advertisements in media other than television and radio, in *The Advertising Association Handbook* (1983).

Thomson, P., The rules governing advertising on television and independent local radio, in *The Advertising Association Handbook* (Holt, Rinehart & Winston, 1983).

Tolliday, S. and Zeitlin J., eds, *Between Fordism and Flexibility: The Automobile Industry and its workers* (Berg, 1992).

Tunstall, J., *The Advertising Man in London Advertising Agencies* (Chapman & Hall 1964).

Turner, E. S., *The Shocking History of Advertising* (Penguin, 1965).

Turner, G., *British Cultural Studies: An Introduction* (Routledge, 1992).

Veblen, T., *The Theory of the Leisure Class* (Macmillan, 1899).

Wachtel, M., Richter, G. and Ulbrich K., Zur Verkehrssicherheitsrelevanz der Autowerbung, in *Publisistik* 40, Jahrgang, Heft 1, S. 39–66 (1995).

Warde, A., Consumption, identity-formation and uncertainty, in *Sociology* 28(4), 877–97, 1994.

Wernick, A., Resort to nostalgia: mountains, memories and myths of time, in Nava *et al.*, eds, *Buy This Book* (Routledge, 1997).

Wernick, A., *Promotional Culture* (Sage, 1991).

Whitehead, F., Advertising, in Leavis, R. and Thompson, D., eds, *Culture and Environment: The Training of Critical Awareness* (Chatto & Windus, 1964).

Whyte, W., *The Organisation Man* (Penguin, 1956).

Williams, R., *Communications* (Penguin, 1968).

Williams, R., Advertising: the magic system, in *Problems in Materialism and Culture: Selected Essays* (Verso, 1980).

Williams, R., *Writing in society* (Verso, 1983).

Williams, R., *Culture and Society* (Hogarth, 1987).

Williamson, J., *Decoding Advertisments* (Marion Boyars, 1978/1995).

Willis, P., *Common Culture Symbolic Work at Paly in the Everyday Cultures of the Young* (Open University Press, 1990).

Wilson, A., *Advertising and the Community* (Manchester University Press, 1968).

Winnicott, D. W., *Human Nature* (Free Association Books, 1988).

Winnicott, D. W., *Playing and Reality* (Routledge, 1990).

Young, R. M., *Mental Space* (Free Association Books, 1994).

Zizek, S., *Mapping Ideology* (Verso, 1994).

Index

Numbers in italics refer to illustrations